MID-CONT

3 000

D1310731

# MARK WAID · MARCIO TAKARA

# INCORRUPTIBLE

## VOLUME 5

Mid-Continent Public Library
15616 East Highway 24
Independence, MO 64050

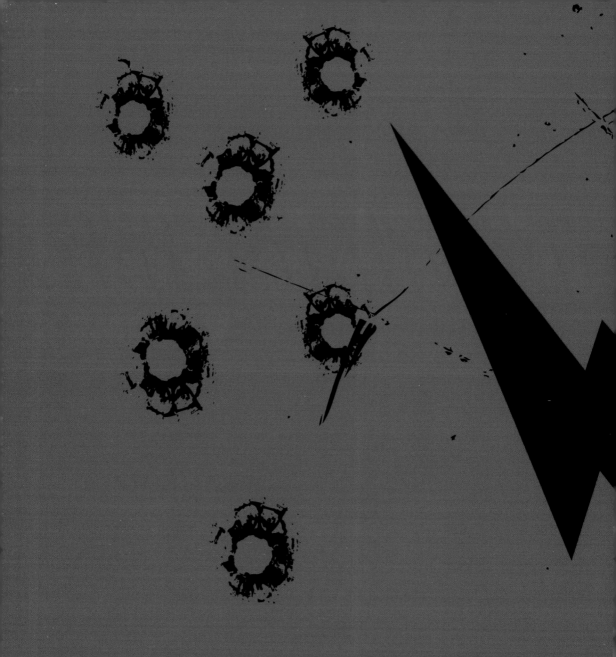

Ross Richie - Chief Executive Officer
Matt Gagnon - Editor-in-Chief
Adam Fortier - VP-New Business
Wes Harris - VP-Publishing
Lance Kreiter - VP-Licensing & Merchandising
Chip Mosher - Marketing & Sales Director
Bryce Carlson - Managing Editor

Ian Brill - Editor
Dafna Pleban - Editor
Christopher Burns - Editor
Shannon Watters - Assistant Editor
Eric Harburn - Assistant Editor
Adam Staffaroni - Assistant Editor

Brian Latimer - Lead Graphic Designer
Stephanie Gonzaga - Graphic Designer
Phil Barbaro - Operations
Ivan Salazar - Marketing Manager
Devin Funches - Marketing & Sales Assistant

**INCORRUPTIBLE Volume Five** — October 2011. Published by BOOM! Studios, a division of Boom Entertainment, Inc. Incorruptible is Copyright © 2011 Boom Entertainment, Inc. Originally published in single magazine form as INCORRUPTIBLE 17-20. Copyright © 2011, Boom Entertainment, Inc. All rights reserved. BOOM! Studios™ and the BOOM! Studios logo are trademarks of Boom Entertainment, Inc., registered in various countries and categories. All characters, events, and institutions depicted herein are fictional. Any similarity between any of the names, characters, persons, events, and/or institutions in this publication to actual names, characters, and persons, whether living or dead, events, and/or institutions is unintended and purely coincidental. BOOM! Studios does not read or accept unsolicited submissions of ideas, stories, or artwork.

A catalog record of this book is available from OCLC and from the BOOM! Studios website, www.boom-studios.com, on the Librarians Page.

BOOM! Studios, 6310 San Vicente Boulevard, Suite 107, Los Angeles, CA 90048-5457. Printed in China. First Printing. ISBN: 978-1-60886-057-9

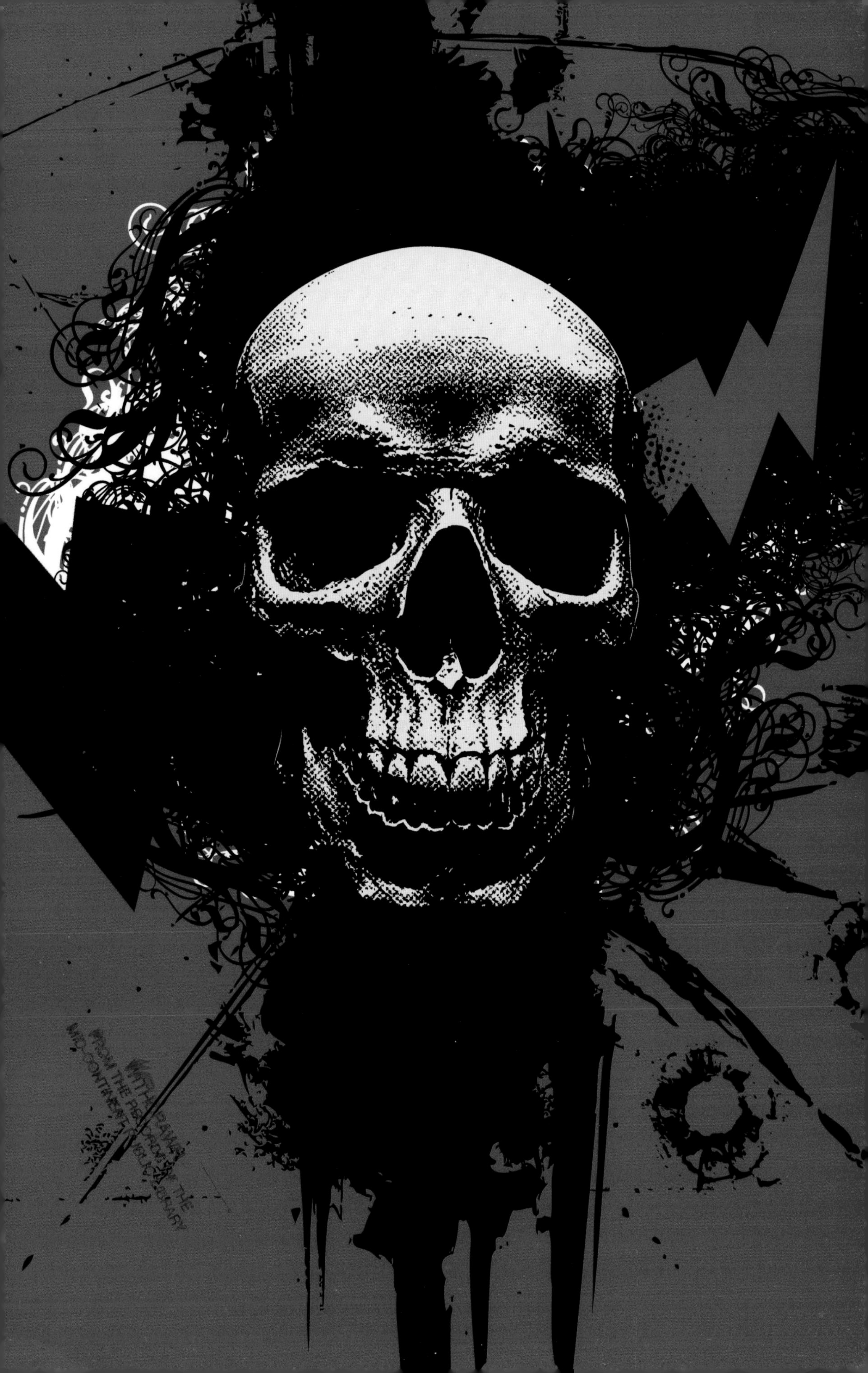

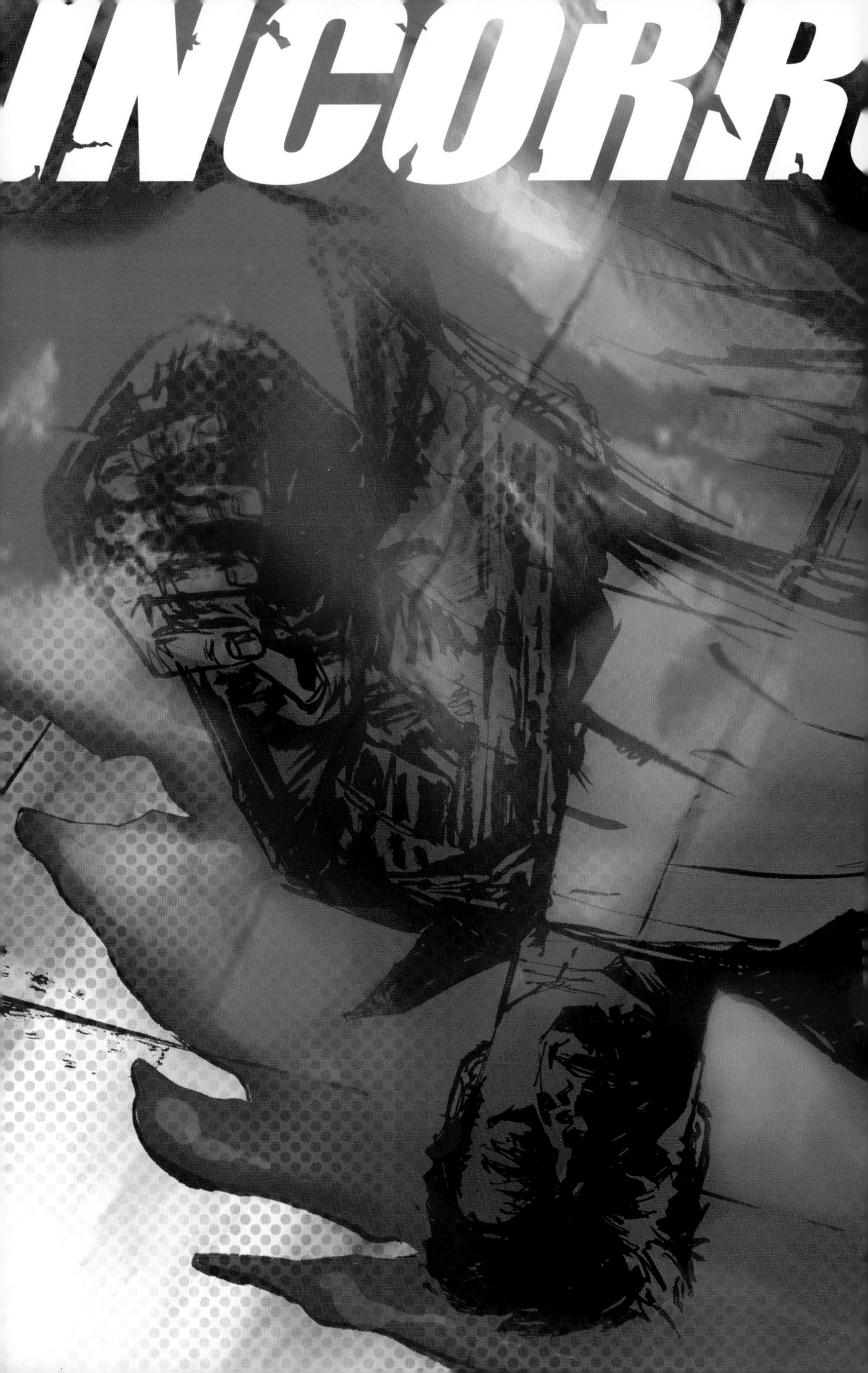
INCORR

# UPTIBLE

**CREATED AND WRITTEN BY**

## MARK WAID

**ARTIST:**

## MARCIO TAKARA

COLORIST: **NOLAN WOODARD**
LETTERER: **ED DUKESHIRE**

EDITOR: **MATT GAGNON**
ASST. EDITOR: **SHANNON WATTERS**

COVER: **GARRY BROWN**

DESIGN: **BRIAN LATIMER**

# CHAPTER 17

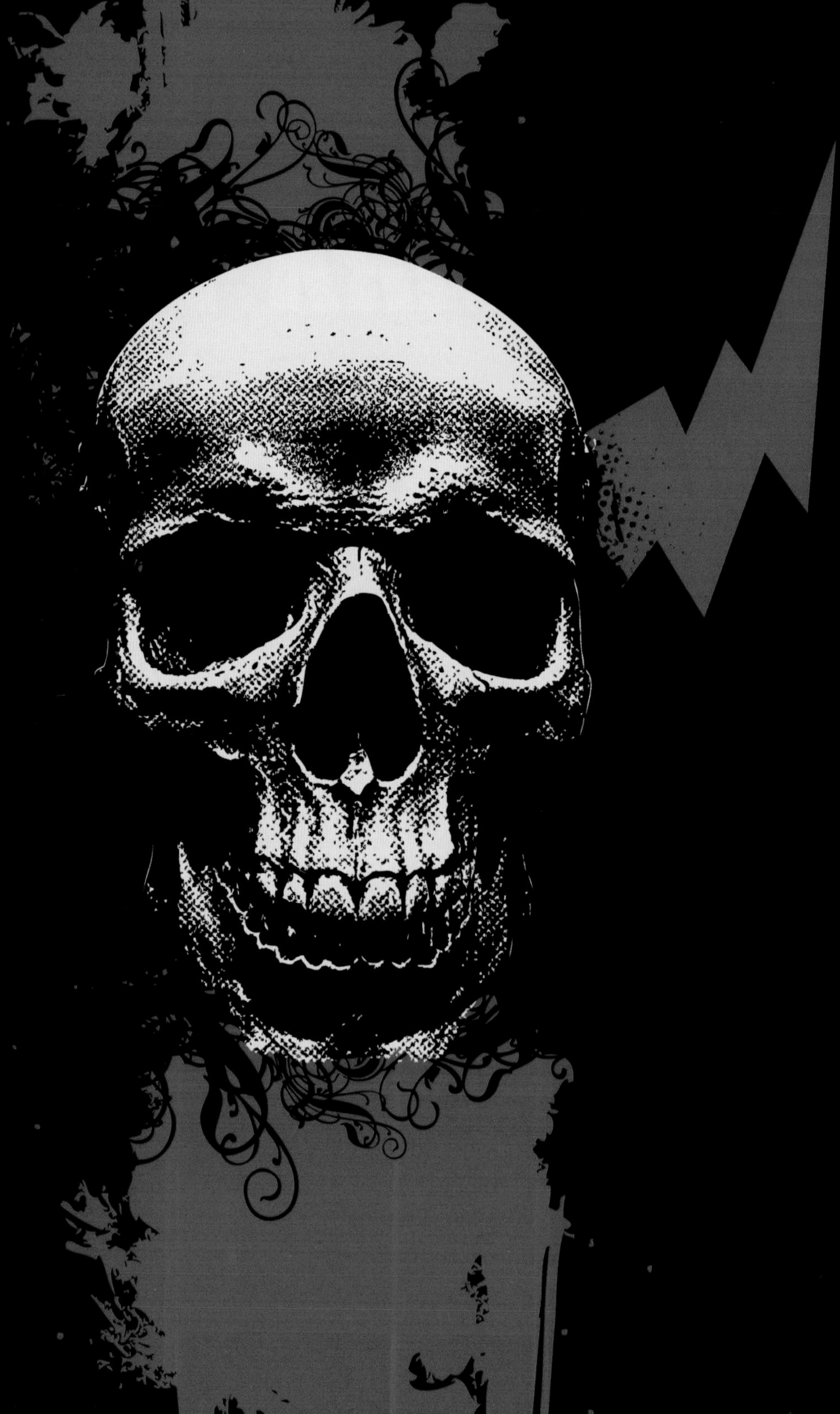

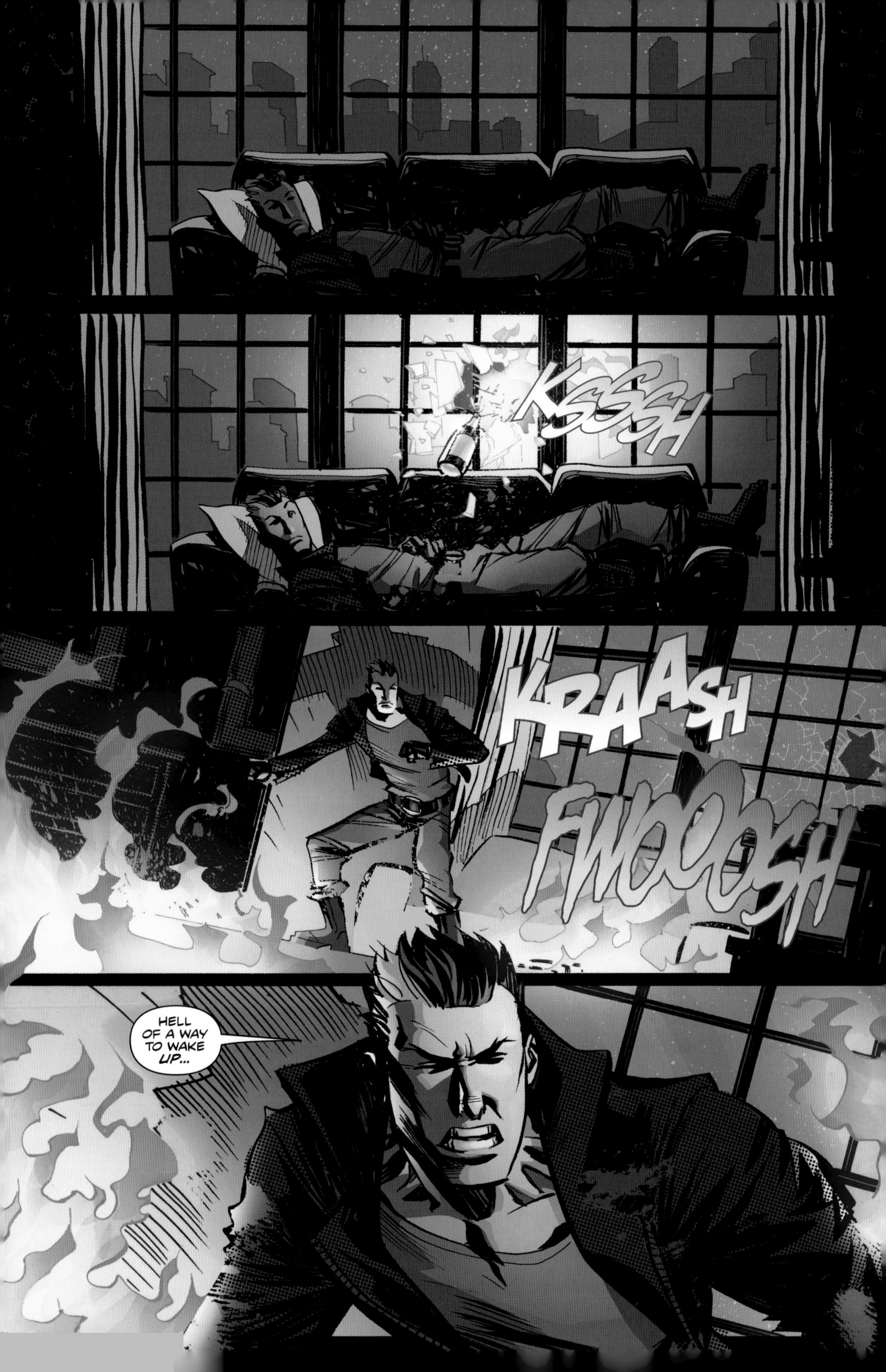
KSSSH
KRAASH
FWOOOSH
HELL OF A WAY TO WAKE UP...

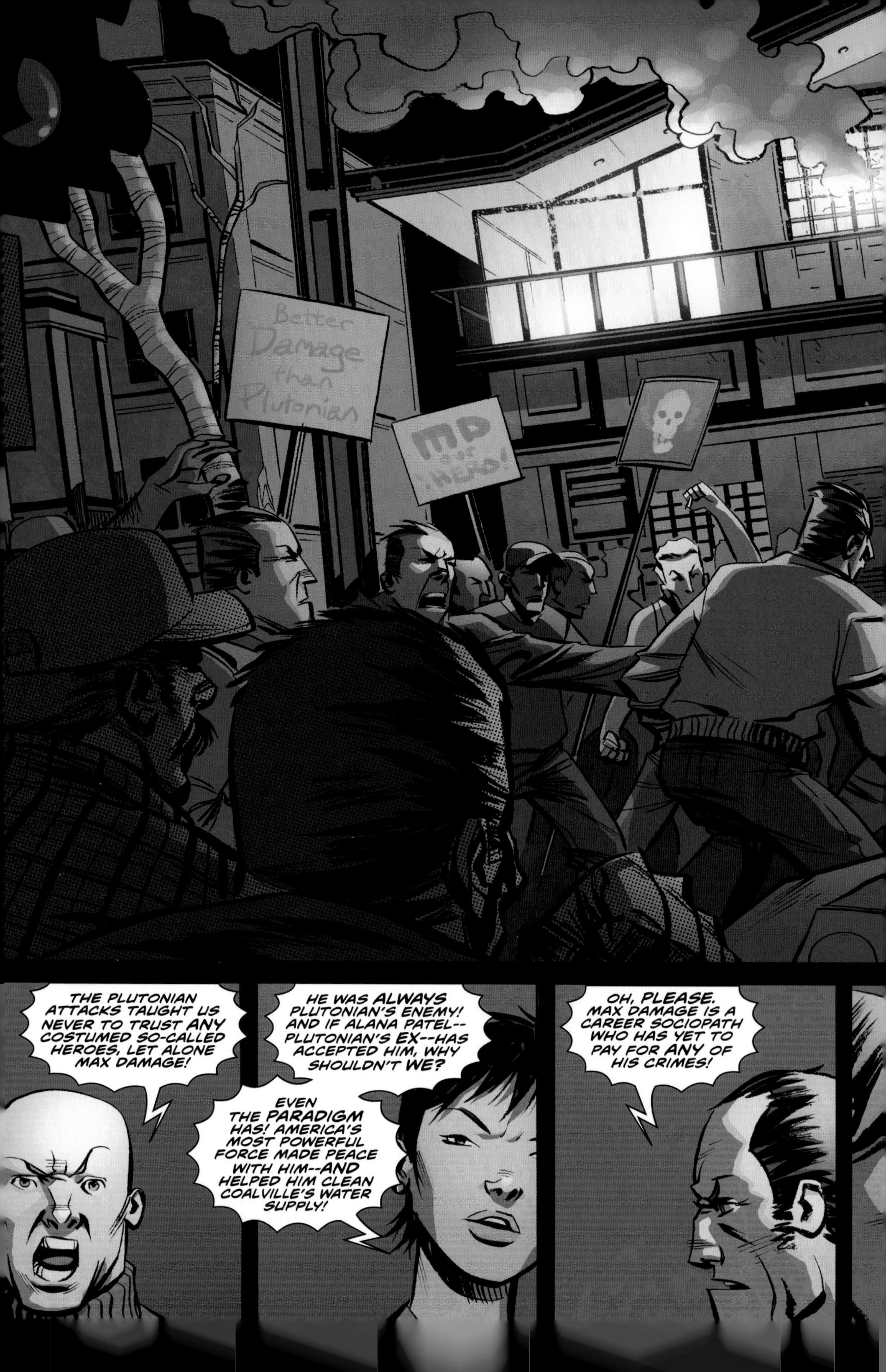
Better Damage than Plutonian
MD our HERO!
THE PLUTONIAN ATTACKS TAUGHT US NEVER TO TRUST ANY COSTUMED SO-CALLED HEROES, LET ALONE MAX DAMAGE!
HE WAS ALWAYS PLUTONIAN'S ENEMY! AND IF ALANA PATEL--PLUTONIAN'S EX--HAS ACCEPTED HIM, WHY SHOULDN'T WE?
EVEN THE PARADIGM HAS! AMERICA'S MOST POWERFUL FORCE MADE PEACE WITH HIM--AND HELPED HIM CLEAN COALVILLE'S WATER SUPPLY!
OH, PLEASE. MAX DAMAGE IS A CAREER SOCIOPATH WHO HAS YET TO PAY FOR ANY OF HIS CRIMES!

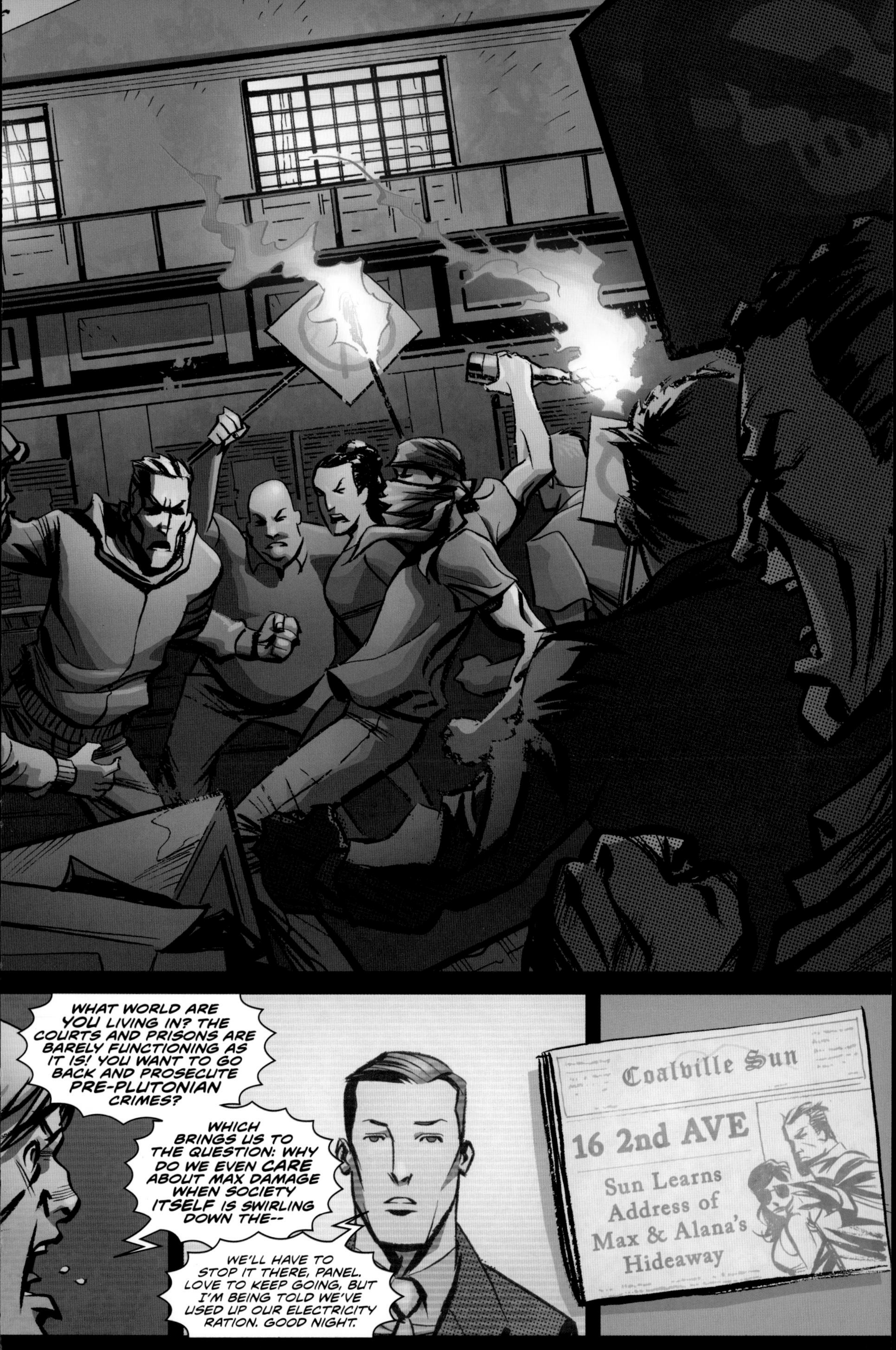
WHAT WORLD ARE YOU LIVING IN? THE COURTS AND PRISONS ARE BARELY FUNCTIONING AS IT IS! YOU WANT TO GO BACK AND PROSECUTE PRE-PLUTONIAN CRIMES?
WHICH BRINGS US TO THE QUESTION: WHY DO WE EVEN CARE ABOUT MAX DAMAGE WHEN SOCIETY ITSELF IS SWIRLING DOWN THE--
WE'LL HAVE TO STOP IT THERE, PANEL. LOVE TO KEEP GOING, BUT I'M BEING TOLD WE'VE USED UP OUR ELECTRICITY RATION. GOOD NIGHT.
Coalville Sun
16 2nd AVE
Sun Learns Address of Max & Alana's Hideaway

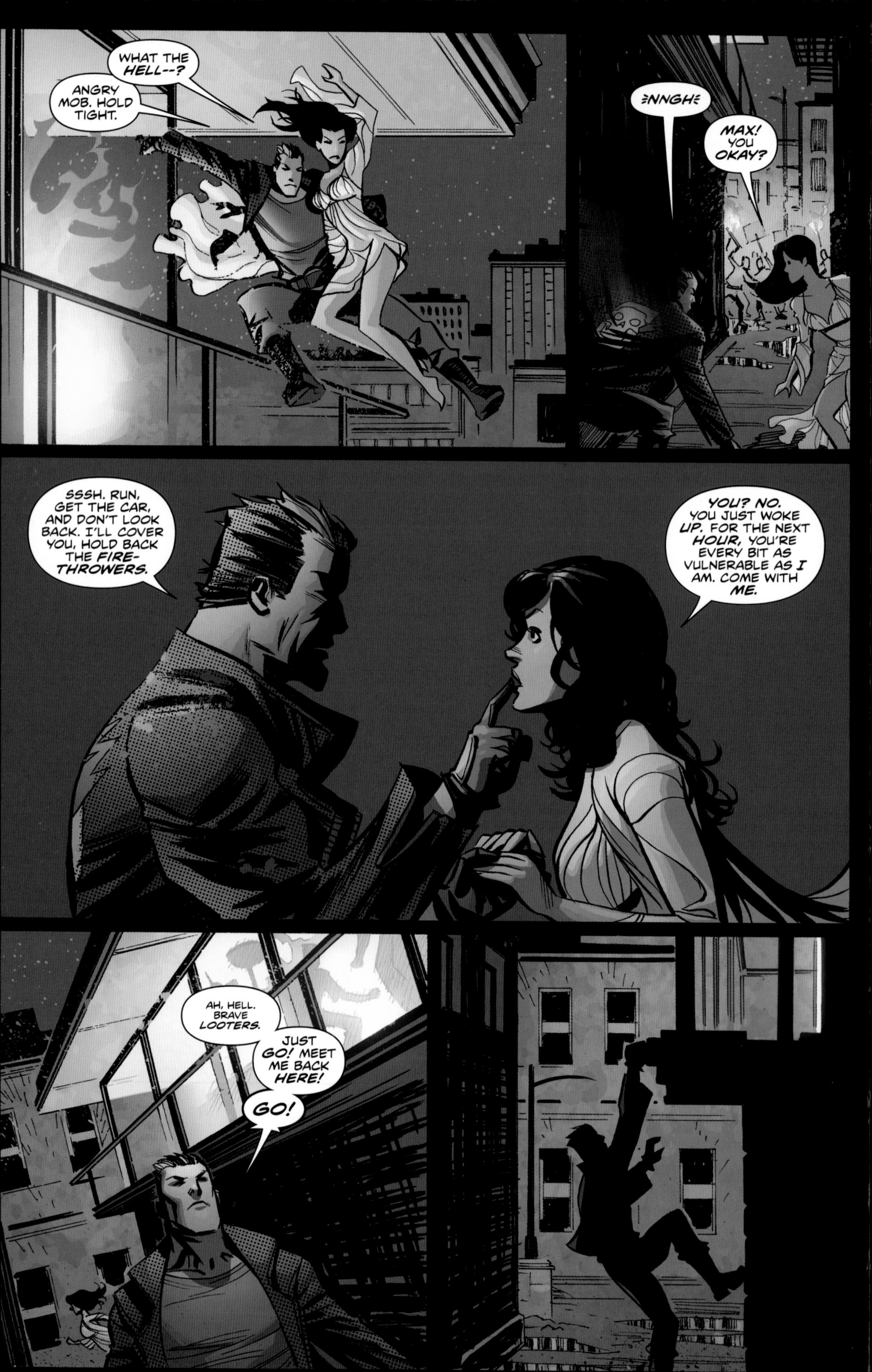
WHAT THE HELL--?
ANGRY MOB. HOLD TIGHT.
NNGH
MAX! YOU OKAY?
SSSH. RUN, GET THE CAR, AND DON'T LOOK BACK. I'LL COVER YOU, HOLD BACK THE FIRE-THROWERS.
YOU? NO. YOU JUST WOKE UP. FOR THE NEXT HOUR, YOU'RE EVERY BIT AS VULNERABLE AS I AM. COME WITH ME.
AH, HELL. BRAVE LOOTERS.
JUST GO! MEET ME BACK HERE!
GO!

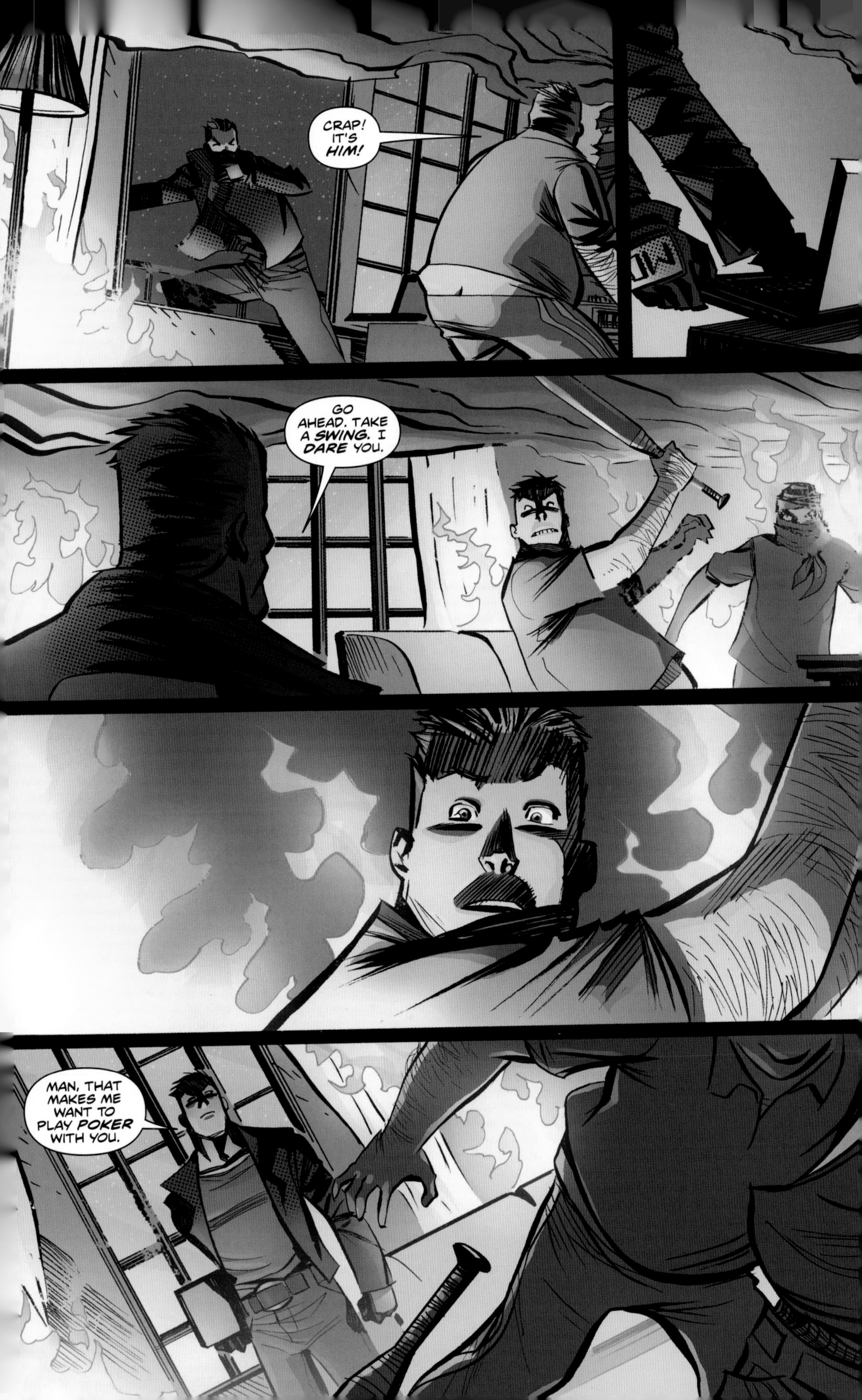
CRAP! IT'S *HIM!*
GO AHEAD. TAKE A *SWING.* I *DARE* YOU.
MAN, THAT MAKES ME WANT TO PLAY *POKER* WITH YOU.

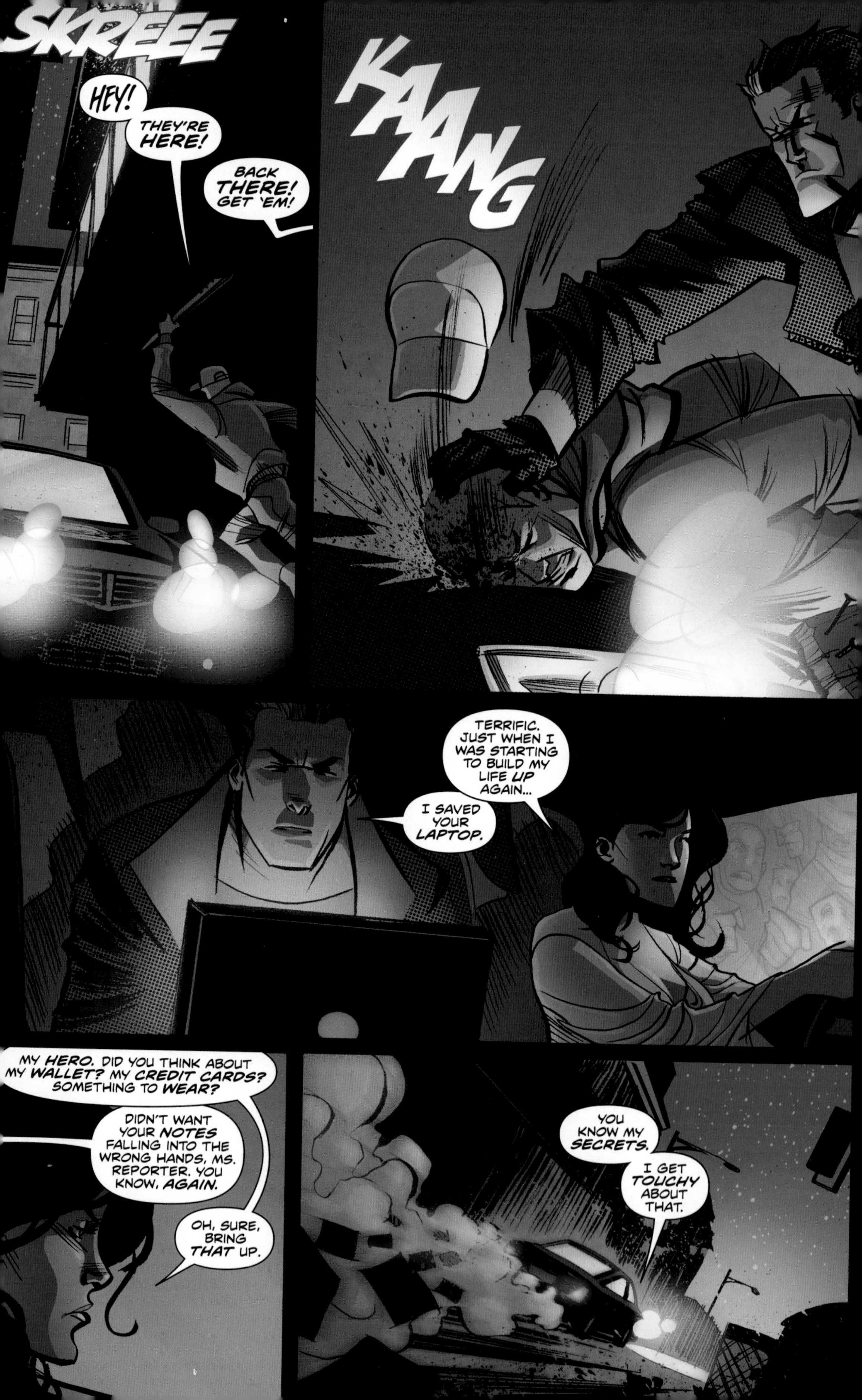
SKREEE
HEY!
THEY'RE HERE!
BACK THERE! GET 'EM!
KAANG
TERRIFIC. JUST WHEN I WAS STARTING TO BUILD MY LIFE UP AGAIN...
I SAVED YOUR LAPTOP.
MY HERO. DID YOU THINK ABOUT MY WALLET? MY CREDIT CARDS? SOMETHING TO WEAR?
DIDN'T WANT YOUR NOTES FALLING INTO THE WRONG HANDS, MS. REPORTER. YOU KNOW, AGAIN.
OH, SURE, BRING THAT UP.
YOU KNOW MY SECRETS.
I GET TOUCHY ABOUT THAT.

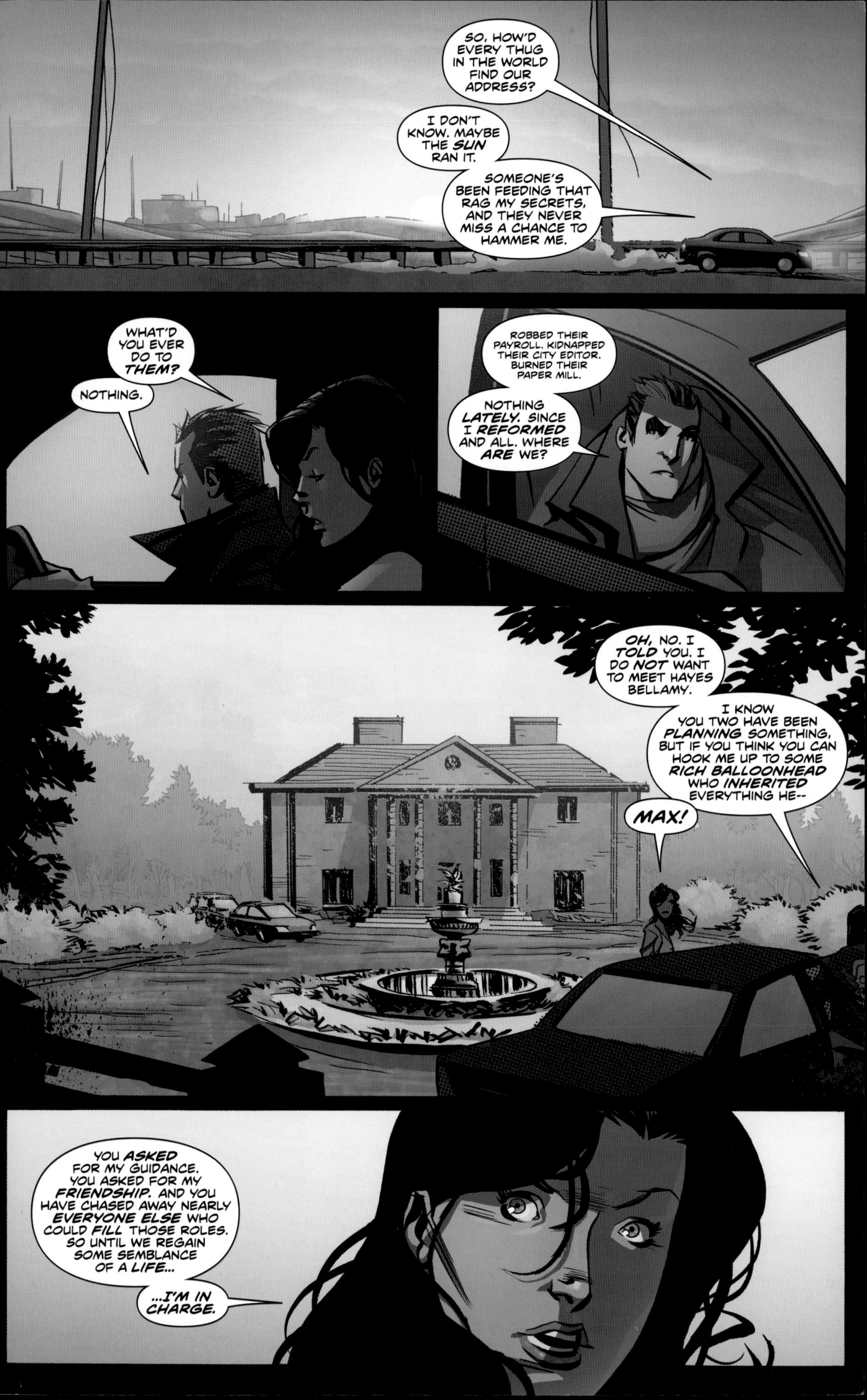
SO, HOW'D EVERY THUG IN THE WORLD FIND OUR ADDRESS?
I DON'T KNOW. MAYBE THE SUN RAN IT.
SOMEONE'S BEEN FEEDING THAT RAG MY SECRETS, AND THEY NEVER MISS A CHANCE TO HAMMER ME.
WHAT'D YOU EVER DO TO THEM?
NOTHING.
ROBBED THEIR PAYROLL. KIDNAPPED THEIR CITY EDITOR. BURNED THEIR PAPER MILL.
NOTHING LATELY. SINCE I REFORMED AND ALL. WHERE ARE WE?
OH, NO. I TOLD YOU. I DO NOT WANT TO MEET HAYES BELLAMY.
I KNOW YOU TWO HAVE BEEN PLANNING SOMETHING, BUT IF YOU THINK YOU CAN HOOK ME UP TO SOME RICH BALLOONHEAD WHO INHERITED EVERYTHING HE--
MAX!
YOU ASKED FOR MY GUIDANCE. YOU ASKED FOR MY FRIENDSHIP. AND YOU HAVE CHASED AWAY NEARLY EVERYONE ELSE WHO COULD FILL THOSE ROLES. SO UNTIL WE REGAIN SOME SEMBLANCE OF A LIFE...
...I'M IN CHARGE.

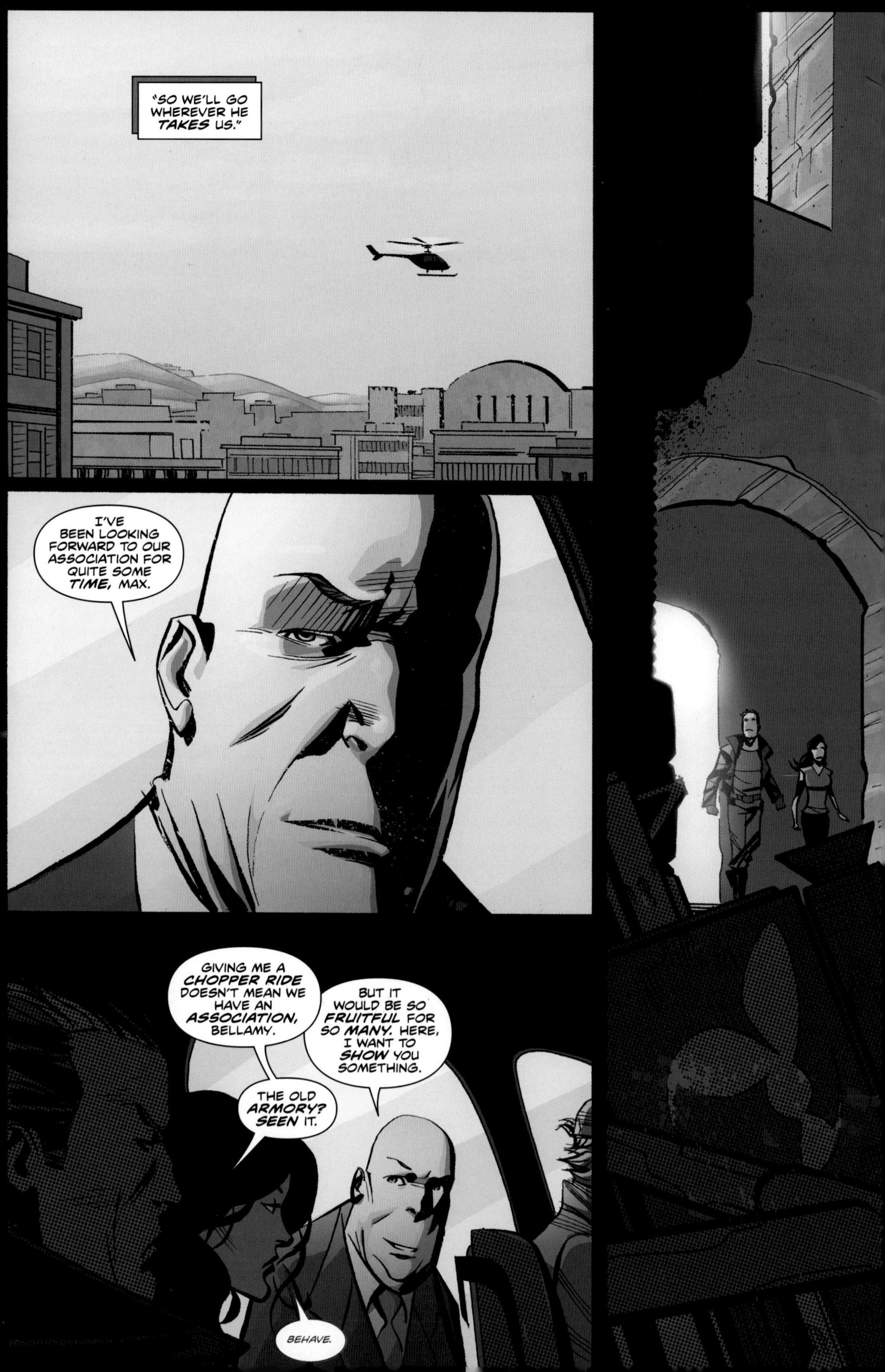
"SO WE'LL GO WHEREVER HE *TAKES* US."
I'VE BEEN LOOKING FORWARD TO OUR ASSOCIATION FOR QUITE SOME *TIME,* MAX.
GIVING ME A *CHOPPER RIDE* DOESN'T MEAN WE HAVE AN *ASSOCIATION,* BELLAMY.
BUT IT WOULD BE SO *FRUITFUL* FOR SO *MANY.* HERE, I WANT TO *SHOW* YOU SOMETHING.
THE OLD *ARMORY? SEEN* IT.
*BEHAVE.*

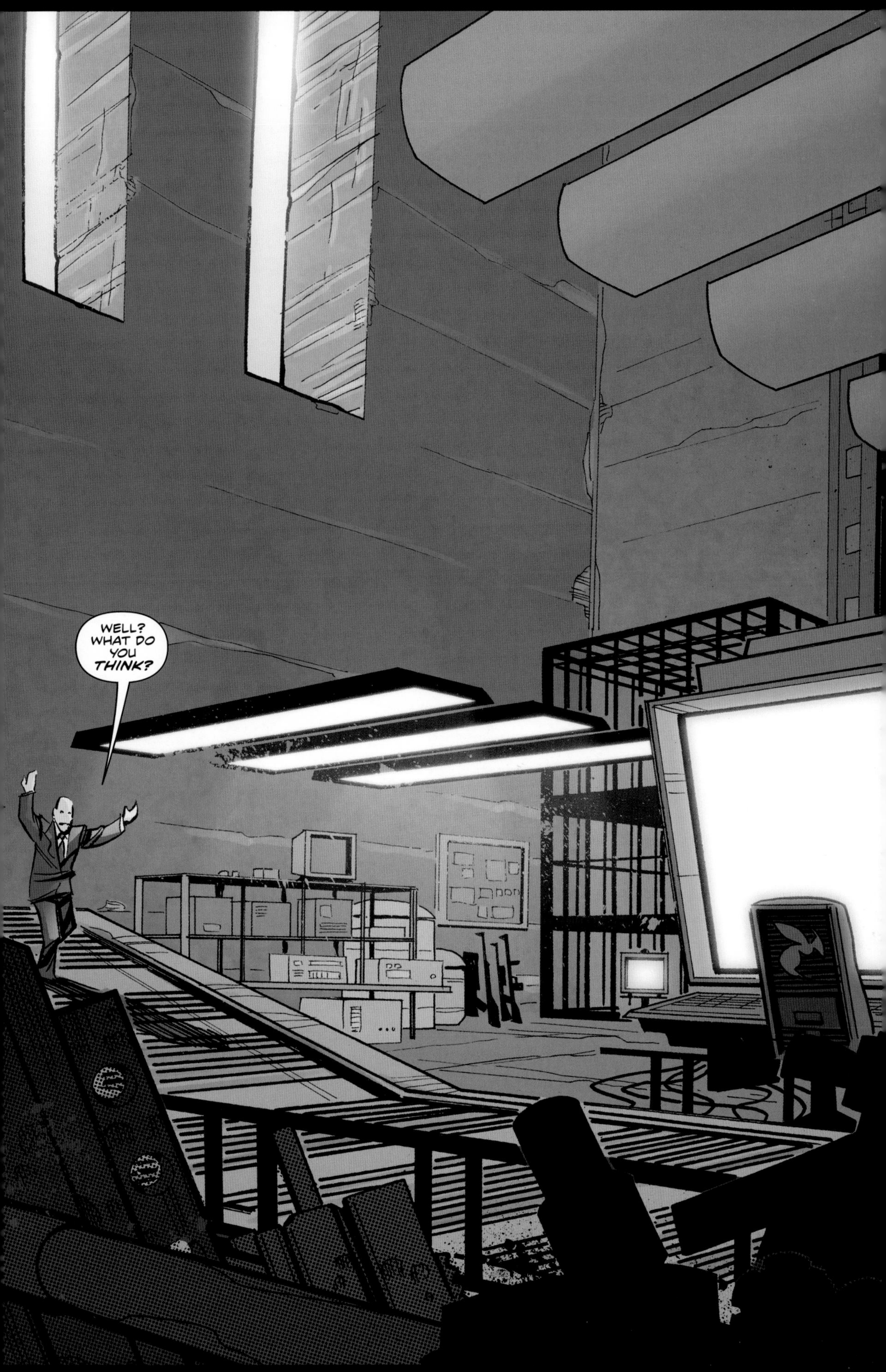
WELL? WHAT DO YOU *THINK?*

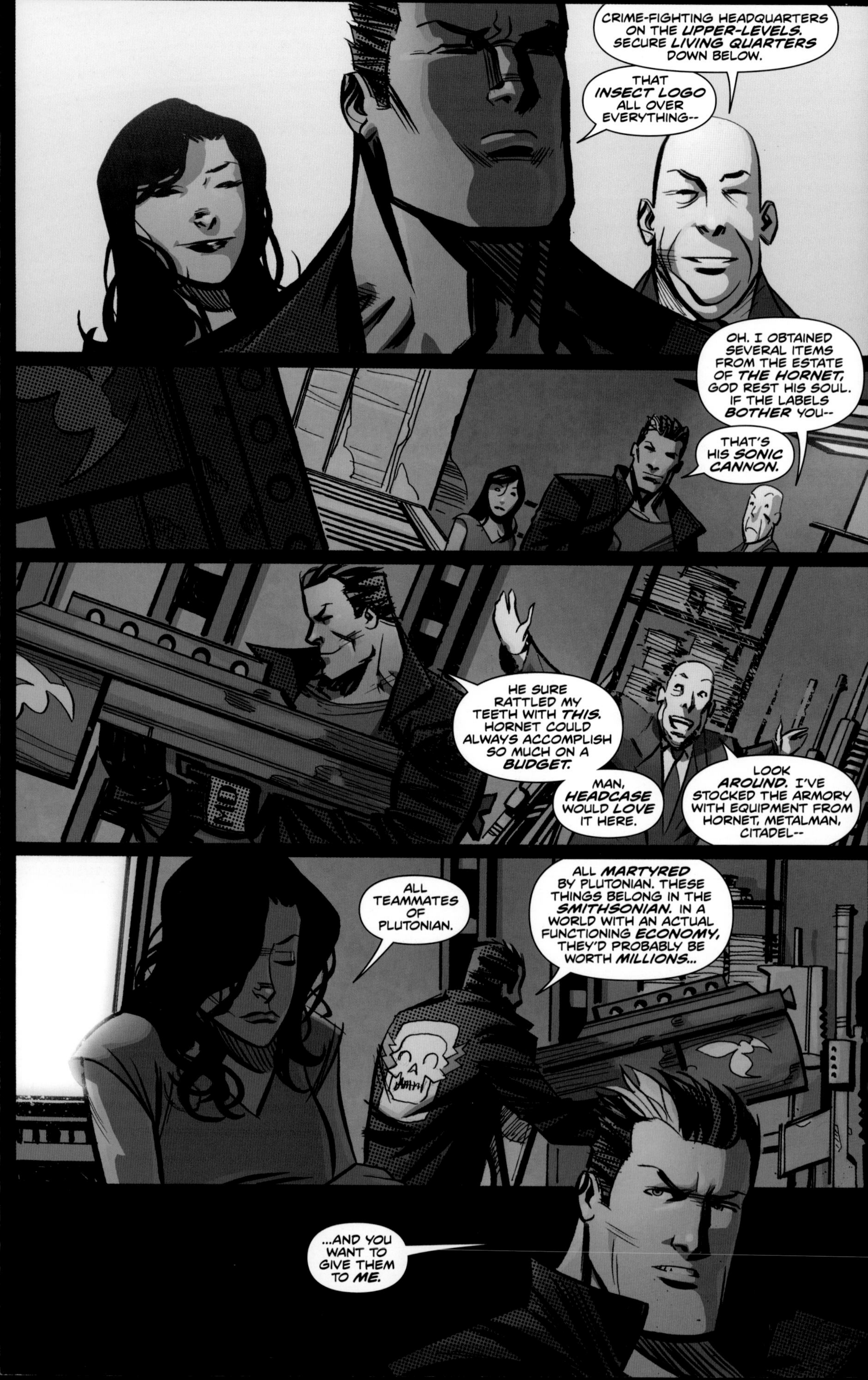
CRIME-FIGHTING HEADQUARTERS ON THE UPPER-LEVELS. SECURE LIVING QUARTERS DOWN BELOW.
THAT INSECT LOGO ALL OVER EVERYTHING--
OH. I OBTAINED SEVERAL ITEMS FROM THE ESTATE OF THE HORNET, GOD REST HIS SOUL. IF THE LABELS BOTHER YOU--
THAT'S HIS SONIC CANNON.
HE SURE RATTLED MY TEETH WITH THIS. HORNET COULD ALWAYS ACCOMPLISH SO MUCH ON A BUDGET.
MAN, HEADCASE WOULD LOVE IT HERE.
LOOK AROUND. I'VE STOCKED THE ARMORY WITH EQUIPMENT FROM HORNET, METALMAN, CITADEL--
ALL TEAMMATES OF PLUTONIAN.
ALL MARTYRED BY PLUTONIAN. THESE THINGS BELONG IN THE SMITHSONIAN. IN A WORLD WITH AN ACTUAL FUNCTIONING ECONOMY, THEY'D PROBABLY BE WORTH MILLIONS...
...AND YOU WANT TO GIVE THEM TO ME.

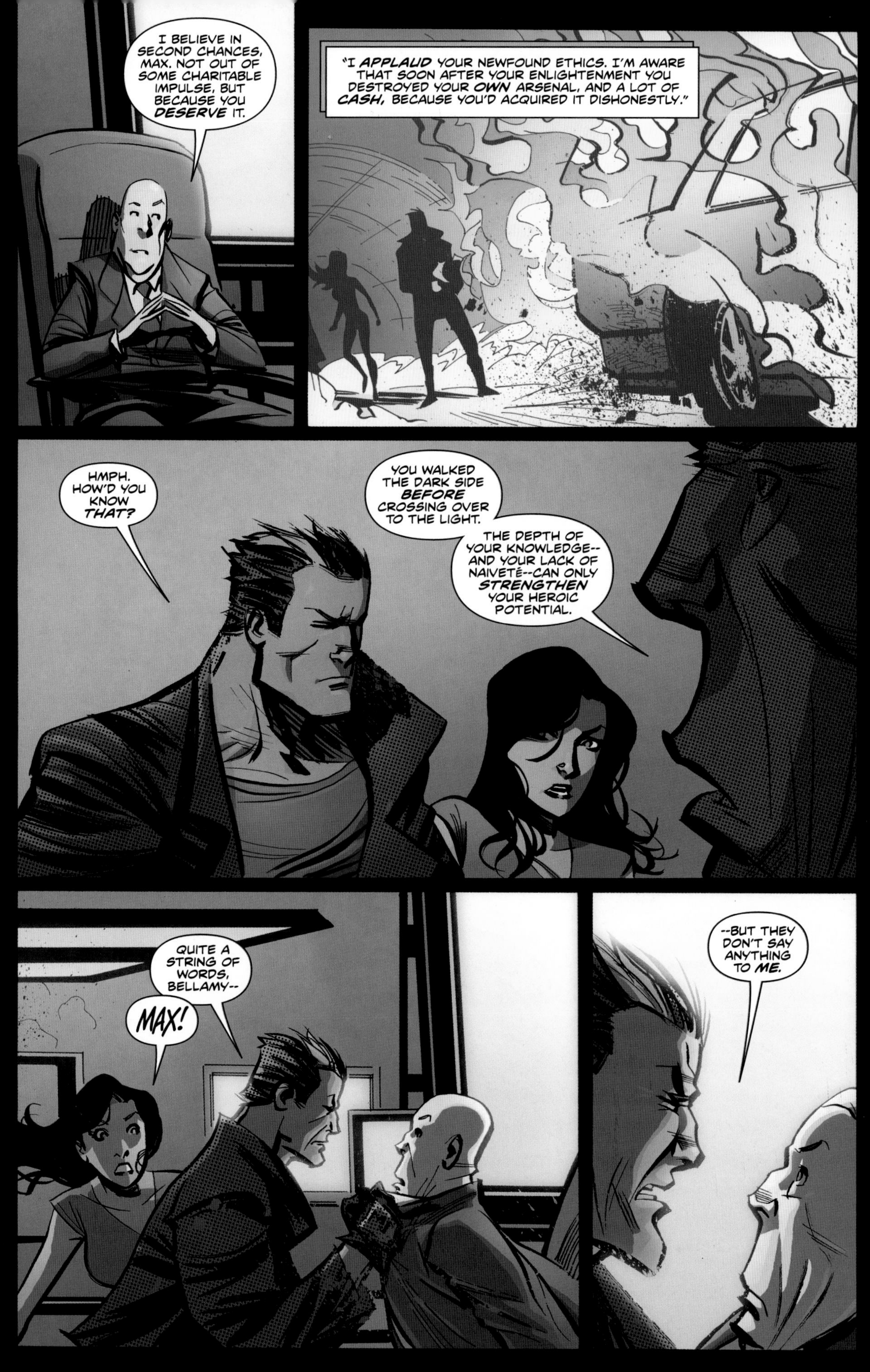
I BELIEVE IN SECOND CHANCES, MAX. NOT OUT OF SOME CHARITABLE IMPULSE, BUT BECAUSE YOU DESERVE IT.
"I APPLAUD YOUR NEWFOUND ETHICS. I'M AWARE THAT SOON AFTER YOUR ENLIGHTENMENT YOU DESTROYED YOUR OWN ARSENAL, AND A LOT OF CASH, BECAUSE YOU'D ACQUIRED IT DISHONESTLY."
HMPH. HOW'D YOU KNOW THAT?
YOU WALKED THE DARK SIDE BEFORE CROSSING OVER TO THE LIGHT.
THE DEPTH OF YOUR KNOWLEDGE--AND YOUR LACK OF NAIVETÉ--CAN ONLY STRENGTHEN YOUR HEROIC POTENTIAL.
QUITE A STRING OF WORDS, BELLAMY--
MAX!
--BUT THEY DON'T SAY ANYTHING TO ME.

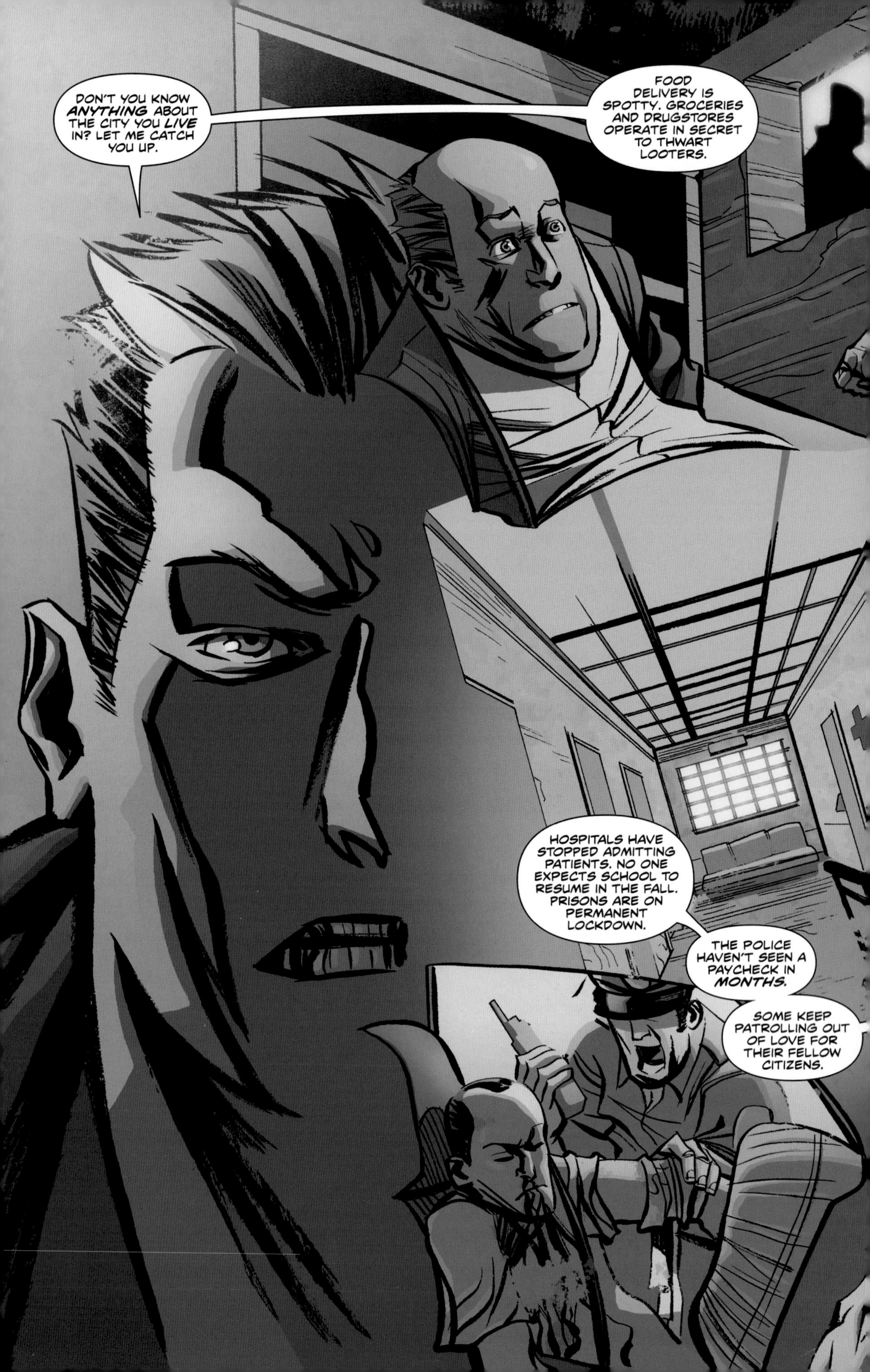
DON'T YOU KNOW *ANYTHING* ABOUT THE CITY YOU *LIVE* IN? LET ME CATCH YOU UP.
FOOD DELIVERY IS SPOTTY. GROCERIES AND DRUGSTORES OPERATE IN SECRET TO THWART LOOTERS.
HOSPITALS HAVE STOPPED ADMITTING PATIENTS. NO ONE EXPECTS SCHOOL TO RESUME IN THE FALL. PRISONS ARE ON PERMANENT LOCKDOWN.
THE POLICE HAVEN'T SEEN A PAYCHECK IN *MONTHS.*
SOME KEEP PATROLLING OUT OF LOVE FOR THEIR FELLOW CITIZENS.

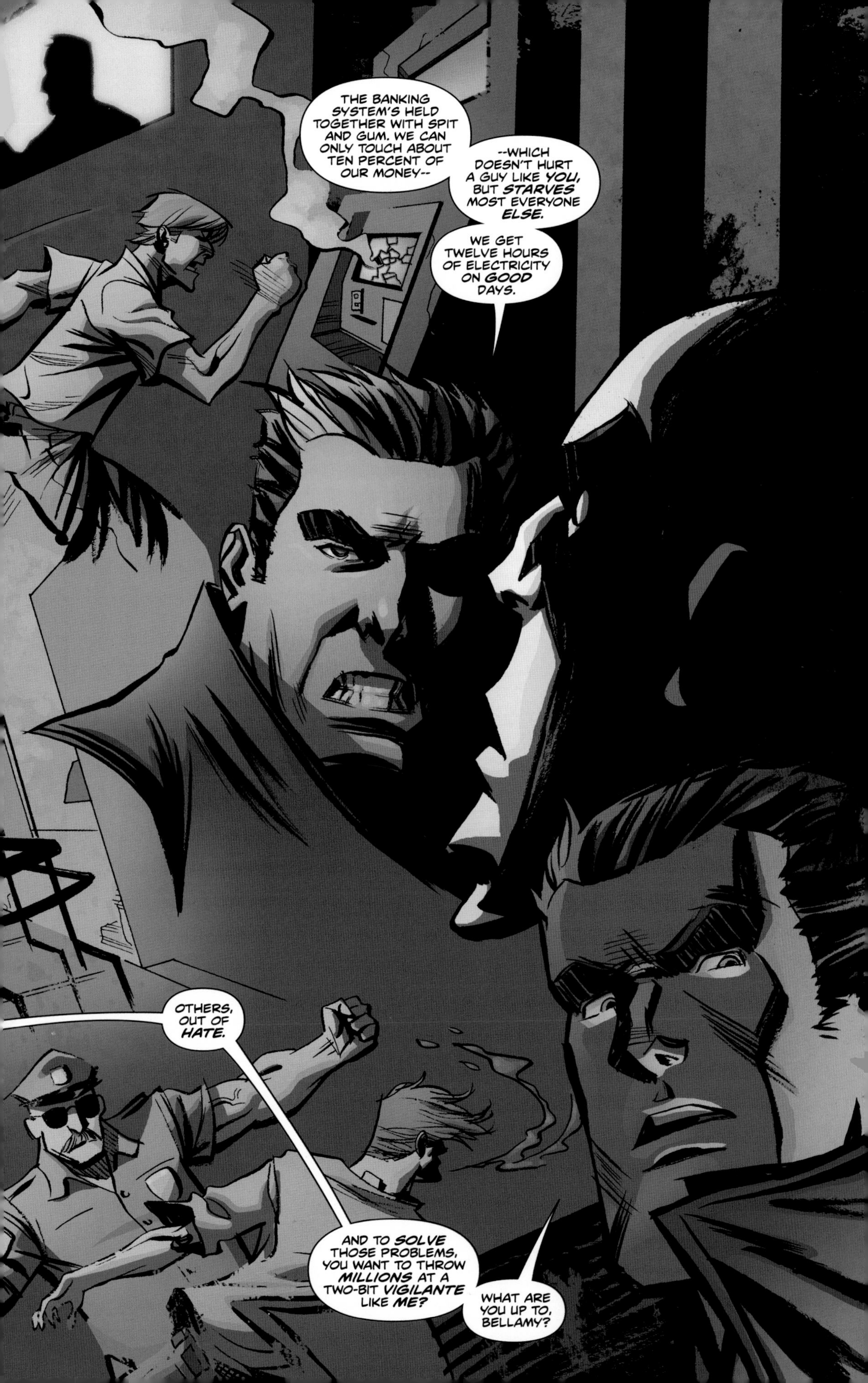
THE BANKING SYSTEM'S HELD TOGETHER WITH SPIT AND GUM. WE CAN ONLY TOUCH ABOUT TEN PERCENT OF OUR MONEY--
--WHICH DOESN'T HURT A GUY LIKE *YOU*, BUT *STARVES* MOST EVERYONE *ELSE*.
WE GET TWELVE HOURS OF ELECTRICITY ON *GOOD* DAYS.
OTHERS, OUT OF *HATE*.
AND TO *SOLVE* THOSE PROBLEMS, YOU WANT TO THROW *MILLIONS* AT A TWO-BIT *VIGILANTE* LIKE *ME*?
WHAT ARE YOU UP TO, BELLAMY?

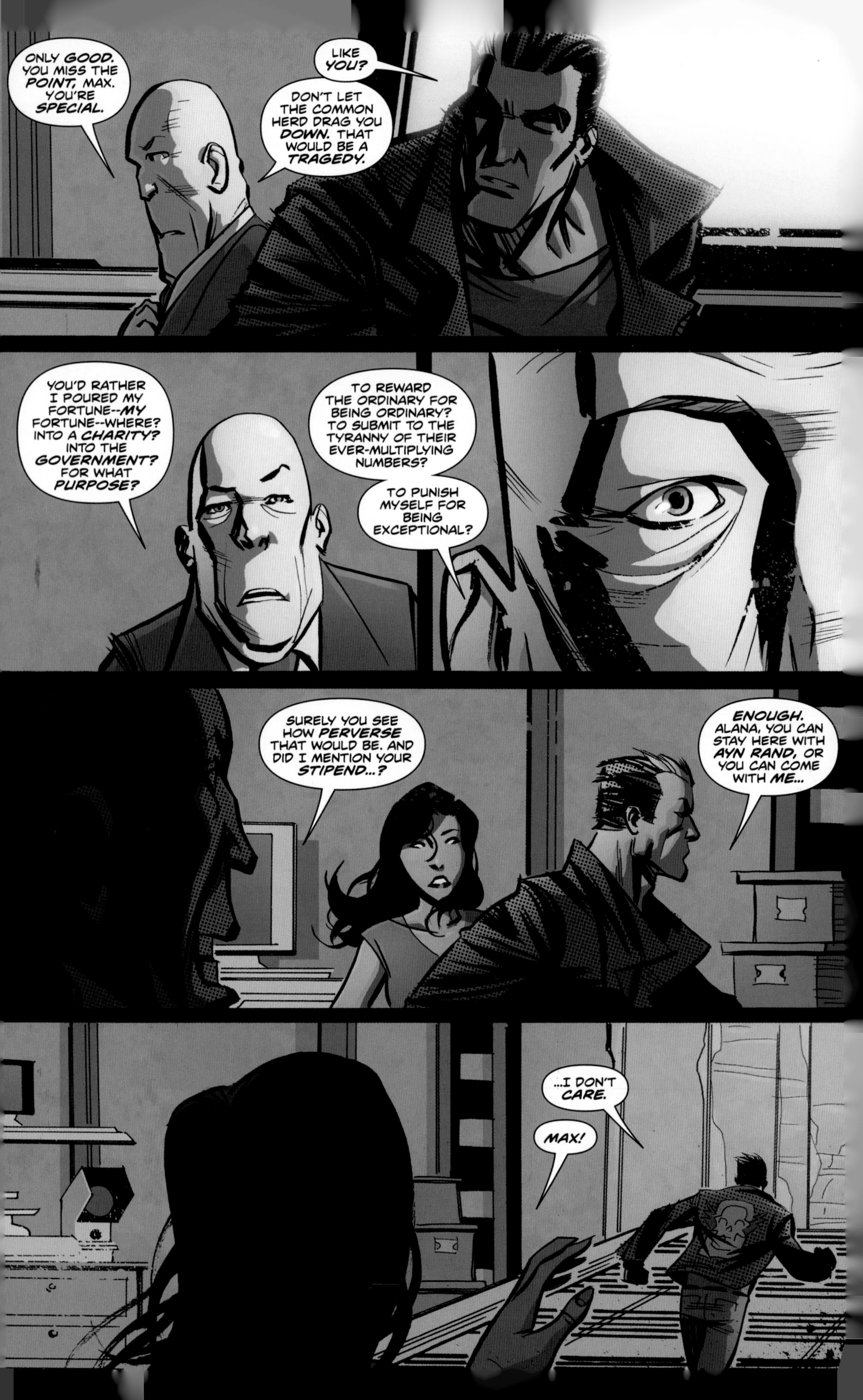
ONLY GOOD. YOU MISS THE POINT, MAX. YOU'RE SPECIAL.
LIKE YOU?
DON'T LET THE COMMON HERD DRAG YOU DOWN. THAT WOULD BE A TRAGEDY.
YOU'D RATHER I POURED MY FORTUNE--MY FORTUNE--WHERE? INTO A CHARITY? INTO THE GOVERNMENT? FOR WHAT PURPOSE?
TO REWARD THE ORDINARY FOR BEING ORDINARY? TO SUBMIT TO THE TYRANNY OF THEIR EVER-MULTIPLYING NUMBERS?
TO PUNISH MYSELF FOR BEING EXCEPTIONAL?
SURELY YOU SEE HOW PERVERSE THAT WOULD BE. AND DID I MENTION YOUR STIPEND...?
ENOUGH. ALANA, YOU CAN STAY HERE WITH AYN RAND, OR YOU CAN COME WITH ME...
...I DON'T CARE.
MAX!

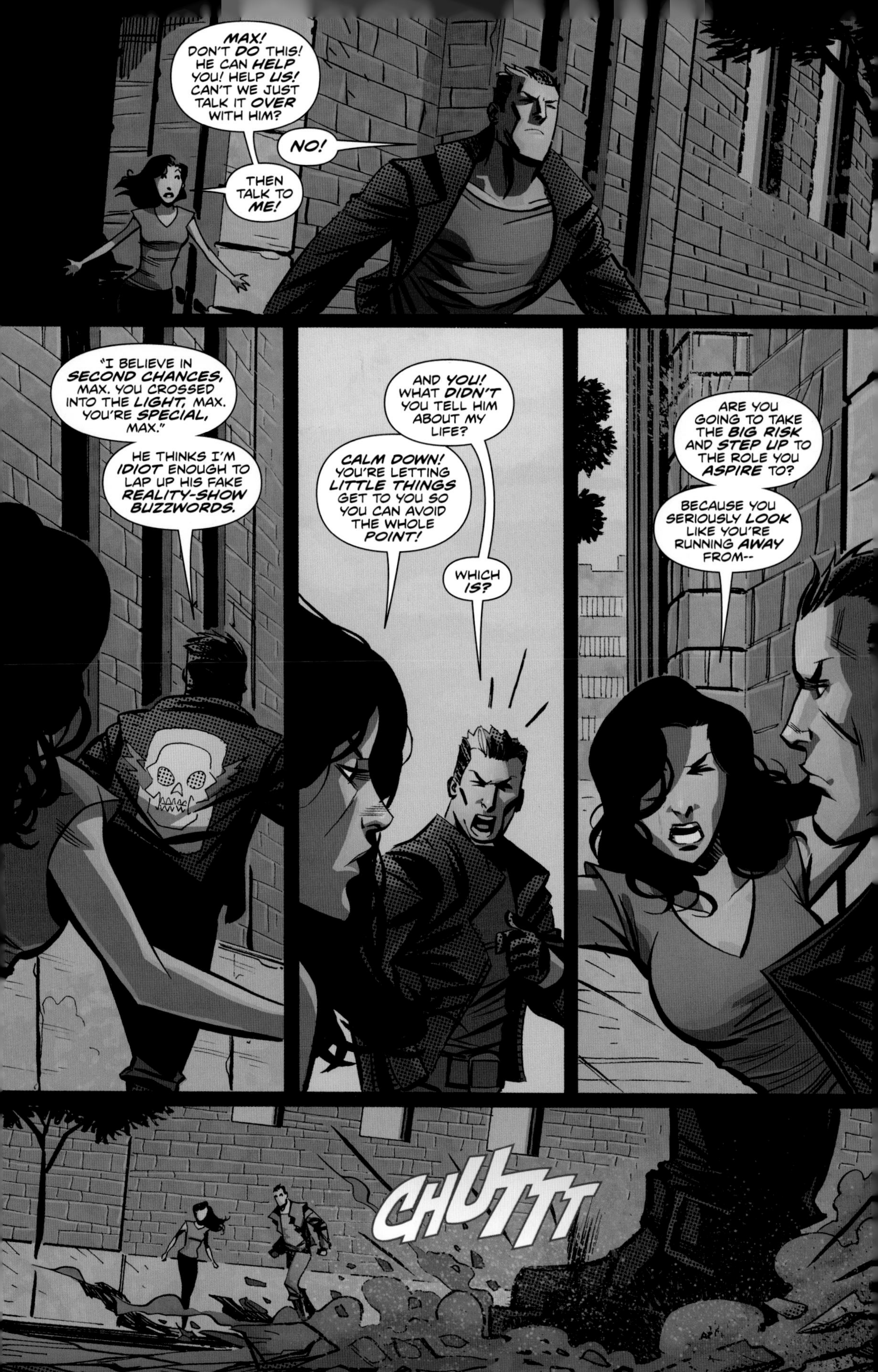
MAX! DON'T DO THIS! HE CAN HELP YOU! HELP US! CAN'T WE JUST TALK IT OVER WITH HIM?
NO!
THEN TALK TO ME!
"I BELIEVE IN SECOND CHANCES, MAX. YOU CROSSED INTO THE LIGHT, MAX. YOU'RE SPECIAL, MAX."
HE THINKS I'M IDIOT ENOUGH TO LAP UP HIS FAKE REALITY-SHOW BUZZWORDS.
AND YOU! WHAT DIDN'T YOU TELL HIM ABOUT MY LIFE?
CALM DOWN! YOU'RE LETTING LITTLE THINGS GET TO YOU SO YOU CAN AVOID THE WHOLE POINT!
WHICH IS?
ARE YOU GOING TO TAKE THE BIG RISK AND STEP UP TO THE ROLE YOU ASPIRE TO?
BECAUSE YOU SERIOUSLY LOOK LIKE YOU'RE RUNNING AWAY FROM--
CHUTTT

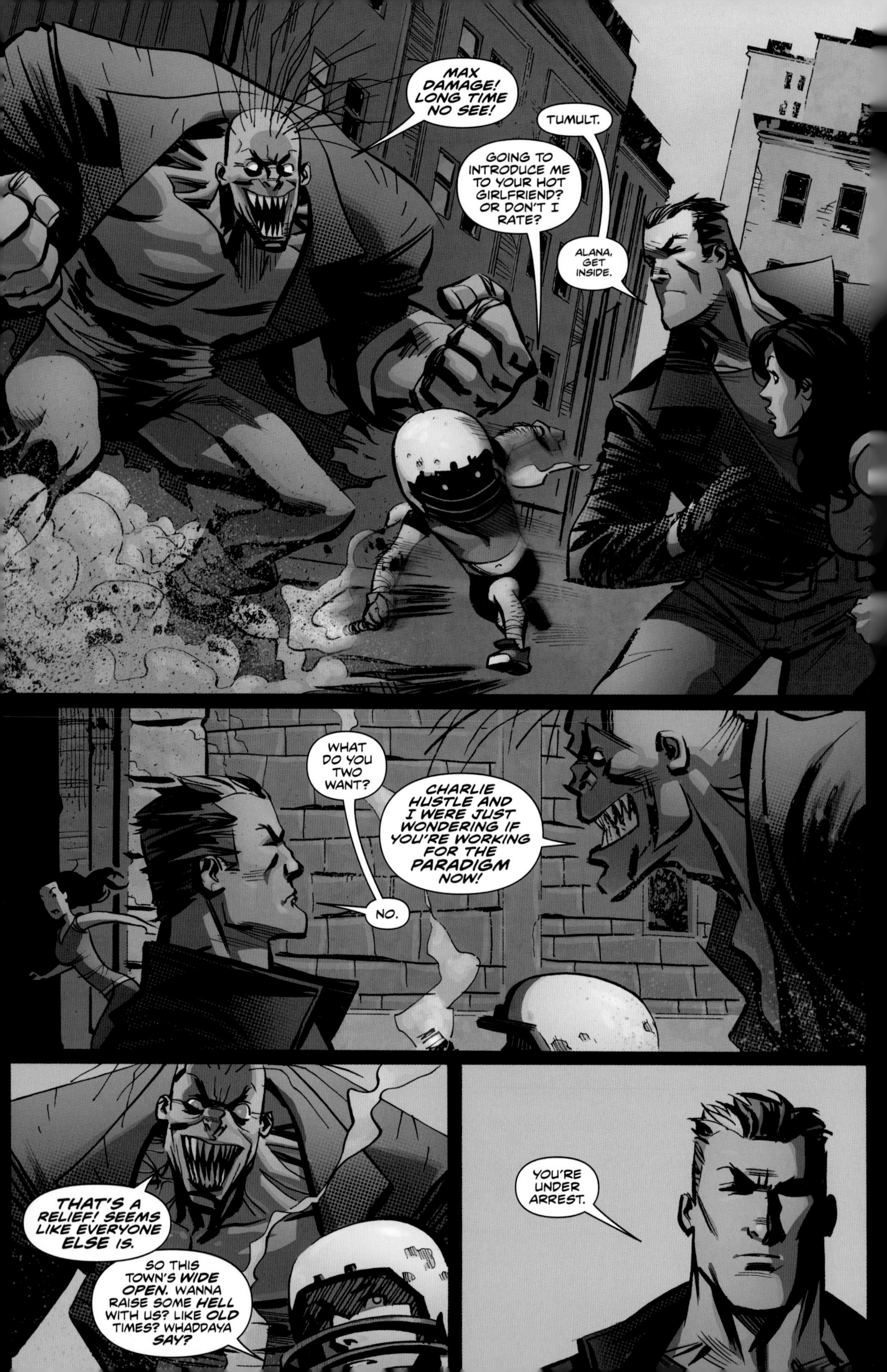
MAX DAMAGE! LONG TIME NO SEE!
TUMULT.
GOING TO INTRODUCE ME TO YOUR HOT GIRLFRIEND? OR DON'T I RATE?
ALANA, GET INSIDE.
WHAT DO YOU TWO WANT?
CHARLIE HUSTLE AND I WERE JUST WONDERING IF YOU'RE WORKING FOR THE PARADIGM NOW!
NO.
THAT'S A RELIEF! SEEMS LIKE EVERYONE ELSE IS.
SO THIS TOWN'S WIDE OPEN. WANNA RAISE SOME HELL WITH US? LIKE OLD TIMES? WHADDAYA SAY?
YOU'RE UNDER ARREST.

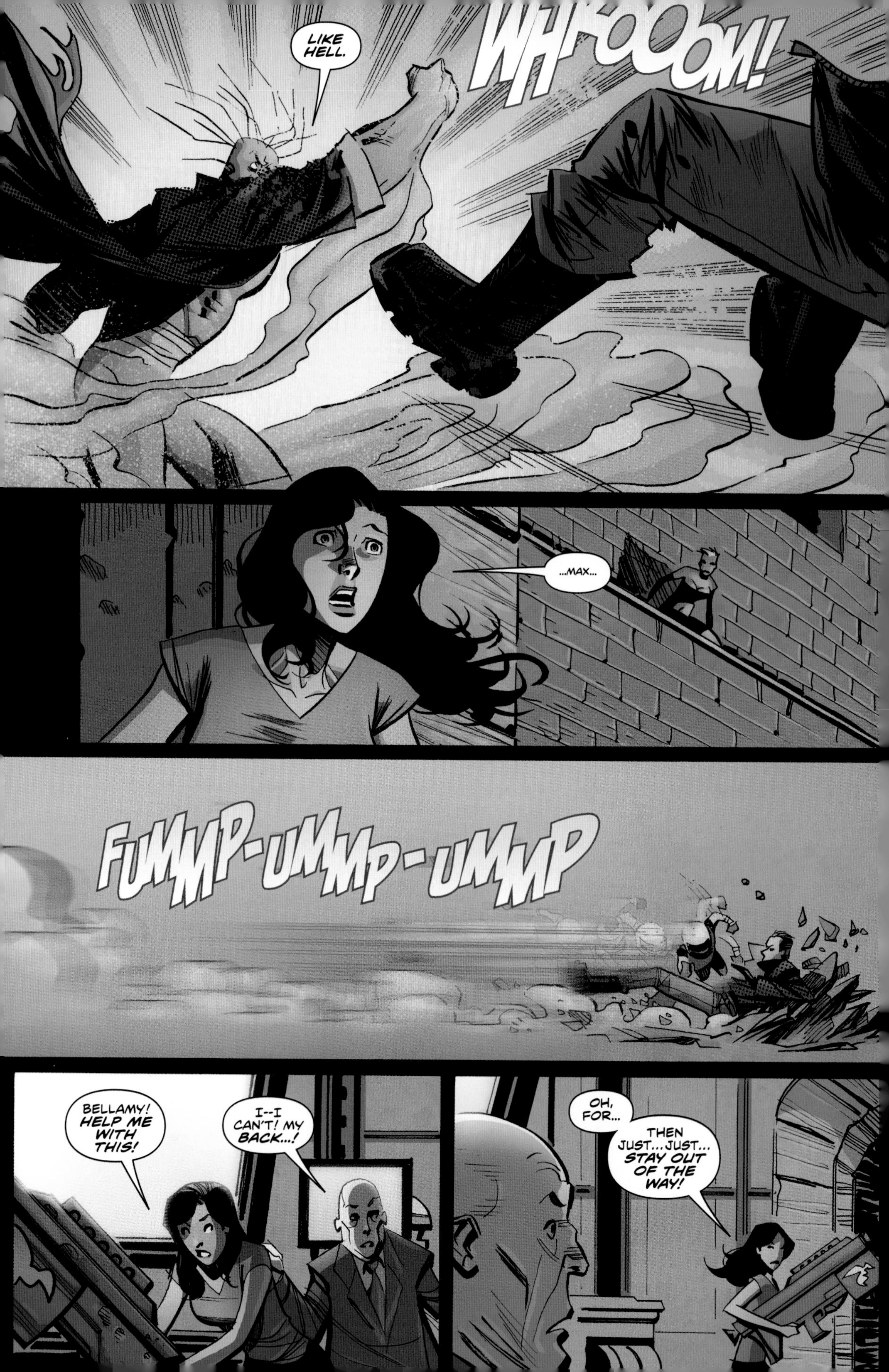
LIKE HELL.
WHOOOOM!
...MAX...
FUMMP-UMMP-UMMP
BELLAMY! HELP ME WITH THIS!
I--I CAN'T! MY BACK...!
OH, FOR...
THEN JUST... JUST... STAY OUT OF THE WAY!

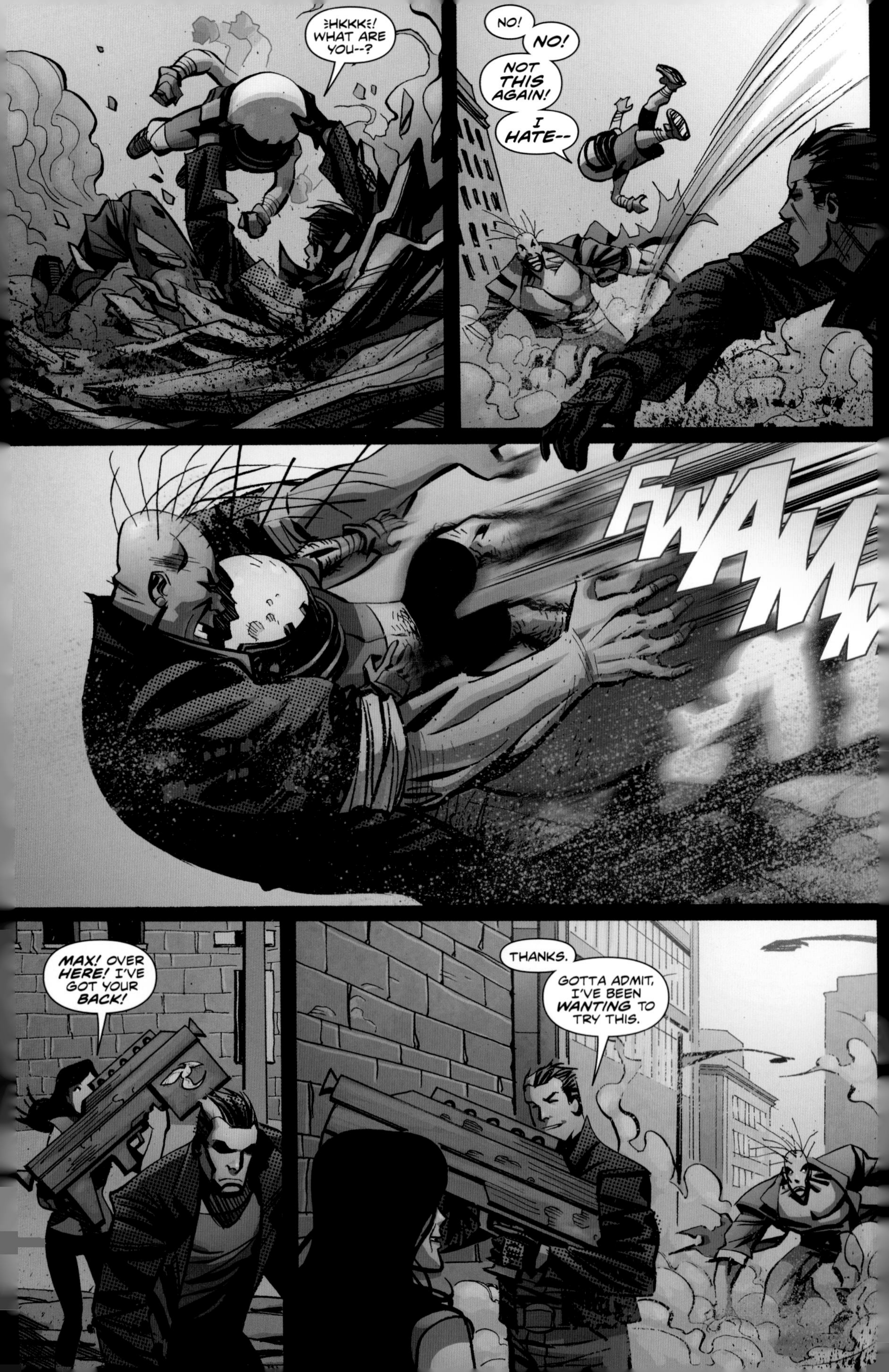
EHKKK! WHAT ARE YOU--?
NO!
NO!
NOT THIS AGAIN!
I HATE--
FWAM
MAX! OVER HERE! I'VE GOT YOUR BACK!
THANKS.
GOTTA ADMIT, I'VE BEEN WANTING TO TRY THIS.

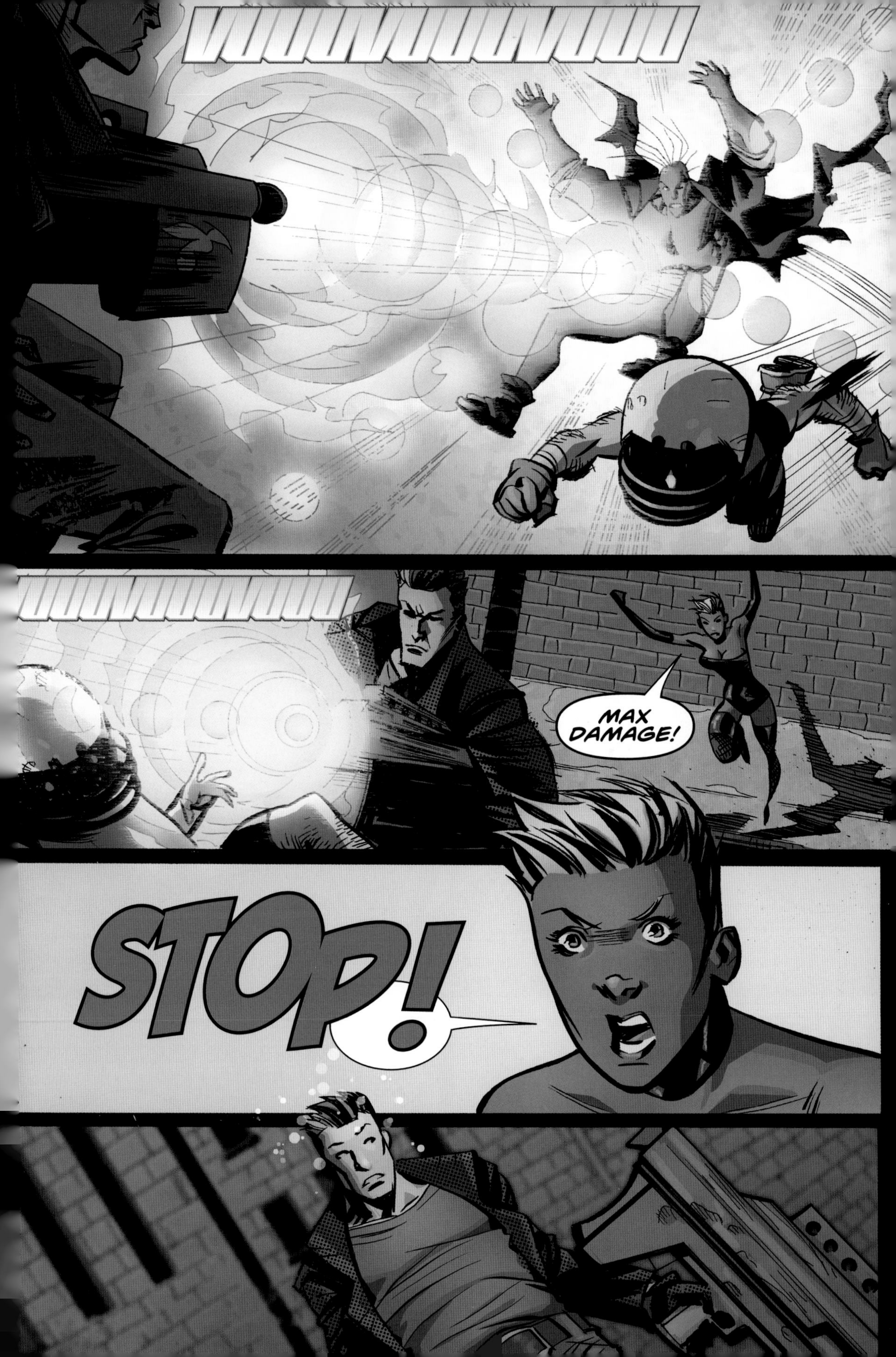
MAX DAMAGE!
STOP!

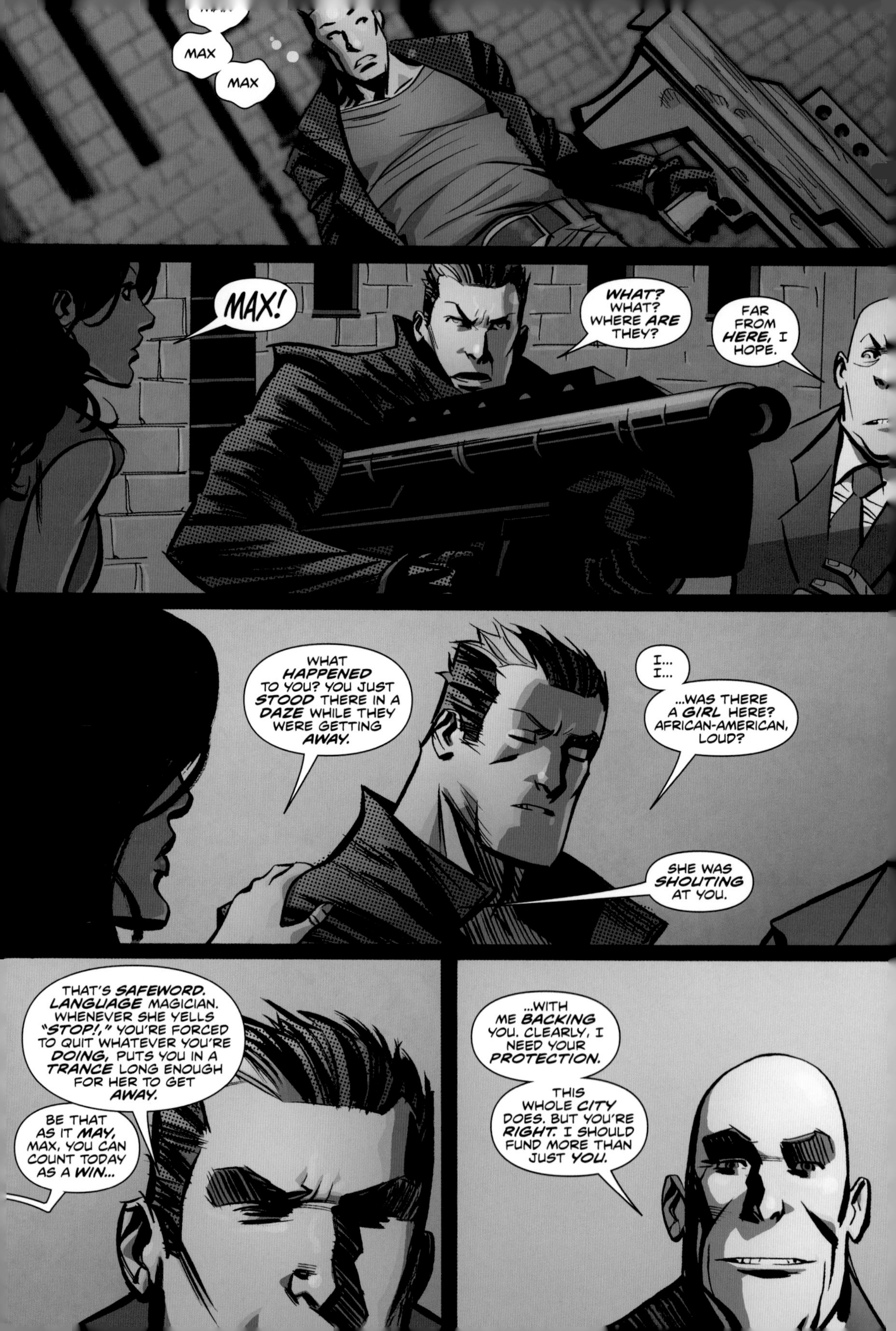
MAX
MAX
MAX!
WHAT? WHAT? WHERE ARE THEY?
FAR FROM HERE, I HOPE.
WHAT HAPPENED TO YOU? YOU JUST STOOD THERE IN A DAZE WHILE THEY WERE GETTING AWAY.
I... I...
...WAS THERE A GIRL HERE? AFRICAN-AMERICAN, LOUD?
SHE WAS SHOUTING AT YOU.
THAT'S SAFEWORD. LANGUAGE MAGICIAN. WHENEVER SHE YELLS "STOP!," YOU'RE FORCED TO QUIT WHATEVER YOU'RE DOING, PUTS YOU IN A TRANCE LONG ENOUGH FOR HER TO GET AWAY.
BE THAT AS IT MAY, MAX, YOU CAN COUNT TODAY AS A WIN...
...WITH ME BACKING YOU. CLEARLY, I NEED YOUR PROTECTION.
THIS WHOLE CITY DOES. BUT YOU'RE RIGHT. I SHOULD FUND MORE THAN JUST YOU.

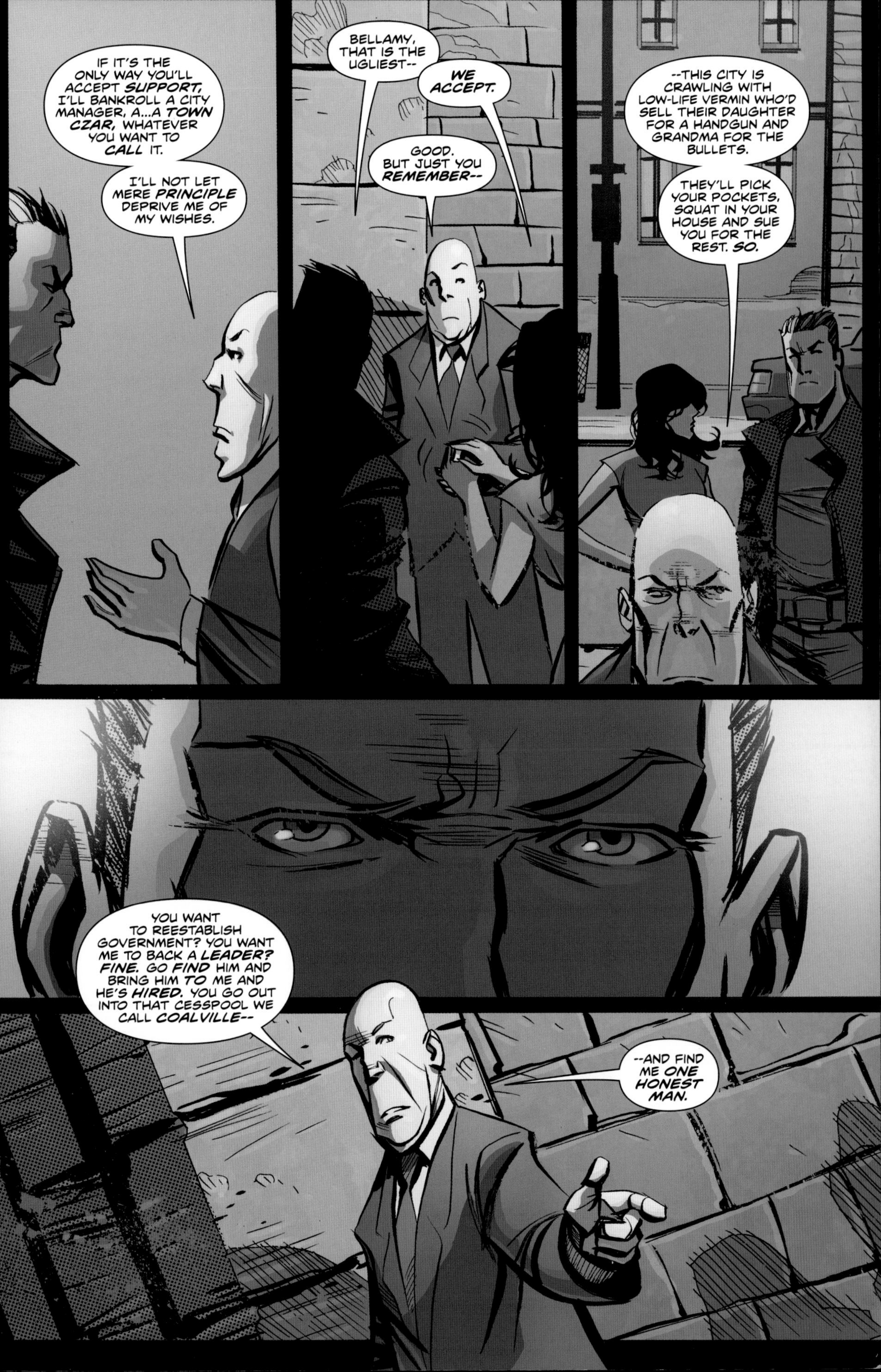
IF IT'S THE ONLY WAY YOU'LL ACCEPT SUPPORT, I'LL BANKROLL A CITY MANAGER, A...A TOWN CZAR, WHATEVER YOU WANT TO CALL IT.
I'LL NOT LET MERE PRINCIPLE DEPRIVE ME OF MY WISHES.
BELLAMY, THAT IS THE UGLIEST--
WE ACCEPT.
GOOD. BUT JUST YOU REMEMBER--
--THIS CITY IS CRAWLING WITH LOW-LIFE VERMIN WHO'D SELL THEIR DAUGHTER FOR A HANDGUN AND GRANDMA FOR THE BULLETS.
THEY'LL PICK YOUR POCKETS, SQUAT IN YOUR HOUSE AND SUE YOU FOR THE REST. SO.
YOU WANT TO REESTABLISH GOVERNMENT? YOU WANT ME TO BACK A LEADER? FINE. GO FIND HIM AND BRING HIM TO ME AND HE'S HIRED. YOU GO OUT INTO THAT CESSPOOL WE CALL COALVILLE--
--AND FIND ME ONE HONEST MAN.

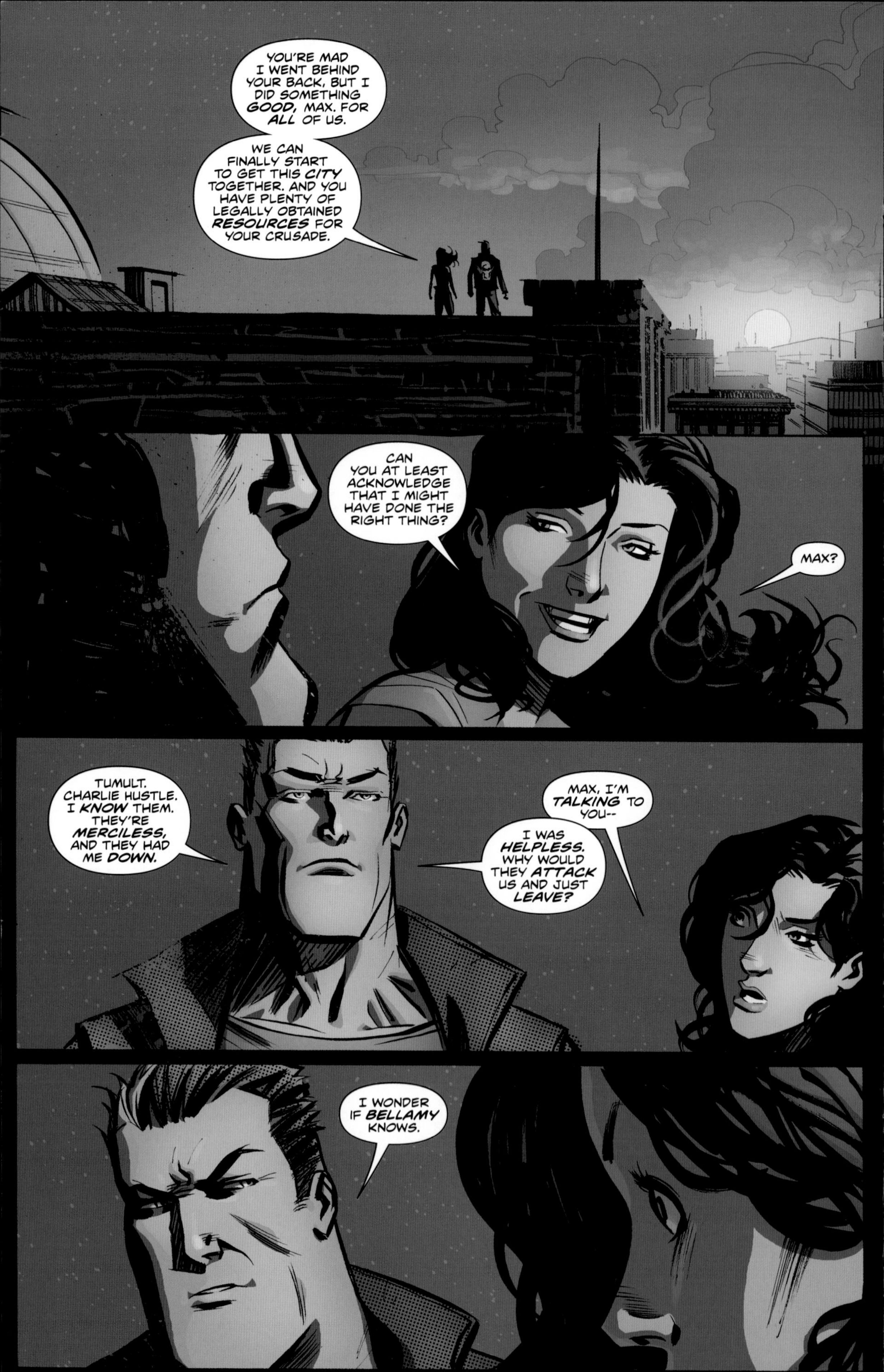
YOU'RE MAD I WENT BEHIND YOUR BACK, BUT I DID SOMETHING GOOD, MAX. FOR ALL OF US.
WE CAN FINALLY START TO GET THIS CITY TOGETHER. AND YOU HAVE PLENTY OF LEGALLY OBTAINED RESOURCES FOR YOUR CRUSADE.
CAN YOU AT LEAST ACKNOWLEDGE THAT I MIGHT HAVE DONE THE RIGHT THING?
MAX?
TUMULT. CHARLIE HUSTLE. I KNOW THEM. THEY'RE MERCILESS, AND THEY HAD ME DOWN.
MAX, I'M TALKING TO YOU--
I WAS HELPLESS. WHY WOULD THEY ATTACK US AND JUST LEAVE?
I WONDER IF BELLAMY KNOWS.

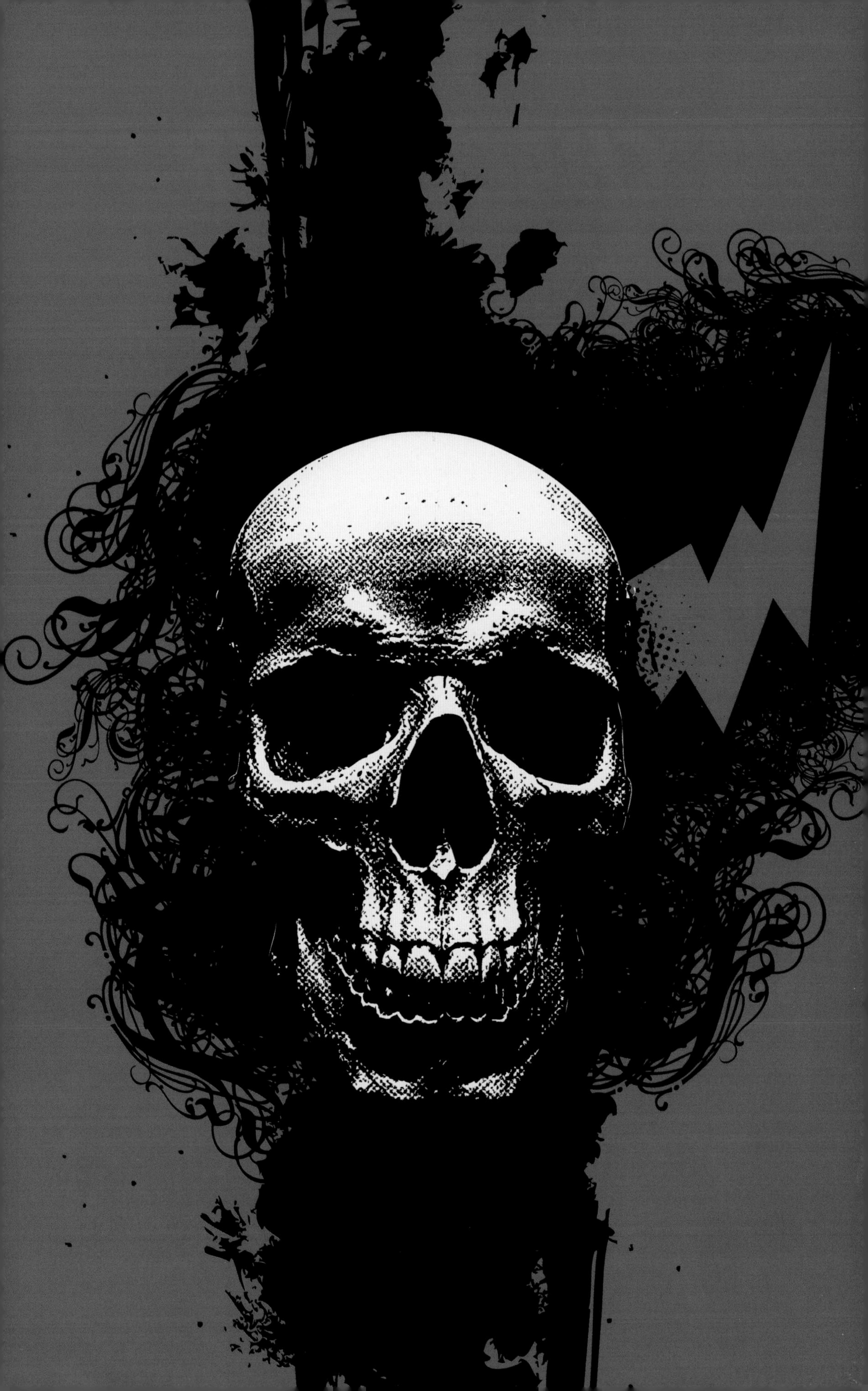

# CHAPTER 18

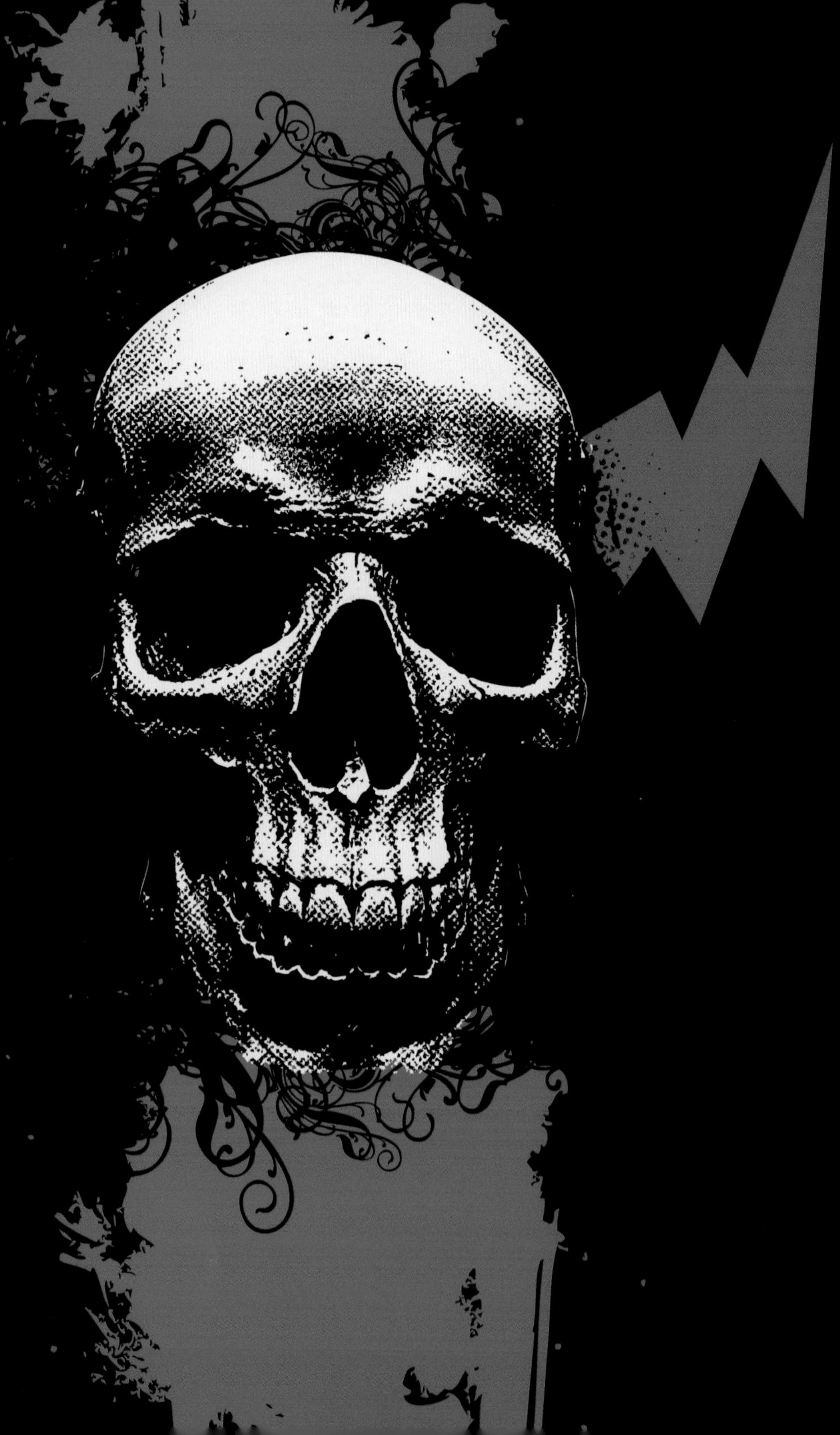

KURRASH

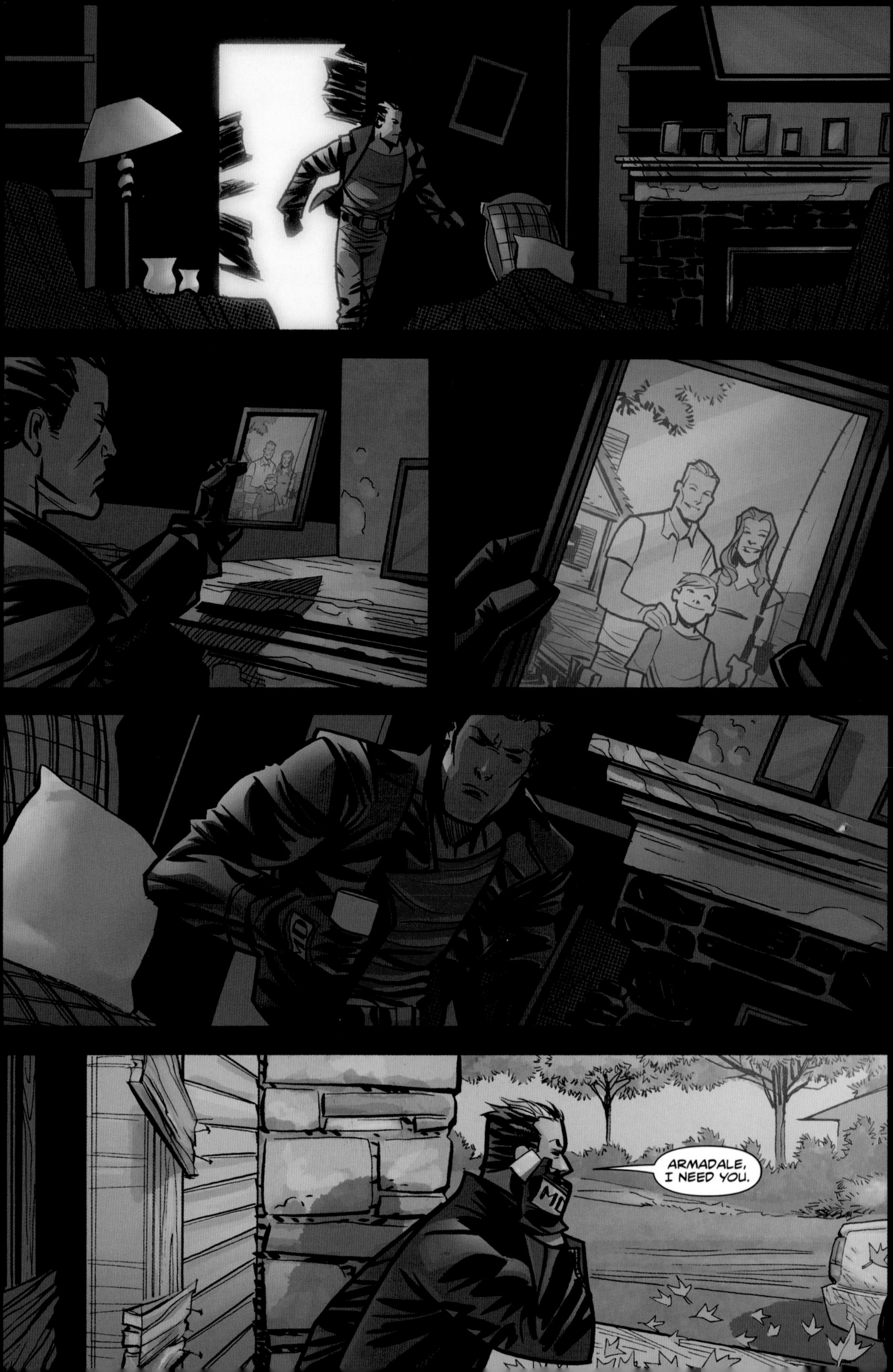
ARMADALE, I NEED YOU.

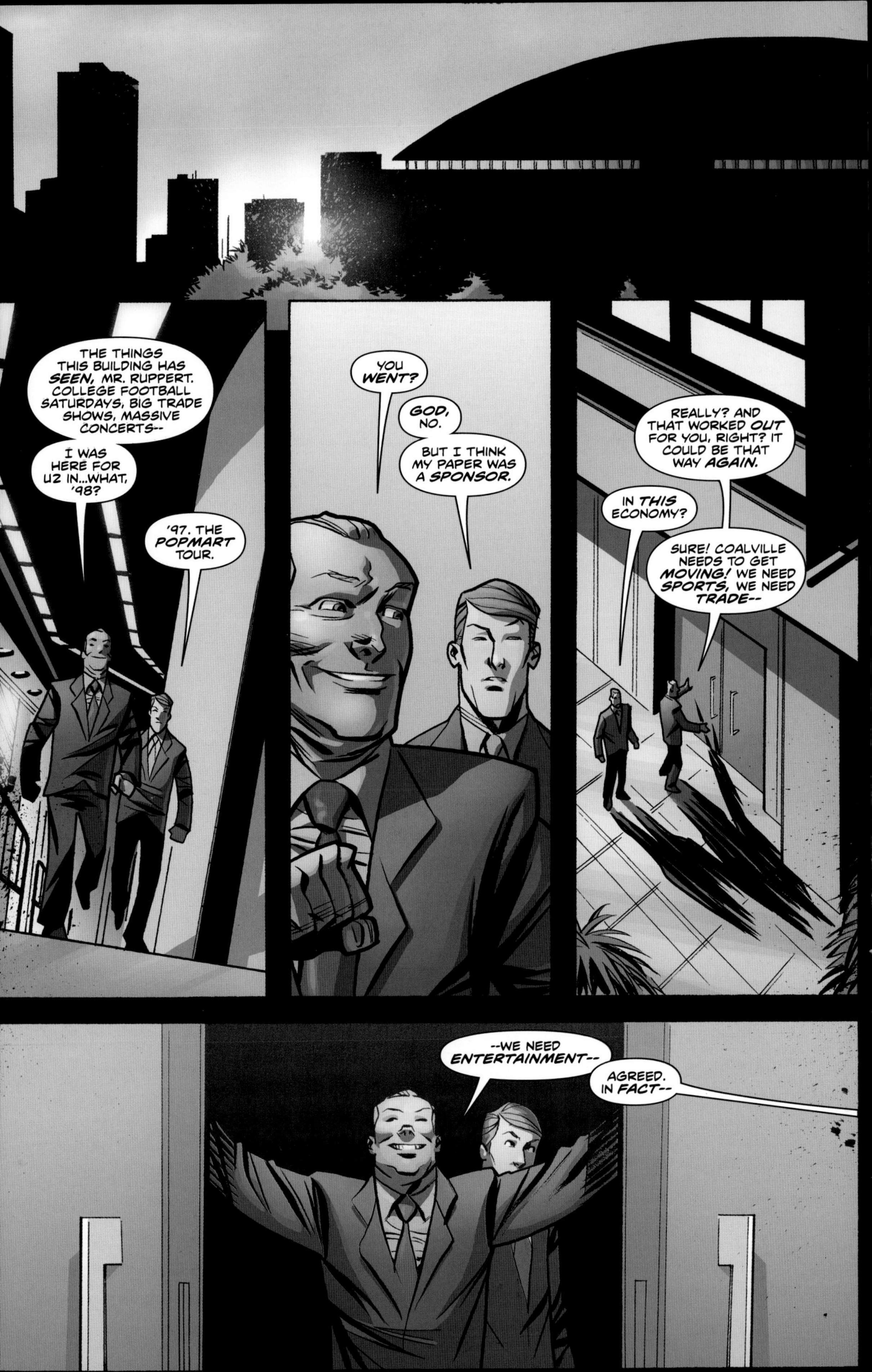
THE THINGS THIS BUILDING HAS SEEN, MR. RUPPERT. COLLEGE FOOTBALL SATURDAYS, BIG TRADE SHOWS, MASSIVE CONCERTS--
I WAS HERE FOR U2 IN...WHAT, '98?
'97. THE POPMART TOUR.
YOU WENT?
GOD, NO.
BUT I THINK MY PAPER WAS A SPONSOR.
REALLY? AND THAT WORKED OUT FOR YOU, RIGHT? IT COULD BE THAT WAY AGAIN.
IN THIS ECONOMY?
SURE! COALVILLE NEEDS TO GET MOVING! WE NEED SPORTS, WE NEED TRADE--
--WE NEED ENTERTAINMENT--
AGREED. IN FACT--

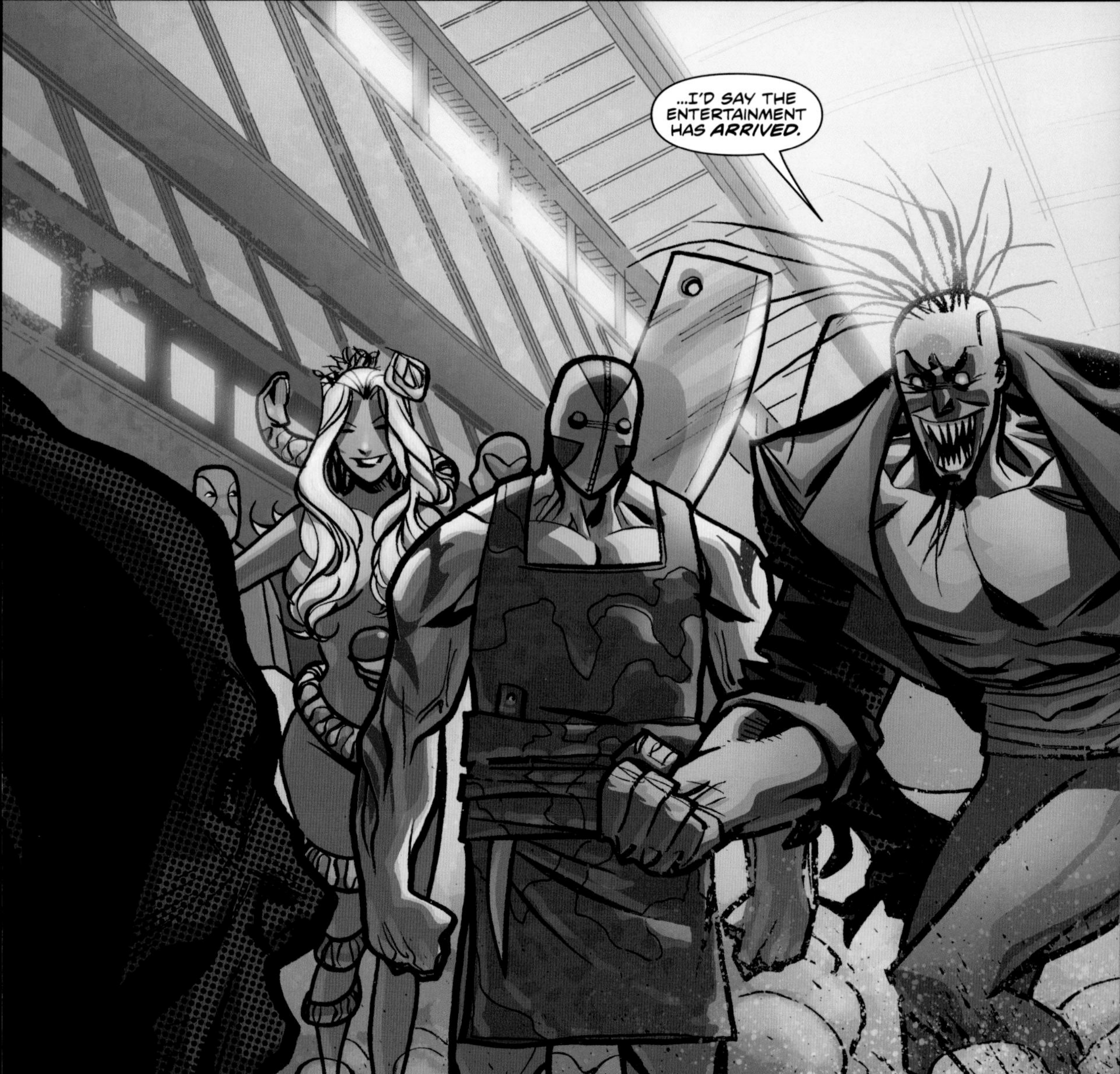
...I'D SAY THE ENTERTAINMENT HAS ARRIVED.

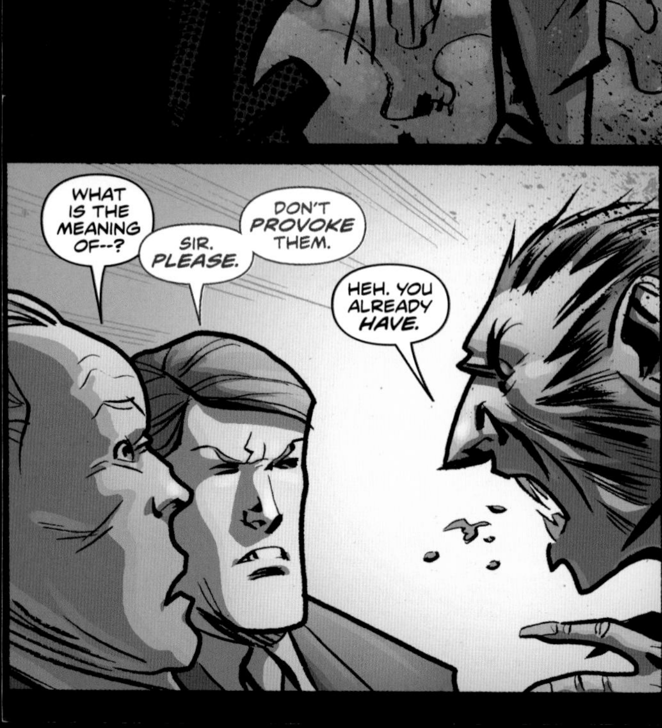
WHAT IS THE MEANING OF--?
SIR. PLEASE.
DON'T PROVOKE THEM.
HEH. YOU ALREADY HAVE.

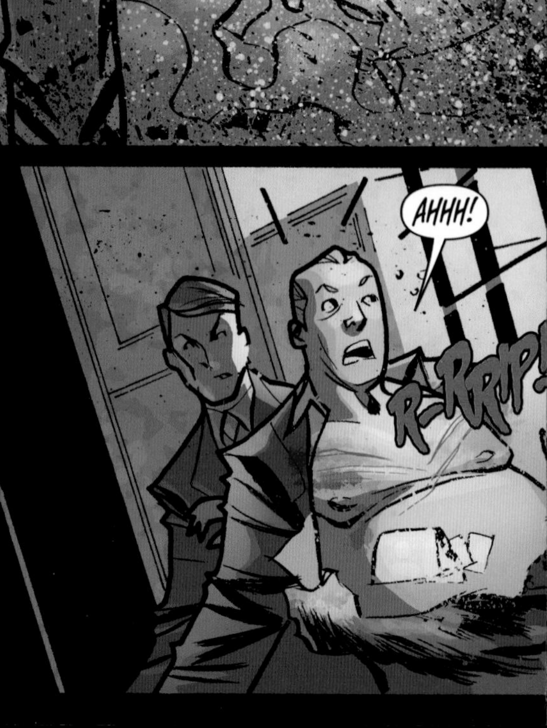
AHHH!
R-RRIP!

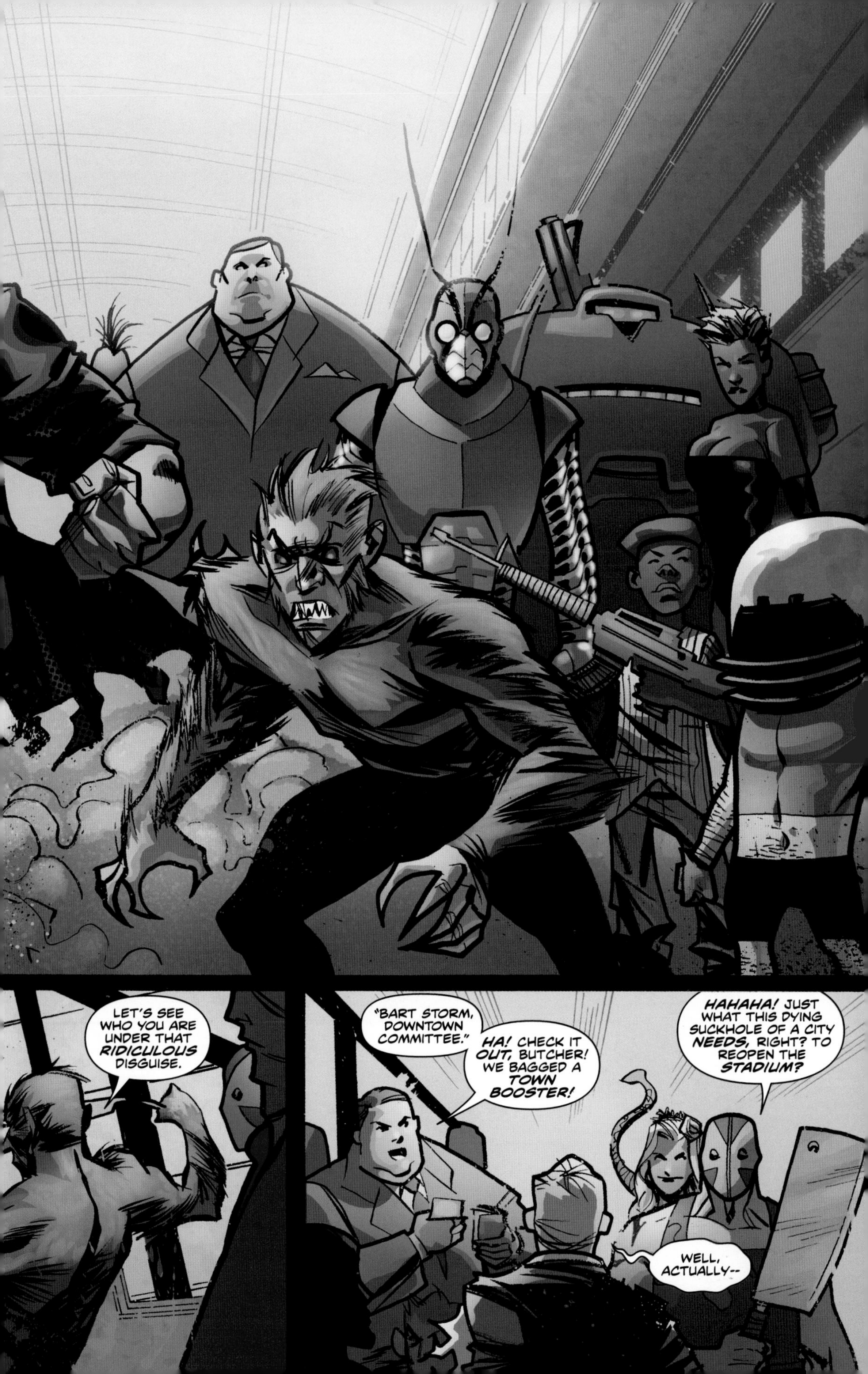

LET'S SEE WHO YOU ARE UNDER THAT RIDICULOUS DISGUISE.
"BART STORM, DOWNTOWN COMMITTEE."
HA! CHECK IT OUT, BUTCHER! WE BAGGED A TOWN BOOSTER!
HAHAHA! JUST WHAT THIS DYING SUCKHOLE OF A CITY NEEDS, RIGHT? TO REOPEN THE STADIUM?
WELL, ACTUALLY--

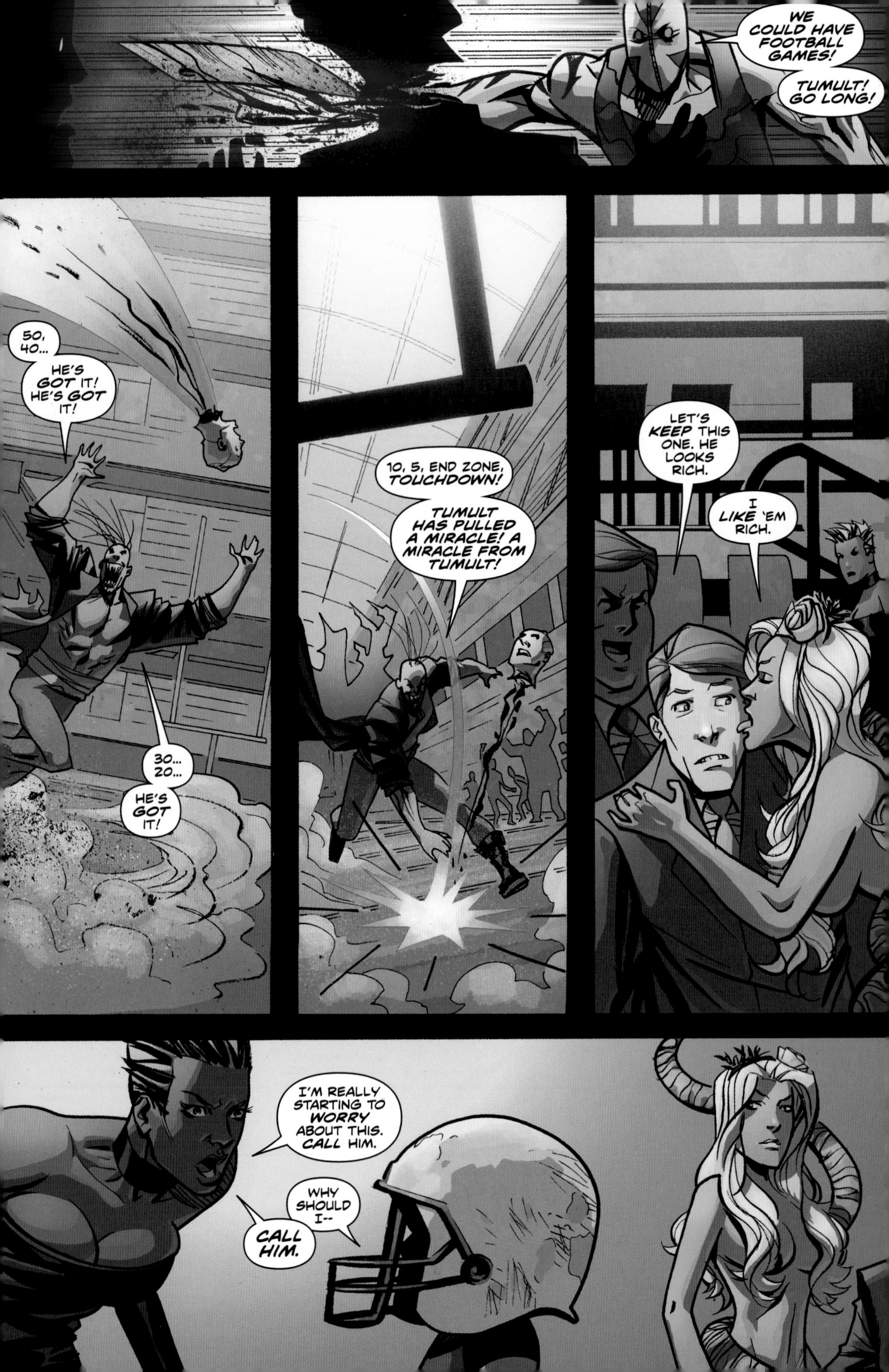
WE COULD HAVE FOOTBALL GAMES!
TUMULT! GO LONG!
50, 40...
HE'S GOT IT! HE'S GOT IT!
30... 20...
HE'S GOT IT!
10, 5, END ZONE, TOUCHDOWN!
TUMULT HAS PULLED A MIRACLE! A MIRACLE FROM TUMULT!
LET'S KEEP THIS ONE. HE LOOKS RICH.
I LIKE 'EM RICH.
I'M REALLY STARTING TO WORRY ABOUT THIS. CALL HIM.
WHY SHOULD I--
CALL HIM.

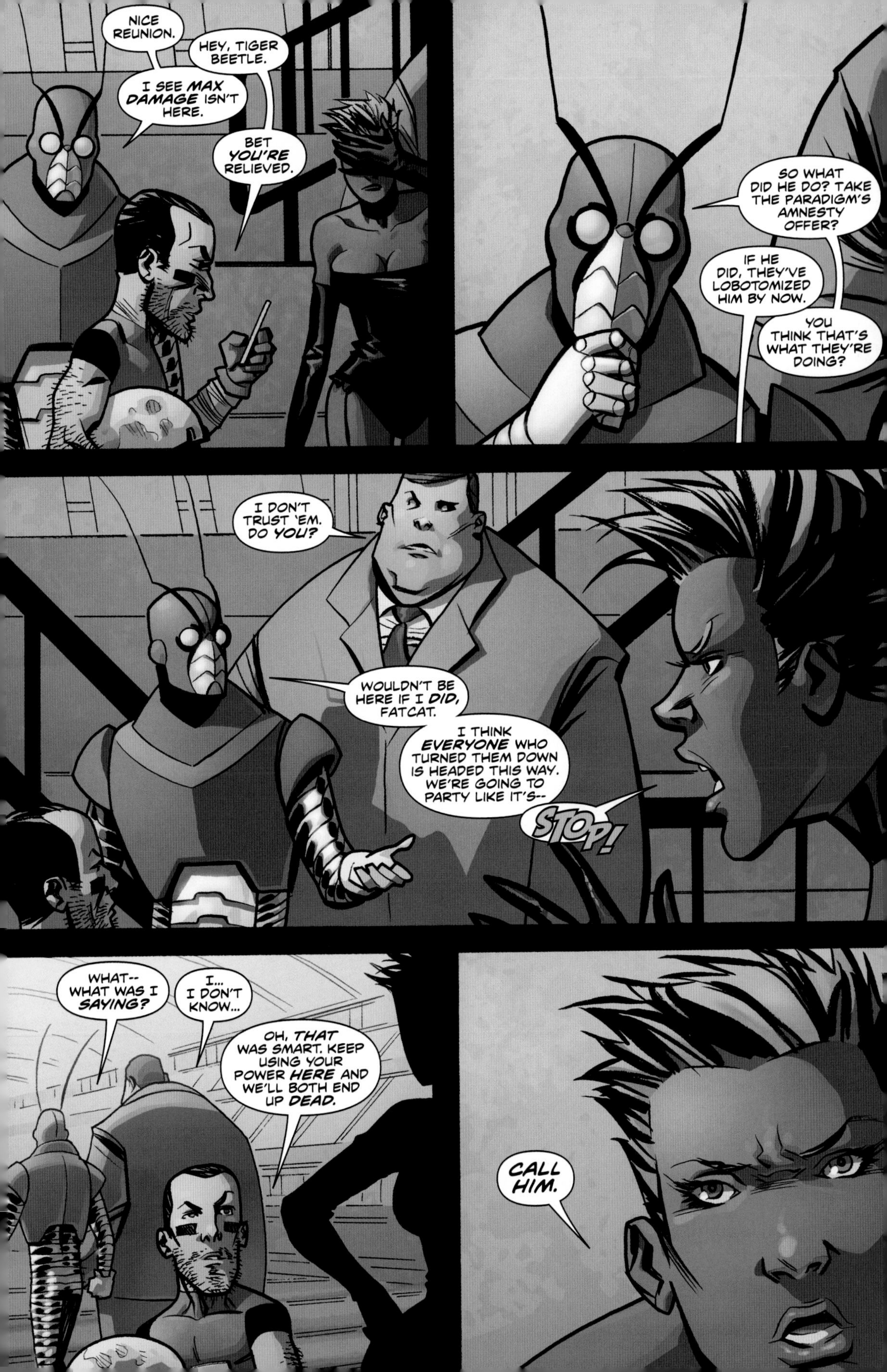

NICE REUNION.
I SEE MAX DAMAGE ISN'T HERE.
HEY, TIGER BEETLE.
BET YOU'RE RELIEVED.
SO WHAT DID HE DO? TAKE THE PARADIGM'S AMNESTY OFFER?
IF HE DID, THEY'VE LOBOTOMIZED HIM BY NOW.
YOU THINK THAT'S WHAT THEY'RE DOING?
I DON'T TRUST 'EM. DO YOU?
WOULDN'T BE HERE IF I DID, FATCAT.
I THINK EVERYONE WHO TURNED THEM DOWN IS HEADED THIS WAY. WE'RE GOING TO PARTY LIKE IT'S--
STOP!
WHAT-- WHAT WAS I SAYING?
I... I DON'T KNOW...
OH, THAT WAS SMART. KEEP USING YOUR POWER HERE AND WE'LL BOTH END UP DEAD.
CALL HIM.

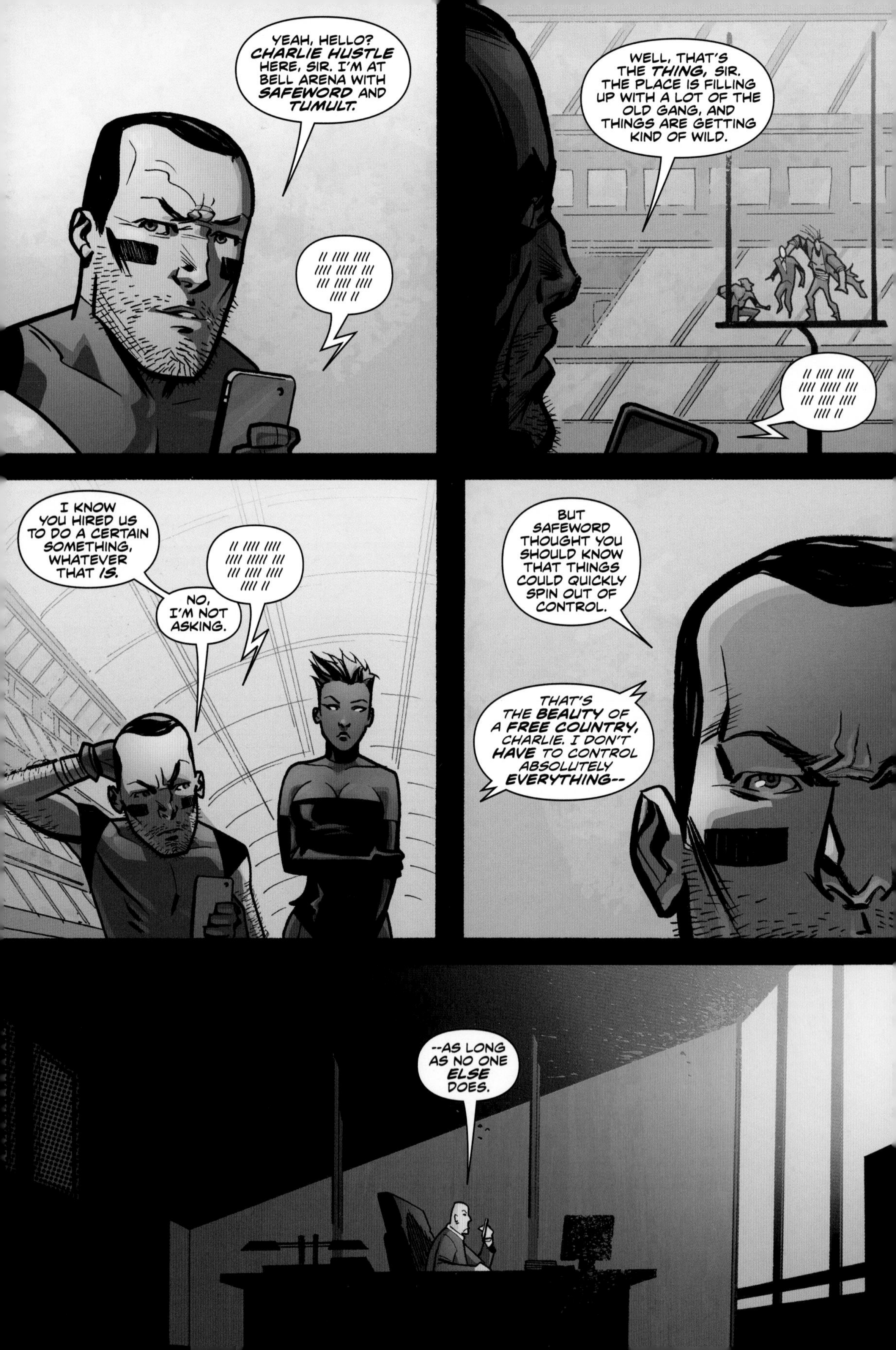
YEAH, HELLO? CHARLIE HUSTLE HERE, SIR. I'M AT BELL ARENA WITH SAFEWORD AND TUMULT.
WELL, THAT'S THE THING, SIR. THE PLACE IS FILLING UP WITH A LOT OF THE OLD GANG, AND THINGS ARE GETTING KIND OF WILD.
I KNOW YOU HIRED US TO DO A CERTAIN SOMETHING, WHATEVER THAT IS.
NO, I'M NOT ASKING.
BUT SAFEWORD THOUGHT YOU SHOULD KNOW THAT THINGS COULD QUICKLY SPIN OUT OF CONTROL.
THAT'S THE BEAUTY OF A FREE COUNTRY, CHARLIE. I DON'T HAVE TO CONTROL ABSOLUTELY EVERYTHING--
--AS LONG AS NO ONE ELSE DOES.

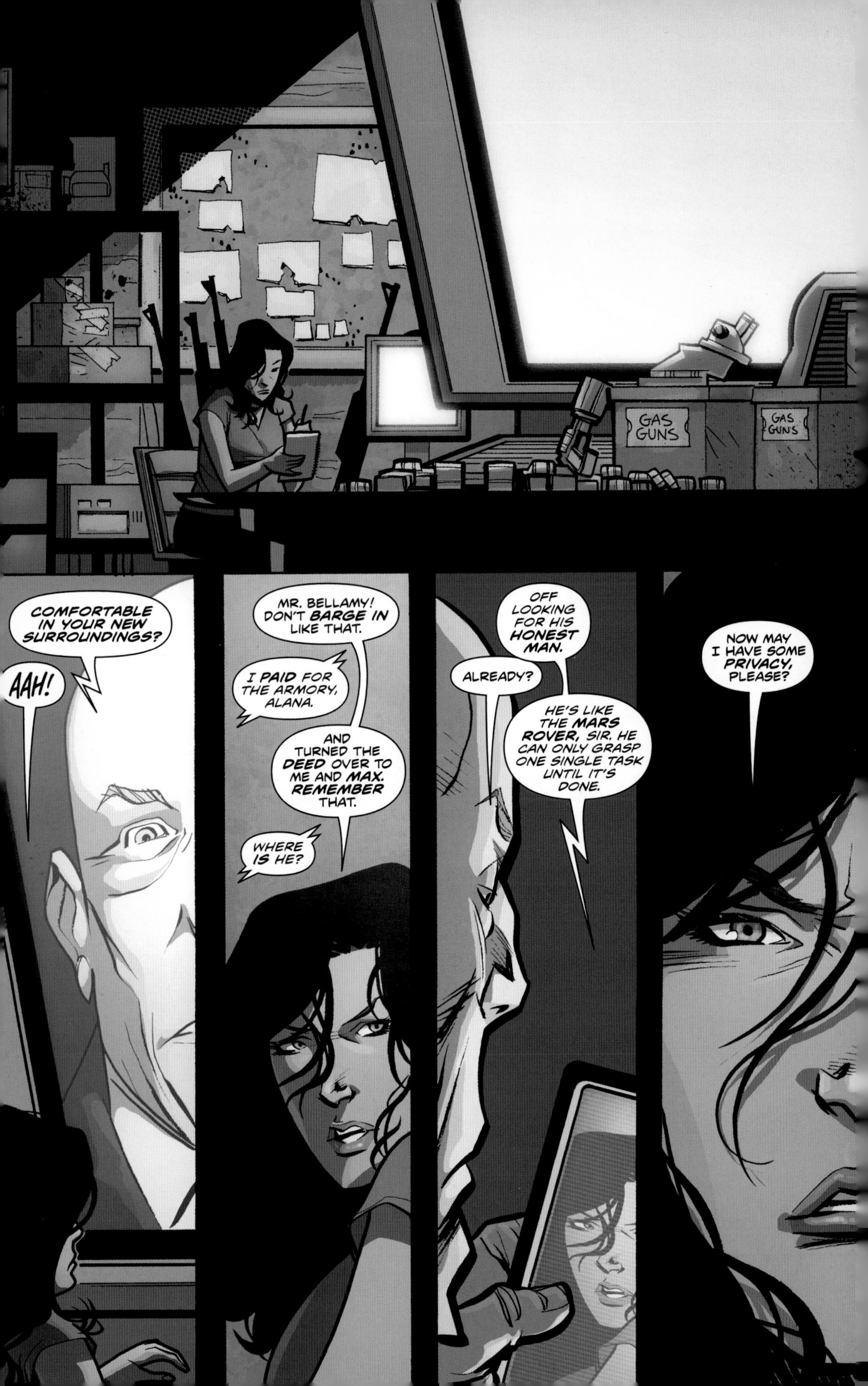
GAS GUNS
GAS GUNS
COMFORTABLE IN YOUR NEW SURROUNDINGS?
AAH!
MR. BELLAMY! DON'T **BARGE IN** LIKE THAT.
I **PAID** FOR THE ARMORY, ALANA.
AND TURNED THE **DEED** OVER TO ME AND **MAX. REMEMBER** THAT.
WHERE **IS** HE?
OFF LOOKING FOR HIS **HONEST MAN.**
ALREADY?
HE'S LIKE THE **MARS ROVER,** SIR. HE CAN ONLY GRASP ONE SINGLE TASK UNTIL IT'S DONE.
NOW MAY I HAVE SOME **PRIVACY,** PLEASE?

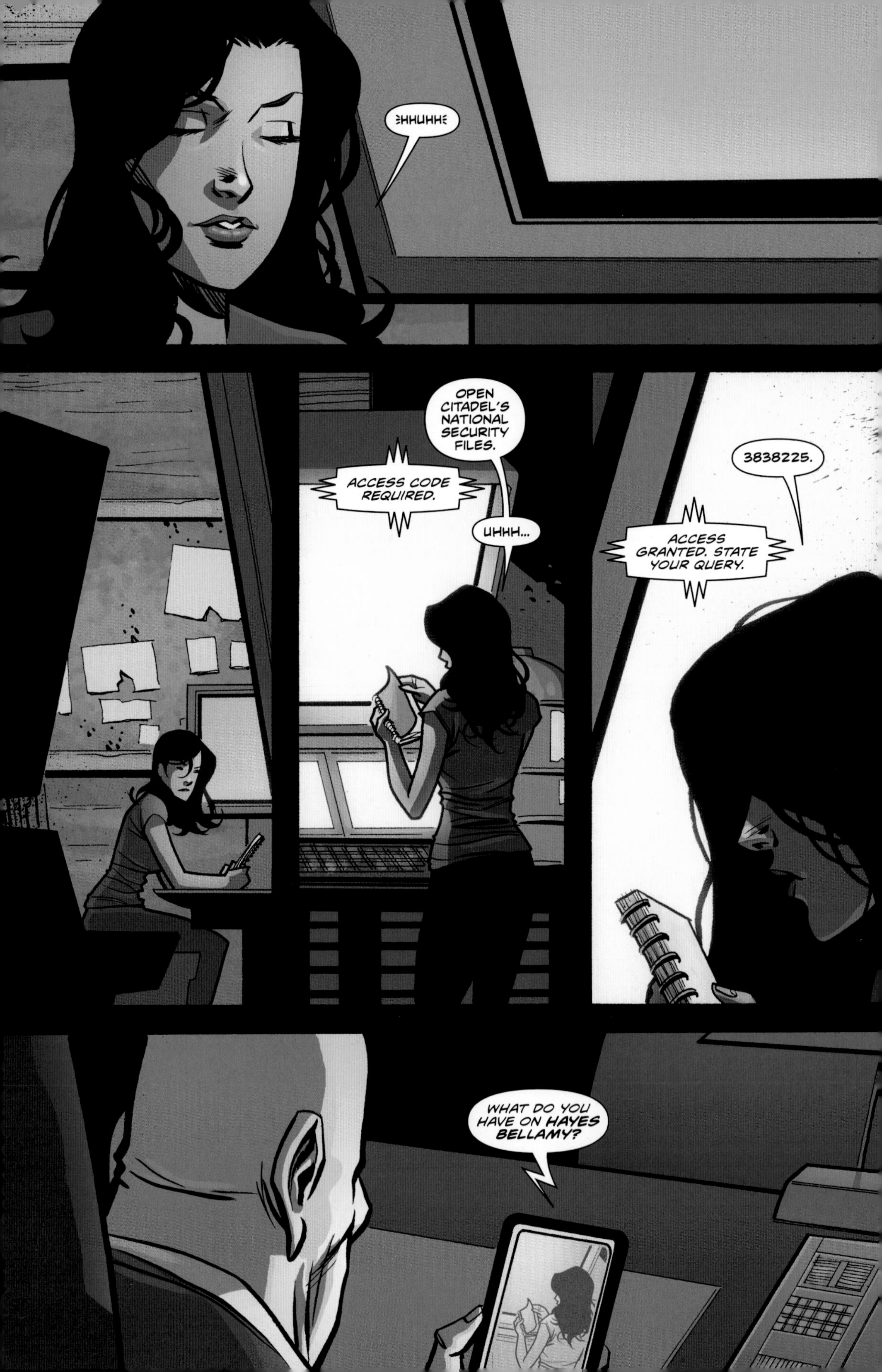
HHUHH
OPEN CITADEL'S NATIONAL SECURITY FILES.
ACCESS CODE REQUIRED.
UHHH...
3838225.
ACCESS GRANTED. STATE YOUR QUERY.
WHAT DO YOU HAVE ON HAYES BELLAMY?

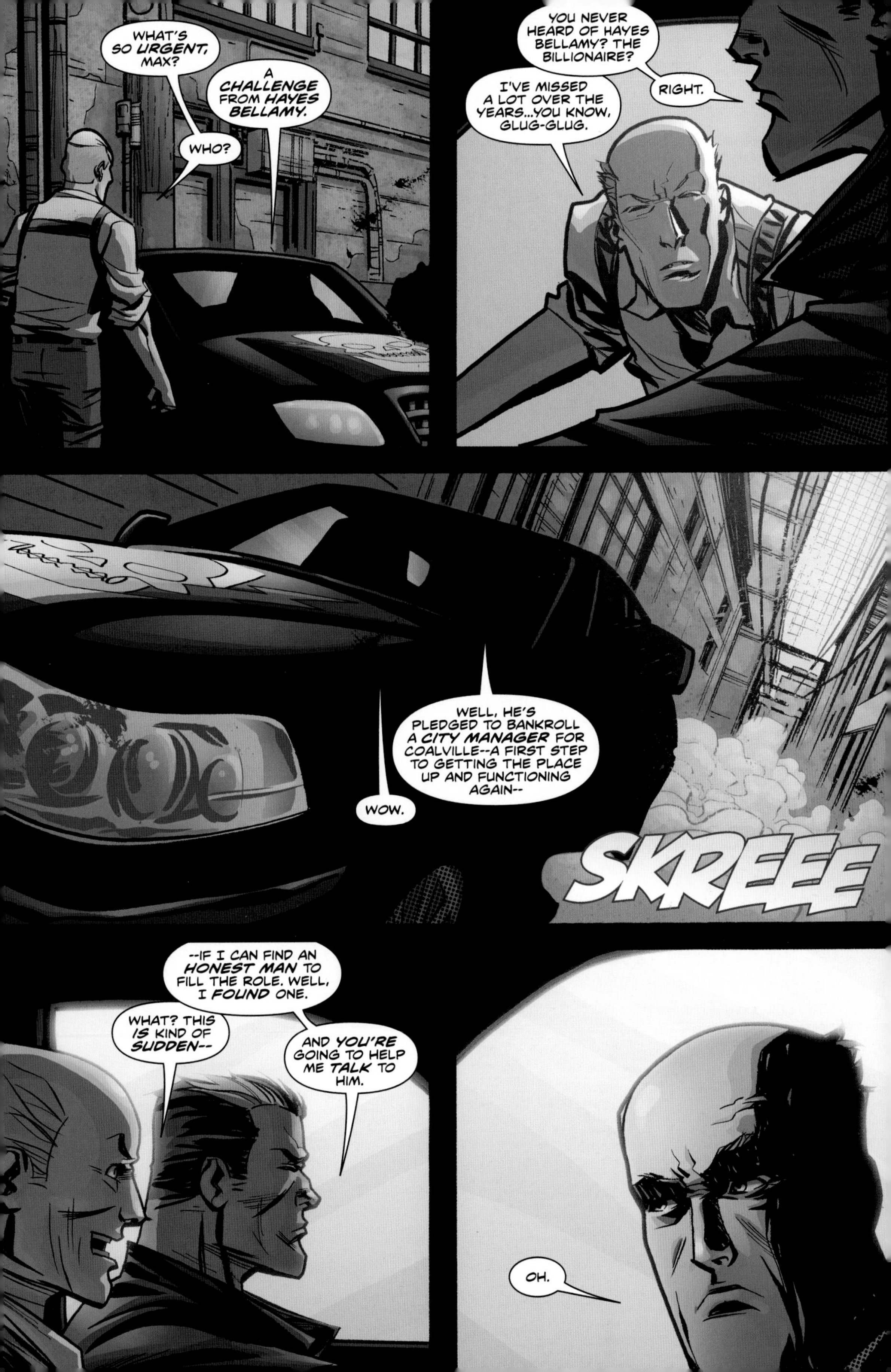
WHAT'S SO URGENT, MAX?
A CHALLENGE FROM HAYES BELLAMY.
WHO?
YOU NEVER HEARD OF HAYES BELLAMY? THE BILLIONAIRE?
I'VE MISSED A LOT OVER THE YEARS...YOU KNOW, GLUG-GLUG.
RIGHT.
WELL, HE'S PLEDGED TO BANKROLL A CITY MANAGER FOR COALVILLE--A FIRST STEP TO GETTING THE PLACE UP AND FUNCTIONING AGAIN--
WOW.
SKREEE
--IF I CAN FIND AN HONEST MAN TO FILL THE ROLE. WELL, I FOUND ONE.
WHAT? THIS IS KIND OF SUDDEN--
AND YOU'RE GOING TO HELP ME TALK TO HIM.
OH.

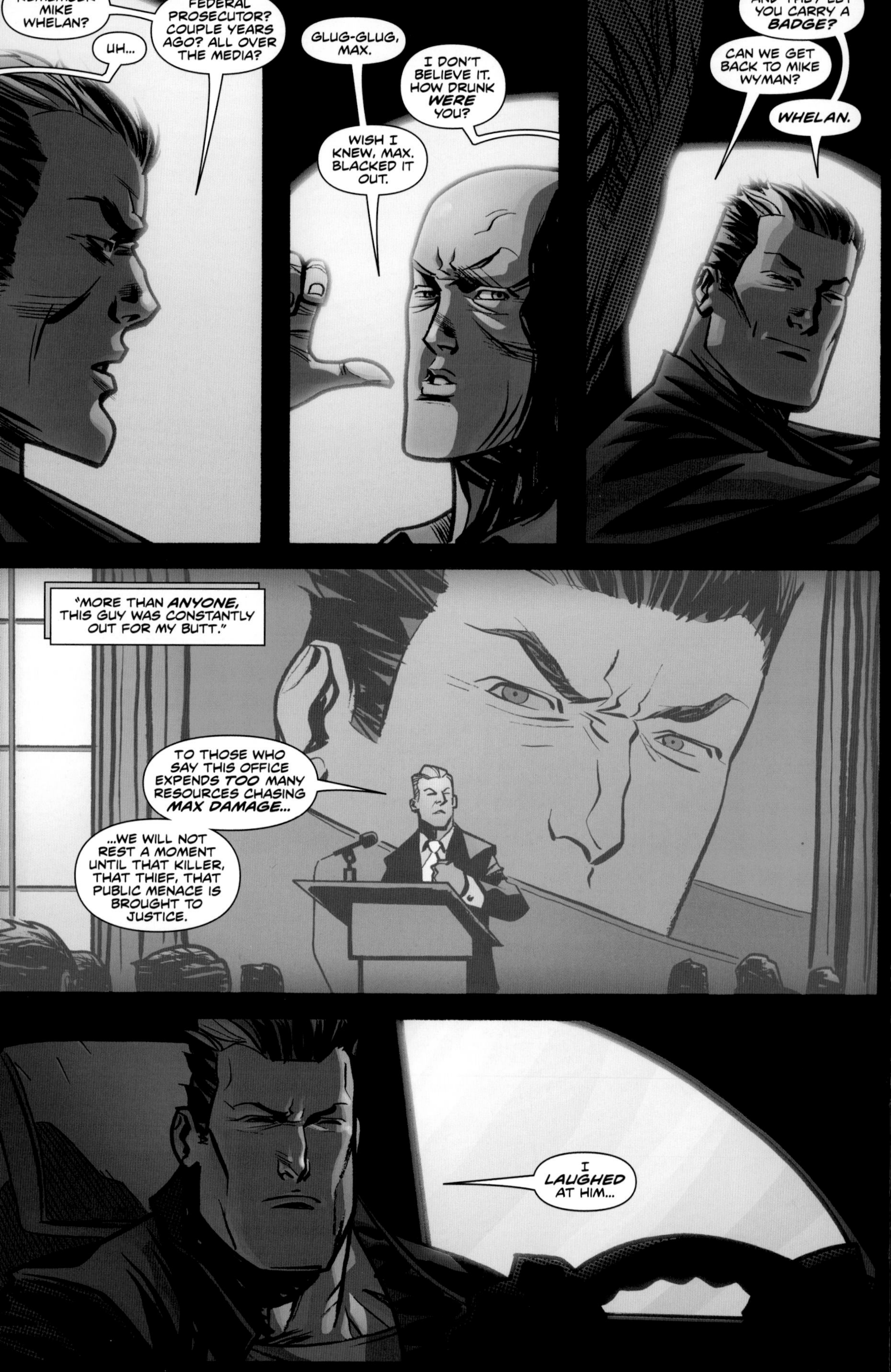
MIKE WHELAN?
UH...
FEDERAL PROSECUTOR? COUPLE YEARS AGO? ALL OVER THE MEDIA?
GLUG-GLUG, MAX.
I DON'T BELIEVE IT. HOW DRUNK *WERE* YOU?
WISH I KNEW, MAX. BLACKED IT OUT.
YOU CARRY A *BADGE?*
CAN WE GET BACK TO MIKE WYMAN?
*WHELAN.*
"MORE THAN *ANYONE,* THIS GUY WAS CONSTANTLY OUT FOR MY BUTT."
TO THOSE WHO SAY THIS OFFICE EXPENDS *TOO* MANY RESOURCES CHASING *MAX DAMAGE...*
...WE WILL NOT REST A MOMENT UNTIL THAT KILLER, THAT THIEF, THAT PUBLIC MENACE IS BROUGHT TO JUSTICE.
I *LAUGHED* AT HIM...

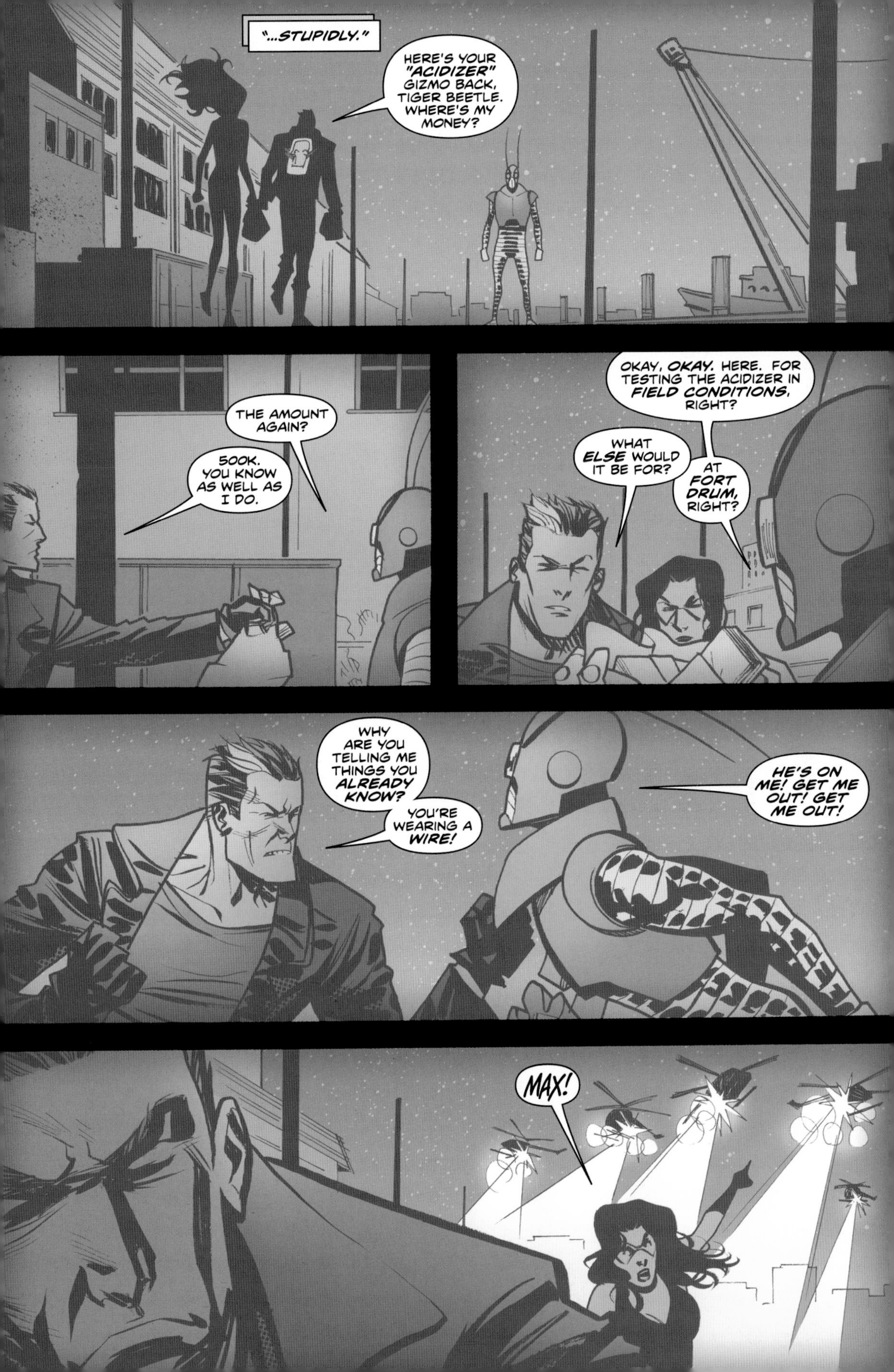
"...STUPIDLY."
HERE'S YOUR "ACIDIZER" GIZMO BACK, TIGER BEETLE. WHERE'S MY MONEY?
THE AMOUNT AGAIN?
500K. YOU KNOW AS WELL AS I DO.
OKAY, OKAY. HERE. FOR TESTING THE ACIDIZER IN FIELD CONDITIONS, RIGHT?
WHAT ELSE WOULD IT BE FOR?
AT FORT DRUM, RIGHT?
WHY ARE YOU TELLING ME THINGS YOU ALREADY KNOW?
YOU'RE WEARING A WIRE!
HE'S ON ME! GET ME OUT! GET ME OUT!
MAX!

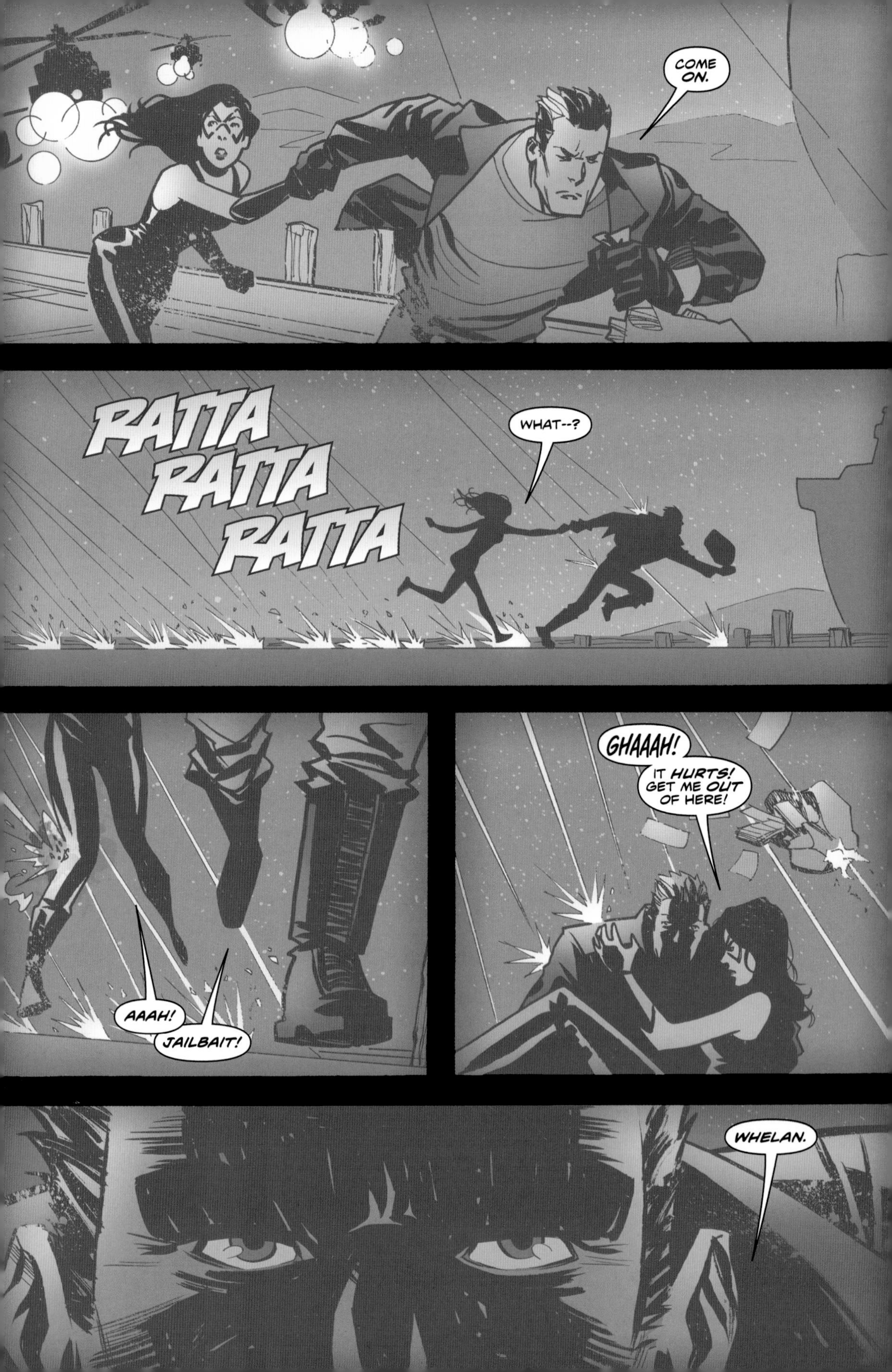
COME ON.
RATTA RATTA RATTA
WHAT--?
AAAH!
JAILBAIT!
GHAAAH!
IT HURTS! GET ME OUT OF HERE!
WHELAN.

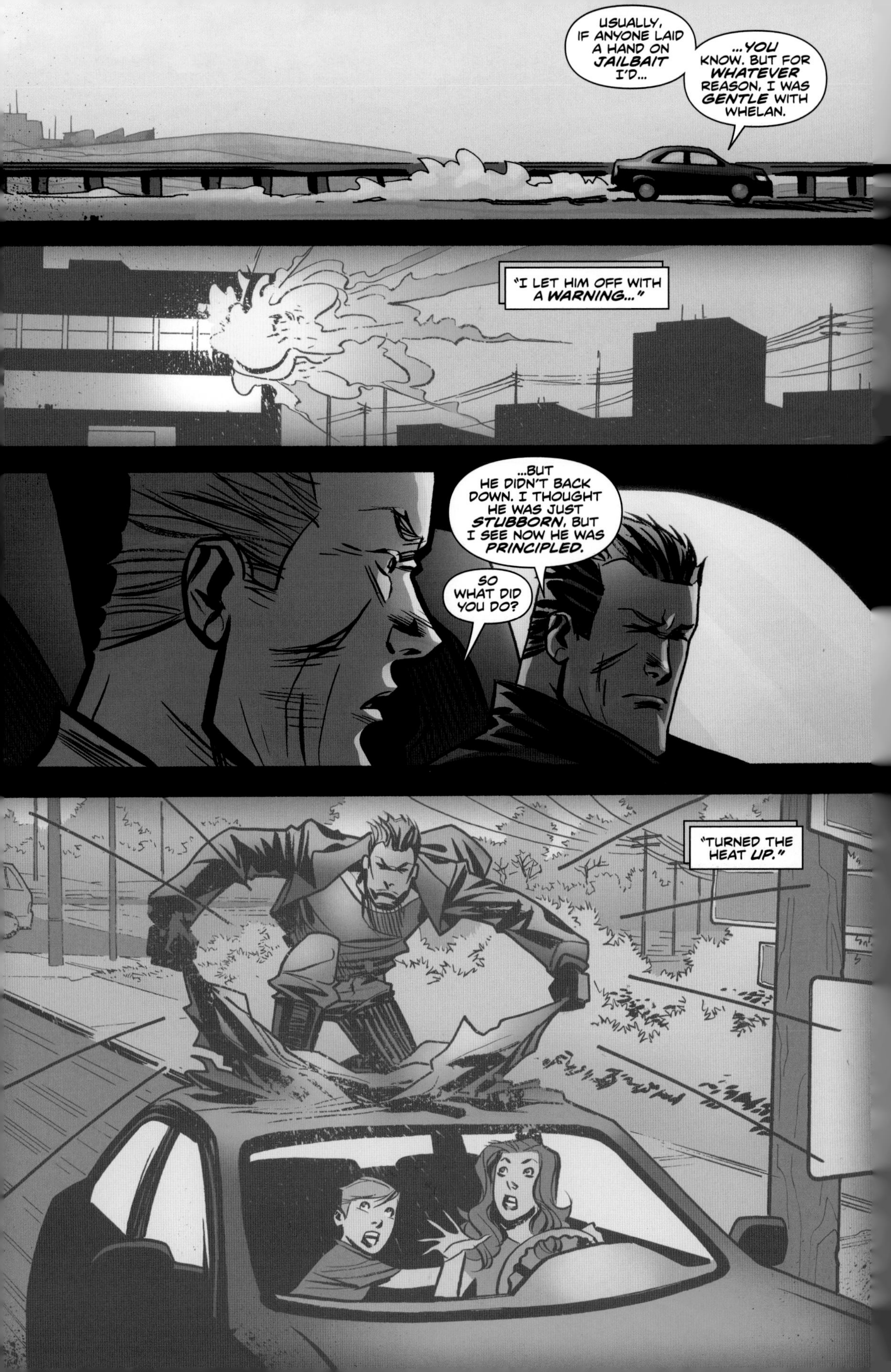
USUALLY, IF ANYONE LAID A HAND ON JAILBAIT I'D...
...YOU KNOW. BUT FOR WHATEVER REASON, I WAS GENTLE WITH WHELAN.
"I LET HIM OFF WITH A WARNING..."
...BUT HE DIDN'T BACK DOWN. I THOUGHT HE WAS JUST STUBBORN, BUT I SEE NOW HE WAS PRINCIPLED.
SO WHAT DID YOU DO?
"TURNED THE HEAT UP."

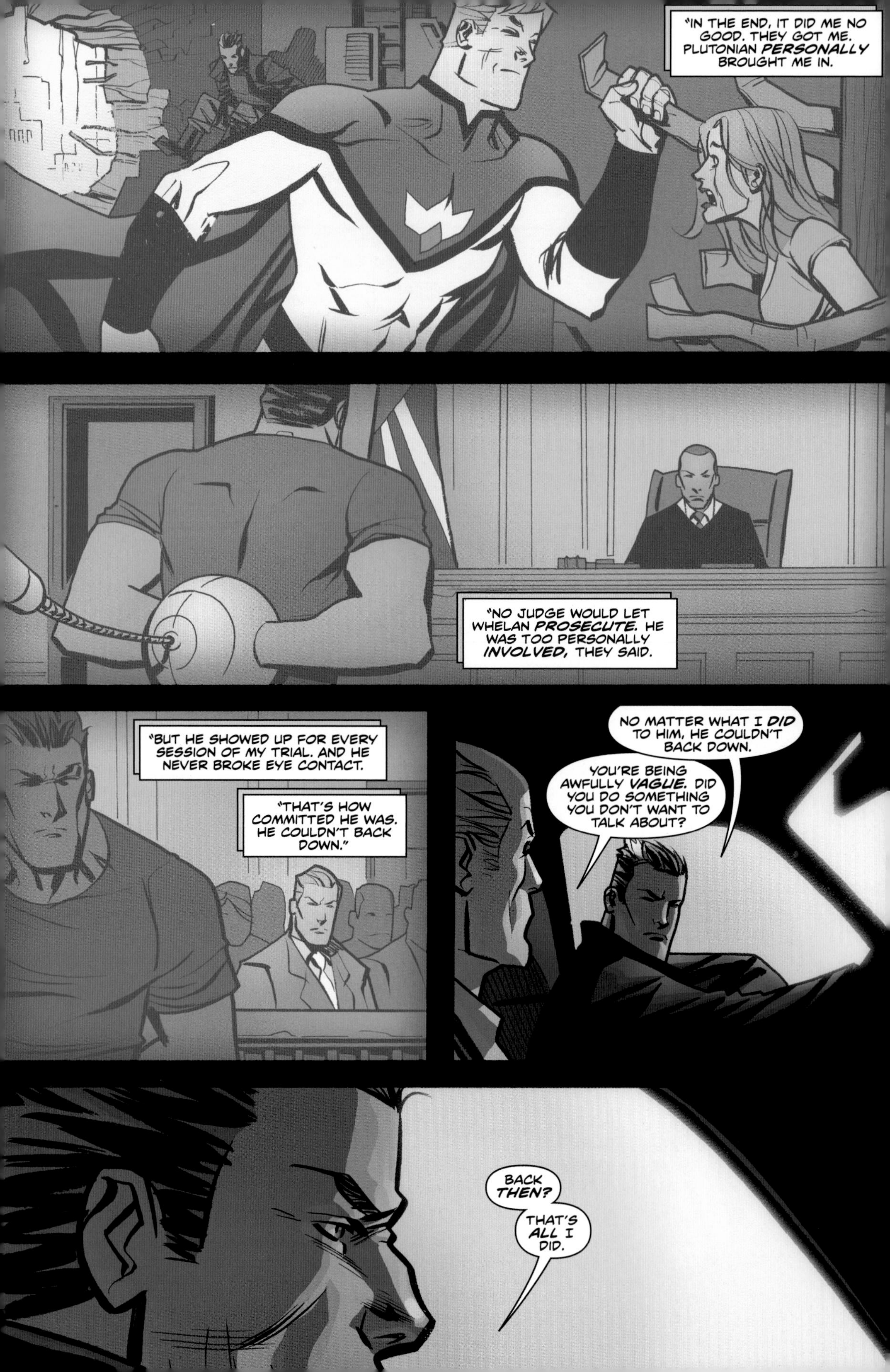
"IN THE END, IT DID ME NO GOOD. THEY GOT ME. PLUTONIAN PERSONALLY BROUGHT ME IN.
"NO JUDGE WOULD LET WHELAN PROSECUTE. HE WAS TOO PERSONALLY INVOLVED, THEY SAID.
"BUT HE SHOWED UP FOR EVERY SESSION OF MY TRIAL. AND HE NEVER BROKE EYE CONTACT.
"THAT'S HOW COMMITTED HE WAS. HE COULDN'T BACK DOWN."
NO MATTER WHAT I DID TO HIM, HE COULDN'T BACK DOWN.
YOU'RE BEING AWFULLY VAGUE. DID YOU DO SOMETHING YOU DON'T WANT TO TALK ABOUT?
BACK THEN?
THAT'S ALL I DID.

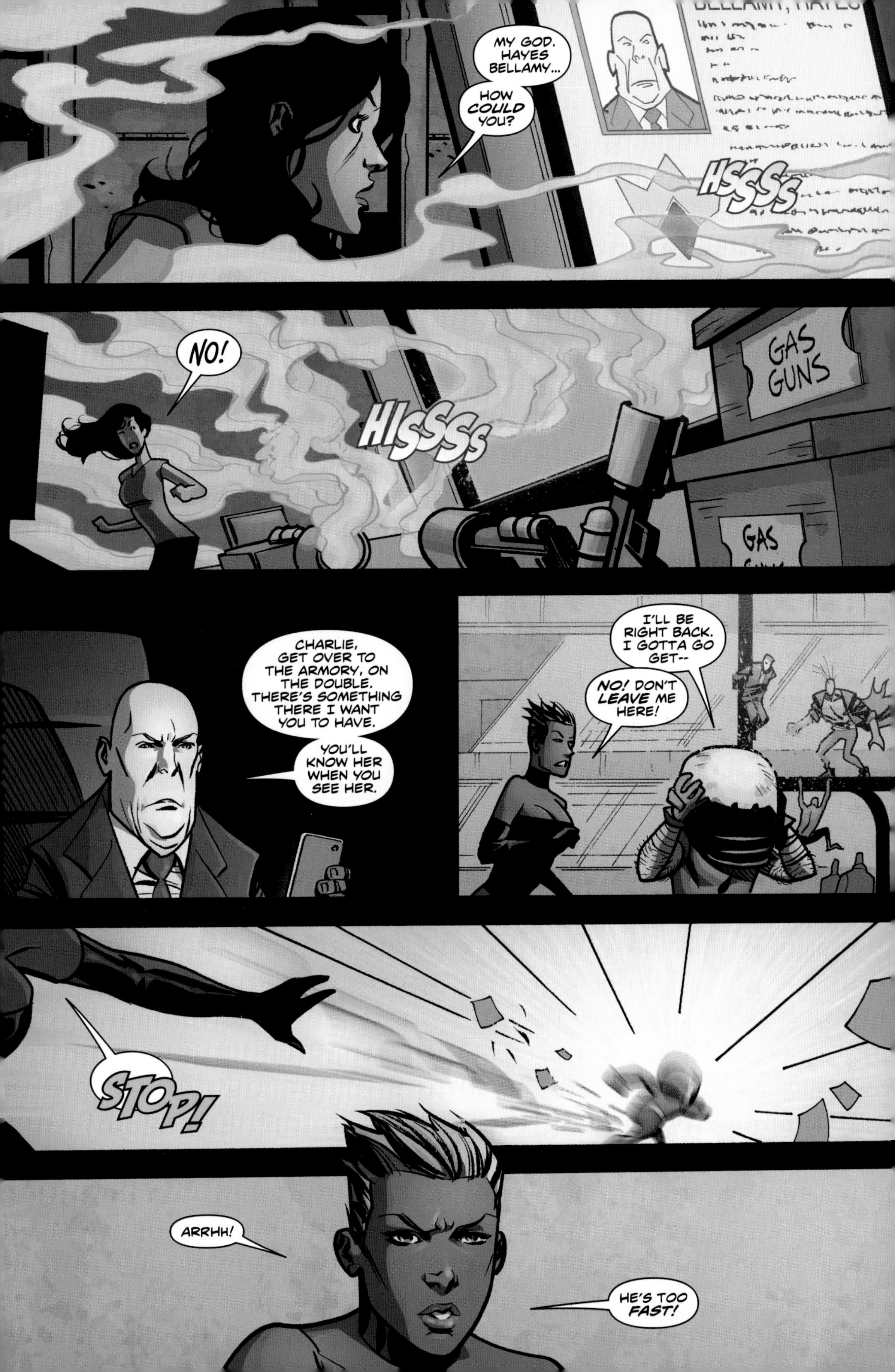
BELLAMY, HAYES
MY GOD. HAYES BELLAMY...
HOW COULD YOU?
HSSSS
NO!
HISSSS
GAS GUNS
GAS
CHARLIE, GET OVER TO THE ARMORY, ON THE DOUBLE. THERE'S SOMETHING THERE I WANT YOU TO HAVE.
YOU'LL KNOW HER WHEN YOU SEE HER.
I'LL BE RIGHT BACK. I GOTTA GO GET--
NO! DON'T LEAVE ME HERE!
STOP!
ARRHH!
HE'S TOO FAST!

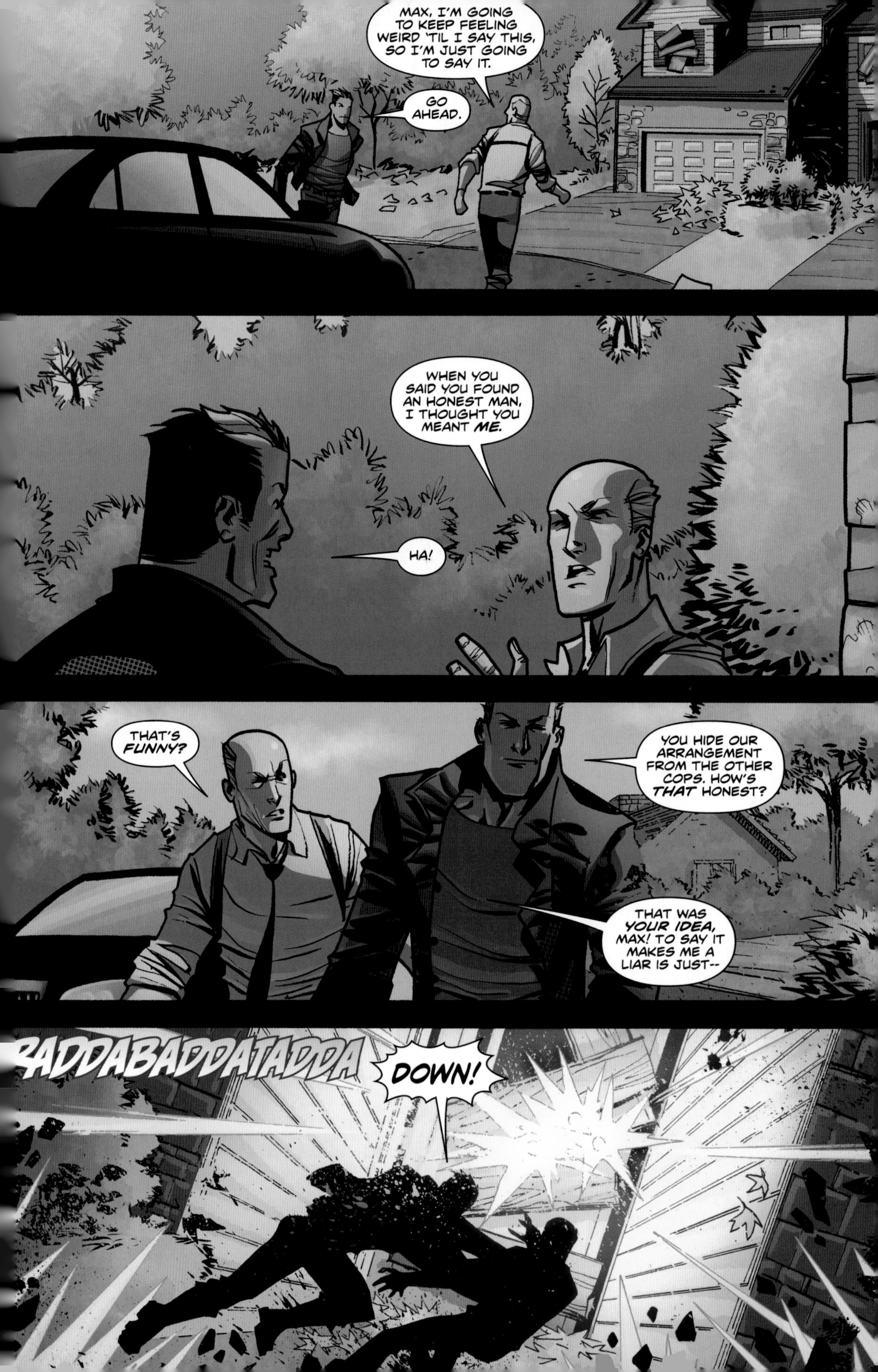
MAX, I'M GOING TO KEEP FEELING WEIRD 'TIL I SAY THIS, SO I'M JUST GOING TO SAY IT.
GO AHEAD.
WHEN YOU SAID YOU FOUND AN HONEST MAN, I THOUGHT YOU MEANT *ME*.
HA!
THAT'S *FUNNY*?
YOU HIDE OUR ARRANGEMENT FROM THE OTHER COPS. HOW'S *THAT* HONEST?
THAT WAS *YOUR IDEA*, MAX! TO SAY IT MAKES ME A LIAR IS JUST--
BADDABADDATADDA
DOWN!

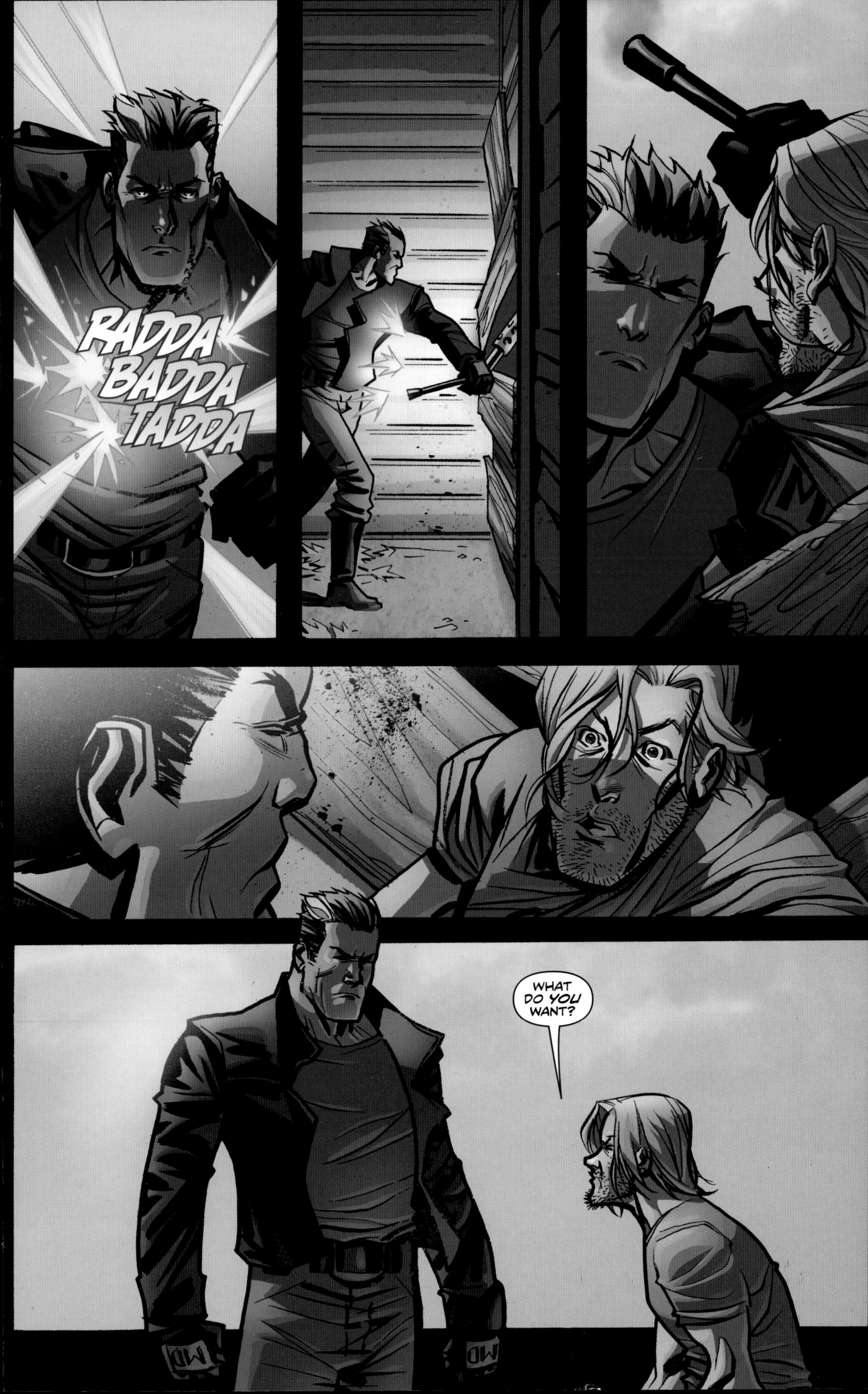
RADDA BADDA TADDA
WHAT DO YOU WANT?

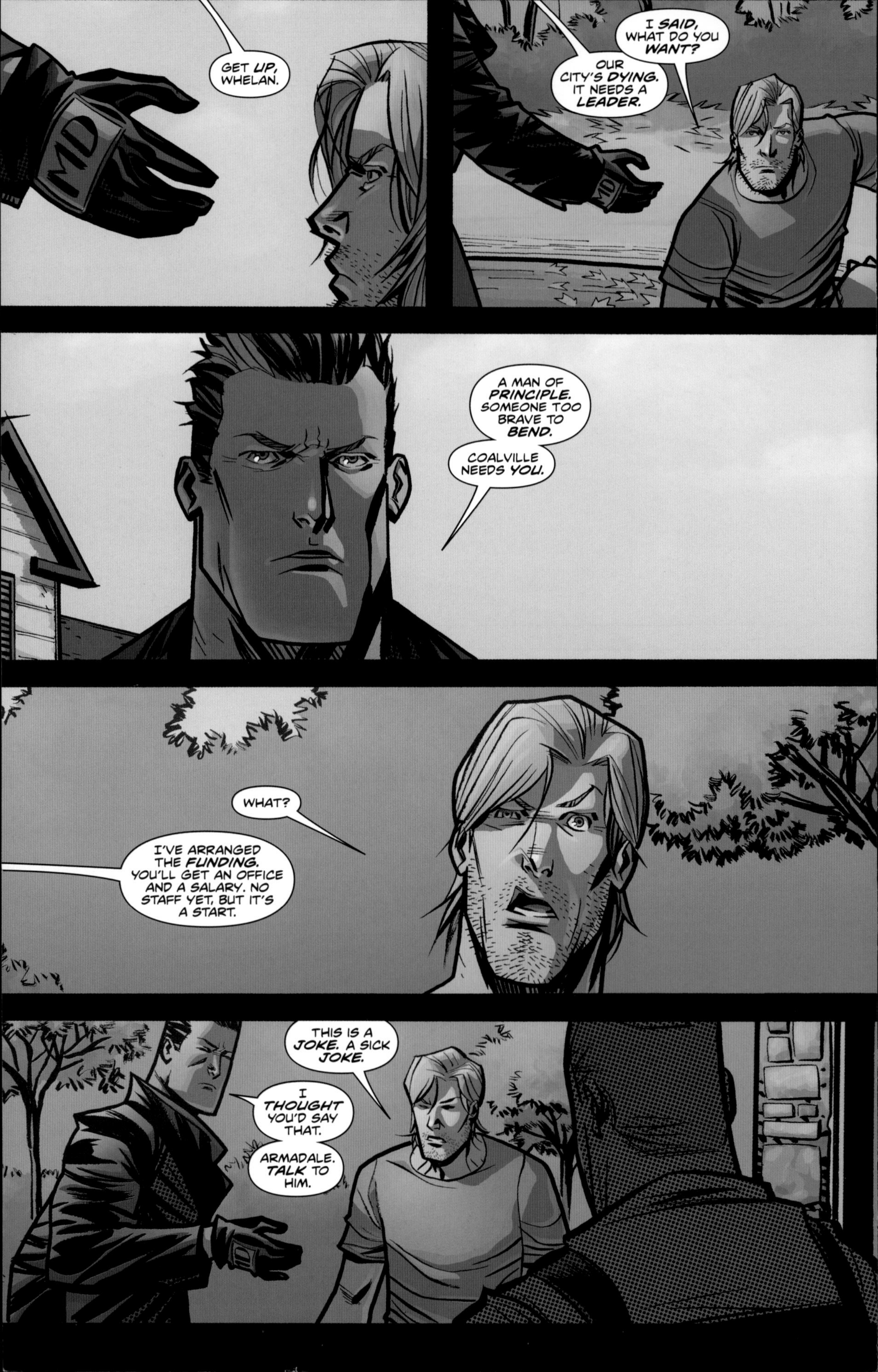
GET UP, WHELAN.
I SAID, WHAT DO YOU WANT?
OUR CITY'S DYING. IT NEEDS A LEADER.
A MAN OF PRINCIPLE. SOMEONE TOO BRAVE TO BEND.
COALVILLE NEEDS YOU.
WHAT?
I'VE ARRANGED THE FUNDING. YOU'LL GET AN OFFICE AND A SALARY. NO STAFF YET, BUT IT'S A START.
THIS IS A JOKE. A SICK JOKE.
I THOUGHT YOU'D SAY THAT.
ARMADALE. TALK TO HIM.

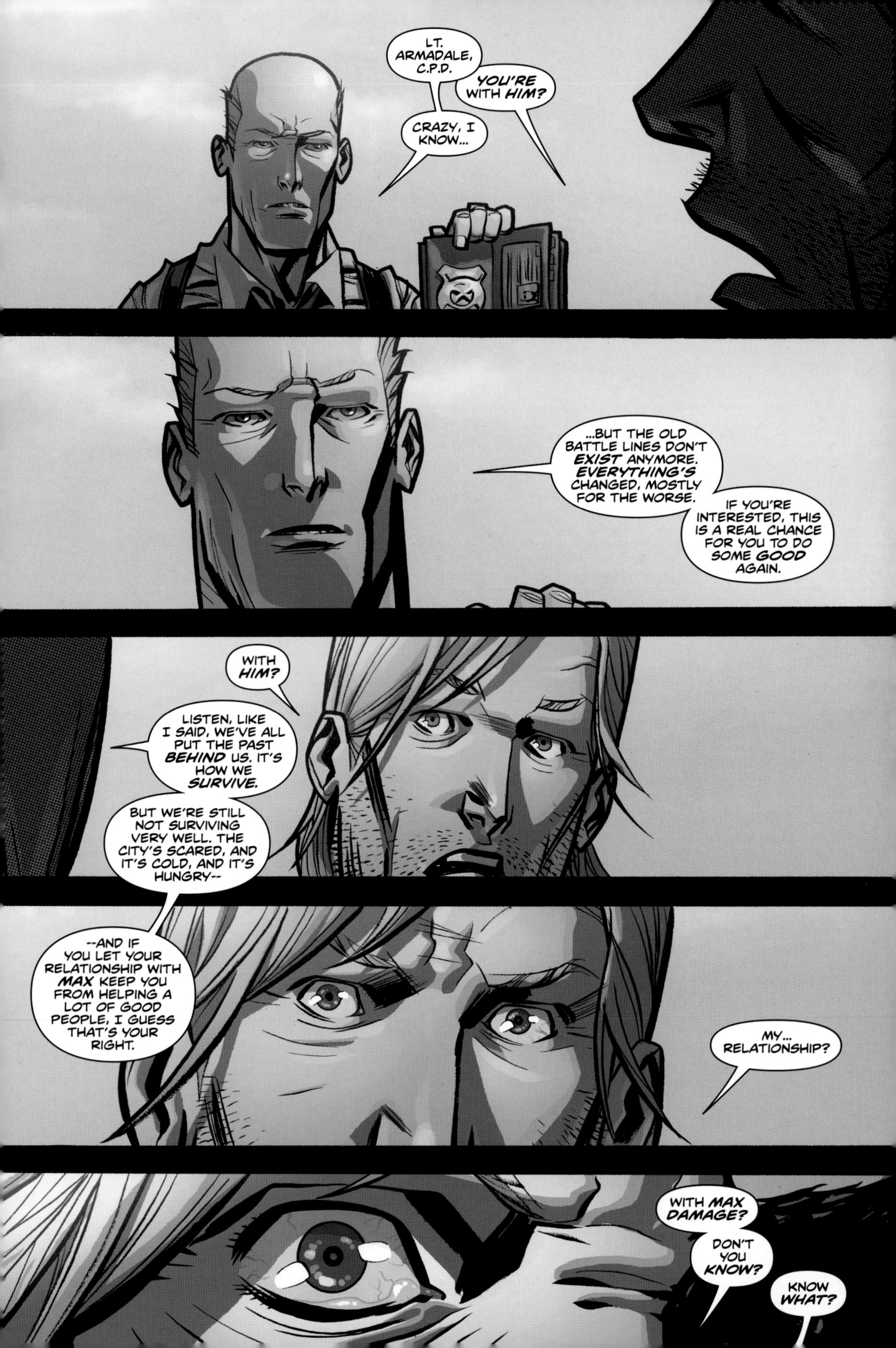
LT. ARMADALE, C.P.D.
YOU'RE WITH HIM?
CRAZY, I KNOW...
...BUT THE OLD BATTLE LINES DON'T EXIST ANYMORE. EVERYTHING'S CHANGED, MOSTLY FOR THE WORSE.
IF YOU'RE INTERESTED, THIS IS A REAL CHANCE FOR YOU TO DO SOME GOOD AGAIN.
WITH HIM?
LISTEN, LIKE I SAID, WE'VE ALL PUT THE PAST BEHIND US. IT'S HOW WE SURVIVE.
BUT WE'RE STILL NOT SURVIVING VERY WELL. THE CITY'S SCARED, AND IT'S COLD, AND IT'S HUNGRY--
--AND IF YOU LET YOUR RELATIONSHIP WITH MAX KEEP YOU FROM HELPING A LOT OF GOOD PEOPLE, I GUESS THAT'S YOUR RIGHT.
MY... RELATIONSHIP?
WITH MAX DAMAGE?
DON'T YOU KNOW?
KNOW WHAT?

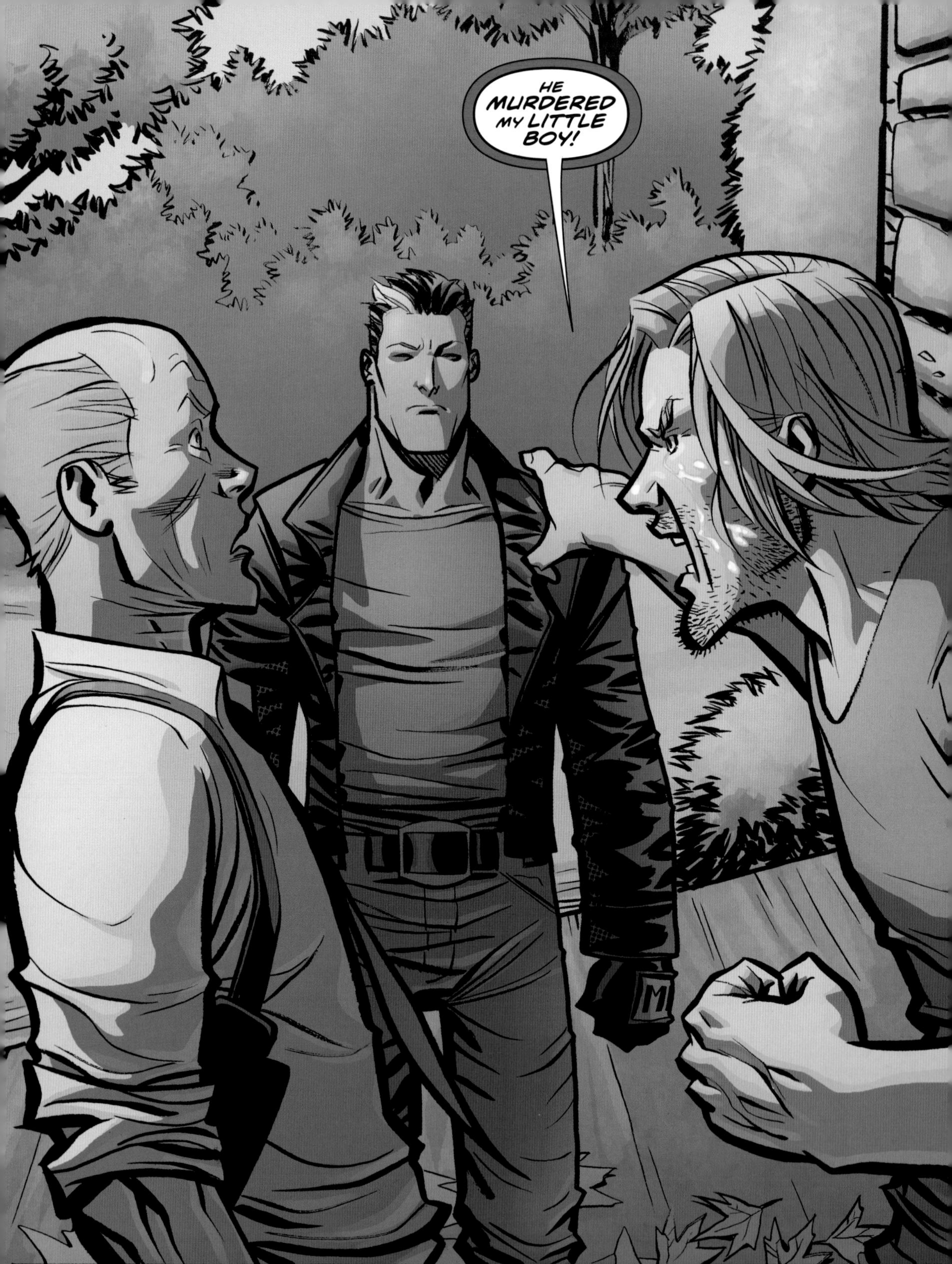
HE MURDERED MY LITTLE BOY!
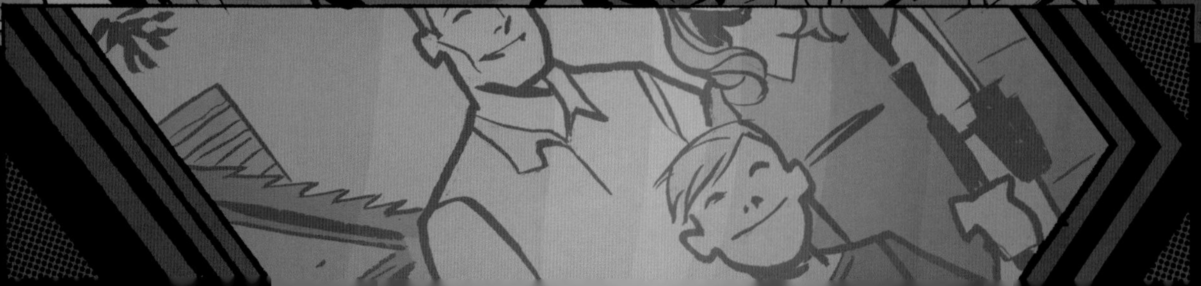

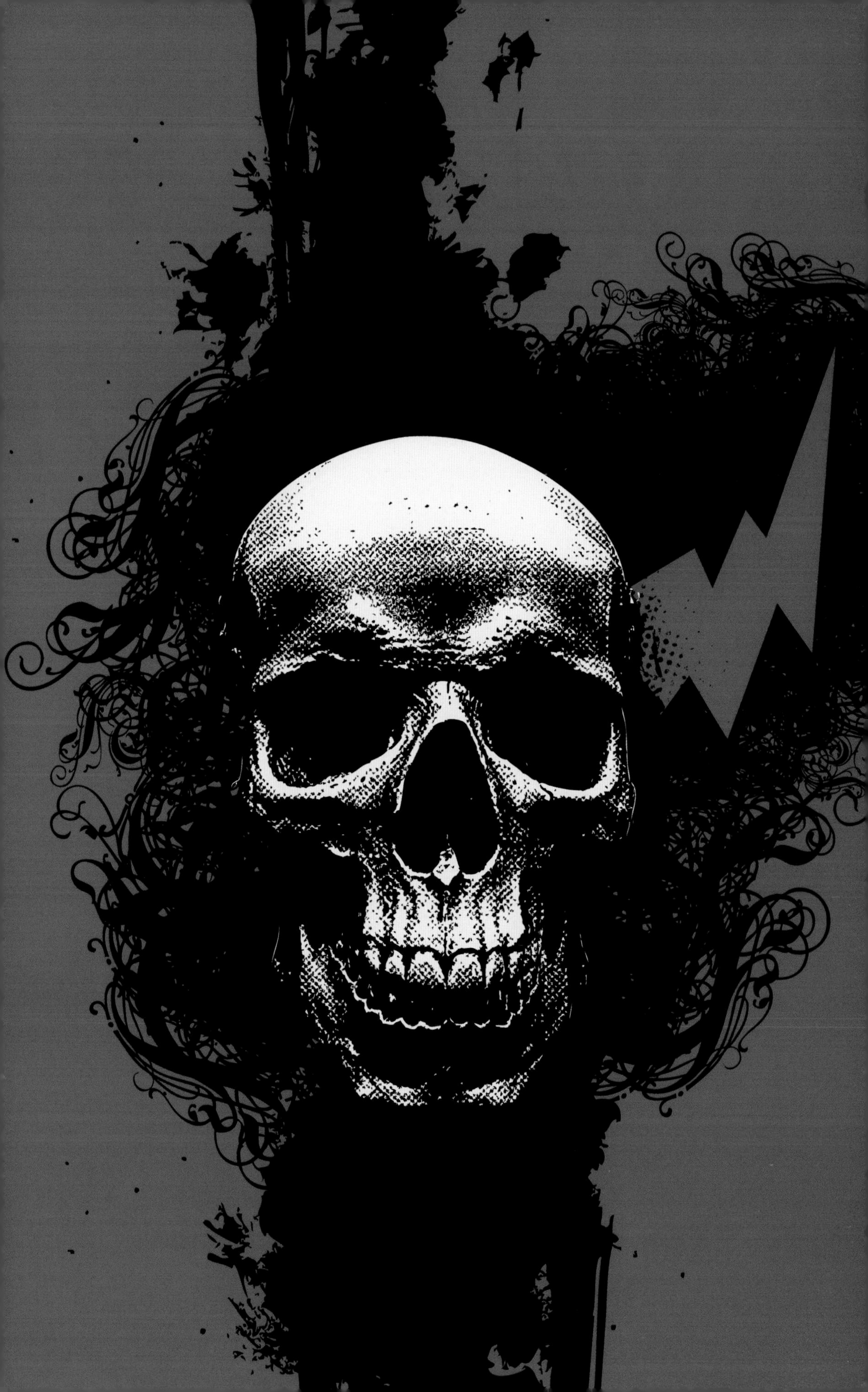

# CHAPTER 19

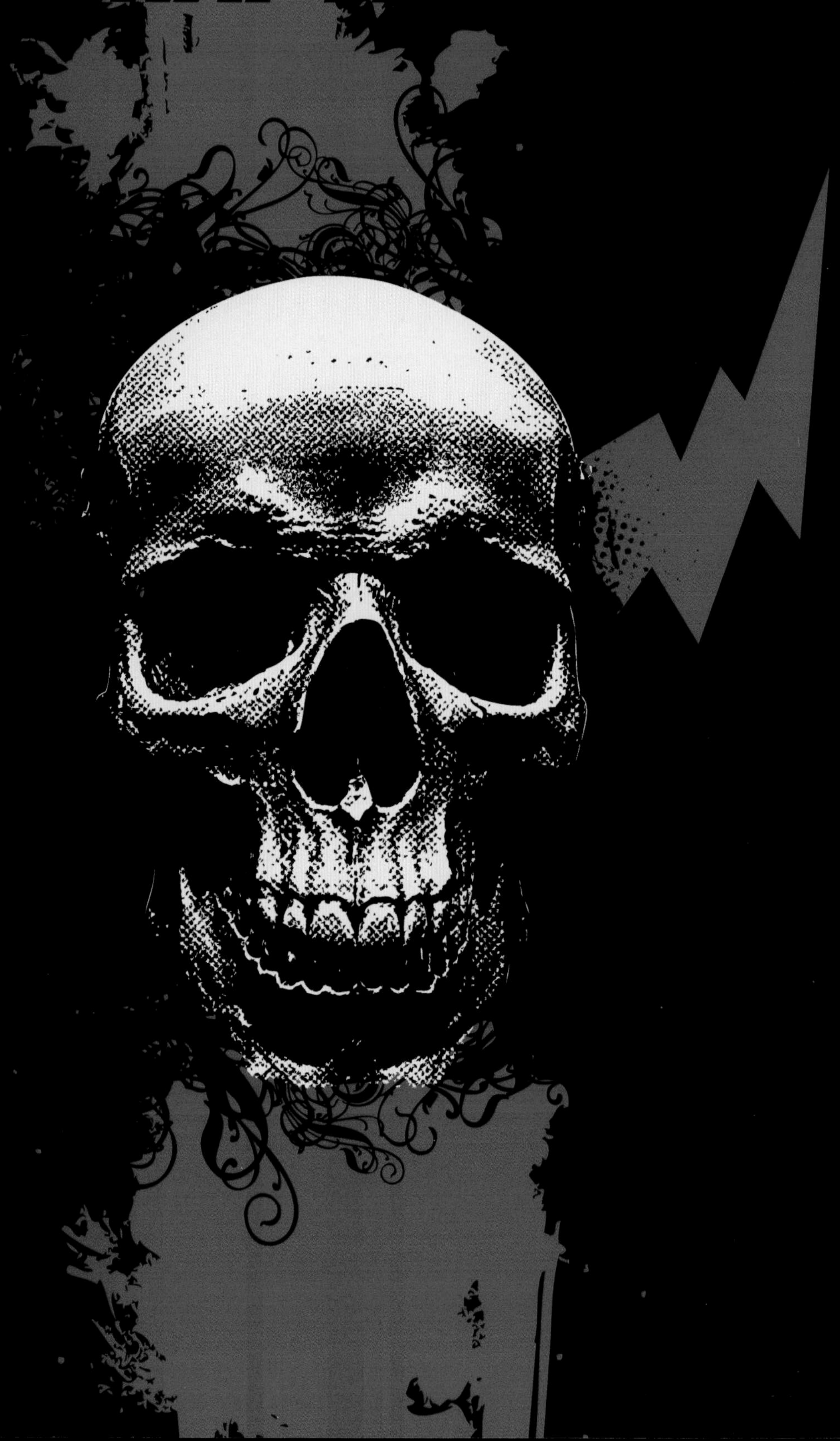

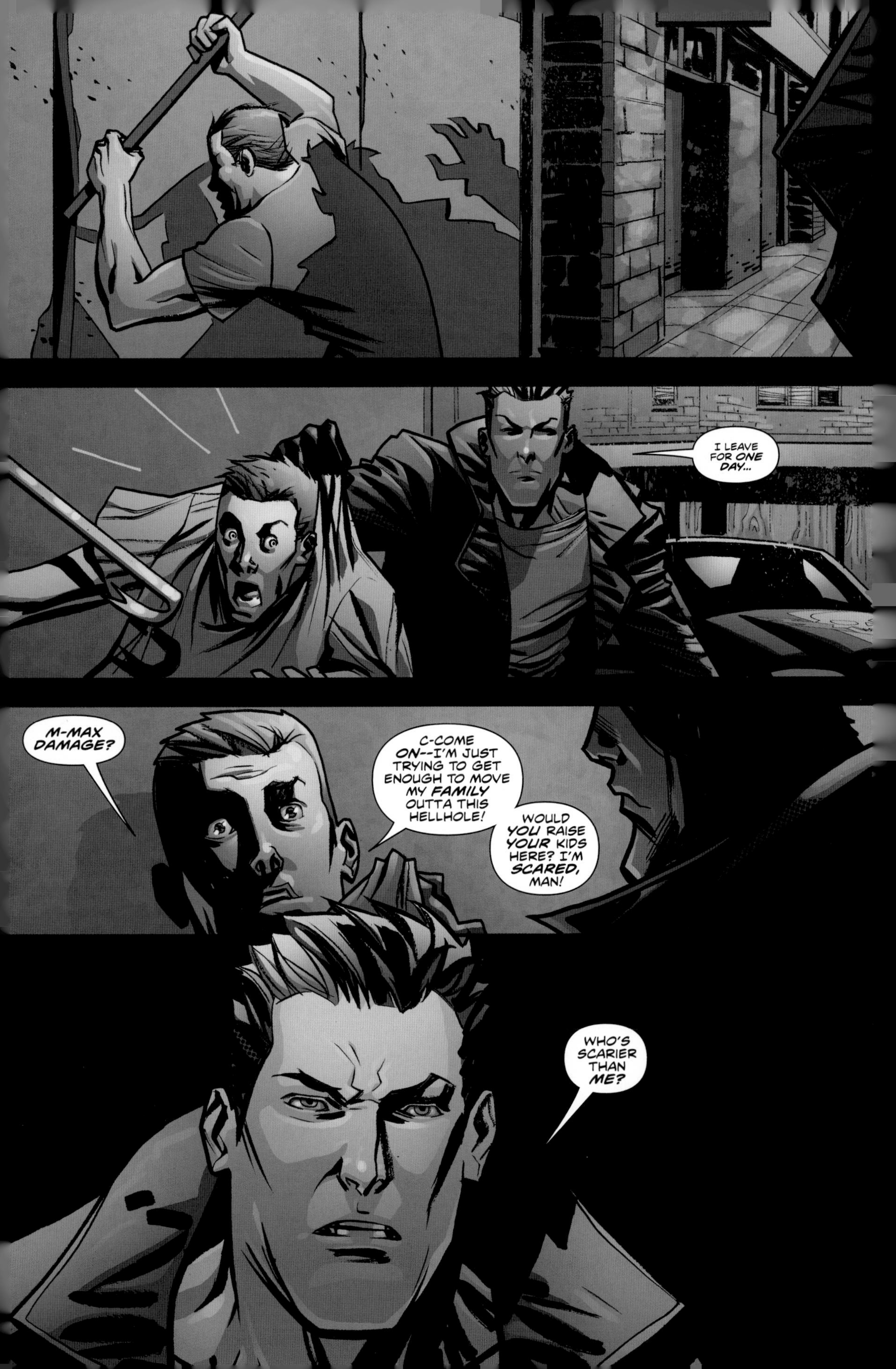

I LEAVE FOR ONE DAY...
M-MAX DAMAGE?
C-COME ON--I'M JUST TRYING TO GET ENOUGH TO MOVE MY FAMILY OUTTA THIS HELLHOLE!
WOULD YOU RAISE YOUR KIDS HERE? I'M SCARED, MAN!
WHO'S SCARIER THAN ME?

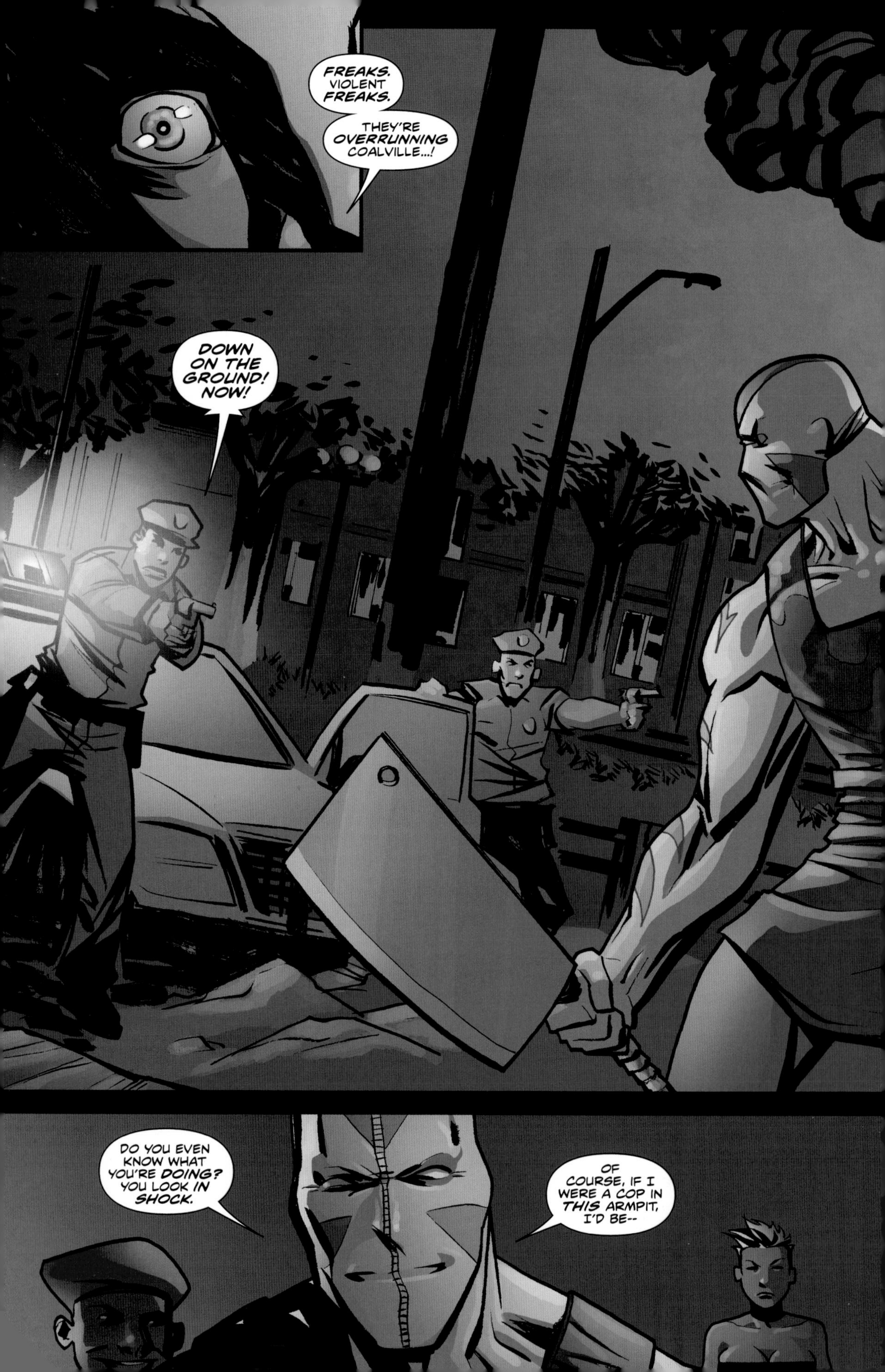

FREAKS. VIOLENT FREAKS.
THEY'RE OVERRUNNING COALVILLE...!
DOWN ON THE GROUND! NOW!
DO YOU EVEN KNOW WHAT YOU'RE DOING? YOU LOOK IN SHOCK.
OF COURSE, IF I WERE A COP IN THIS ARMPIT, I'D BE--

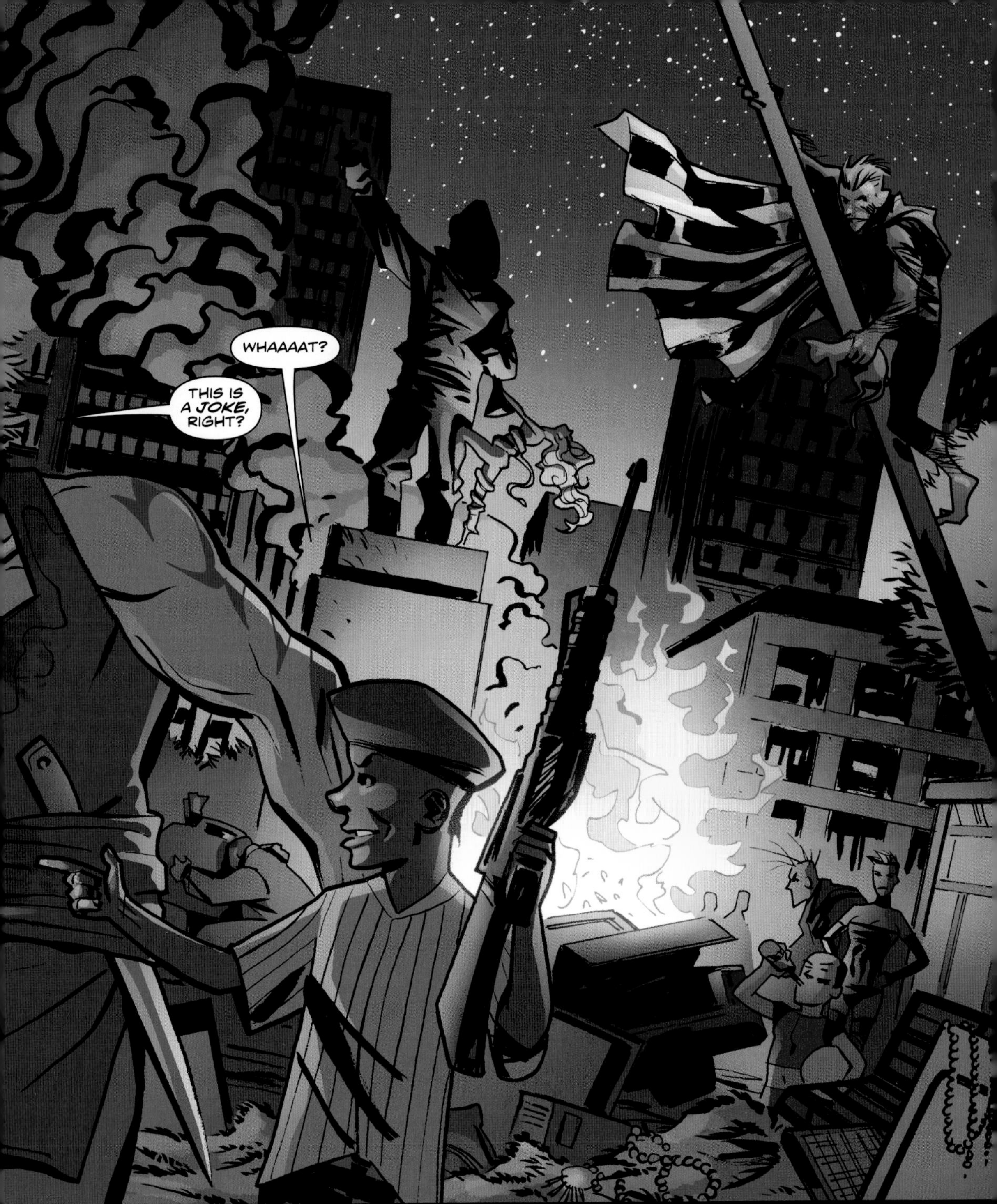
THIS IS A JOKE, RIGHT?
WHAAAAT?
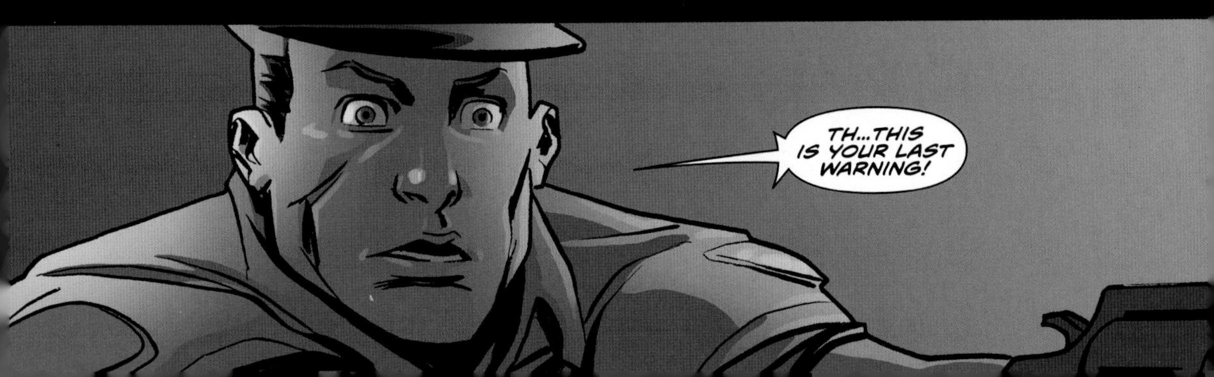
TH...THIS IS YOUR LAST WARNING!

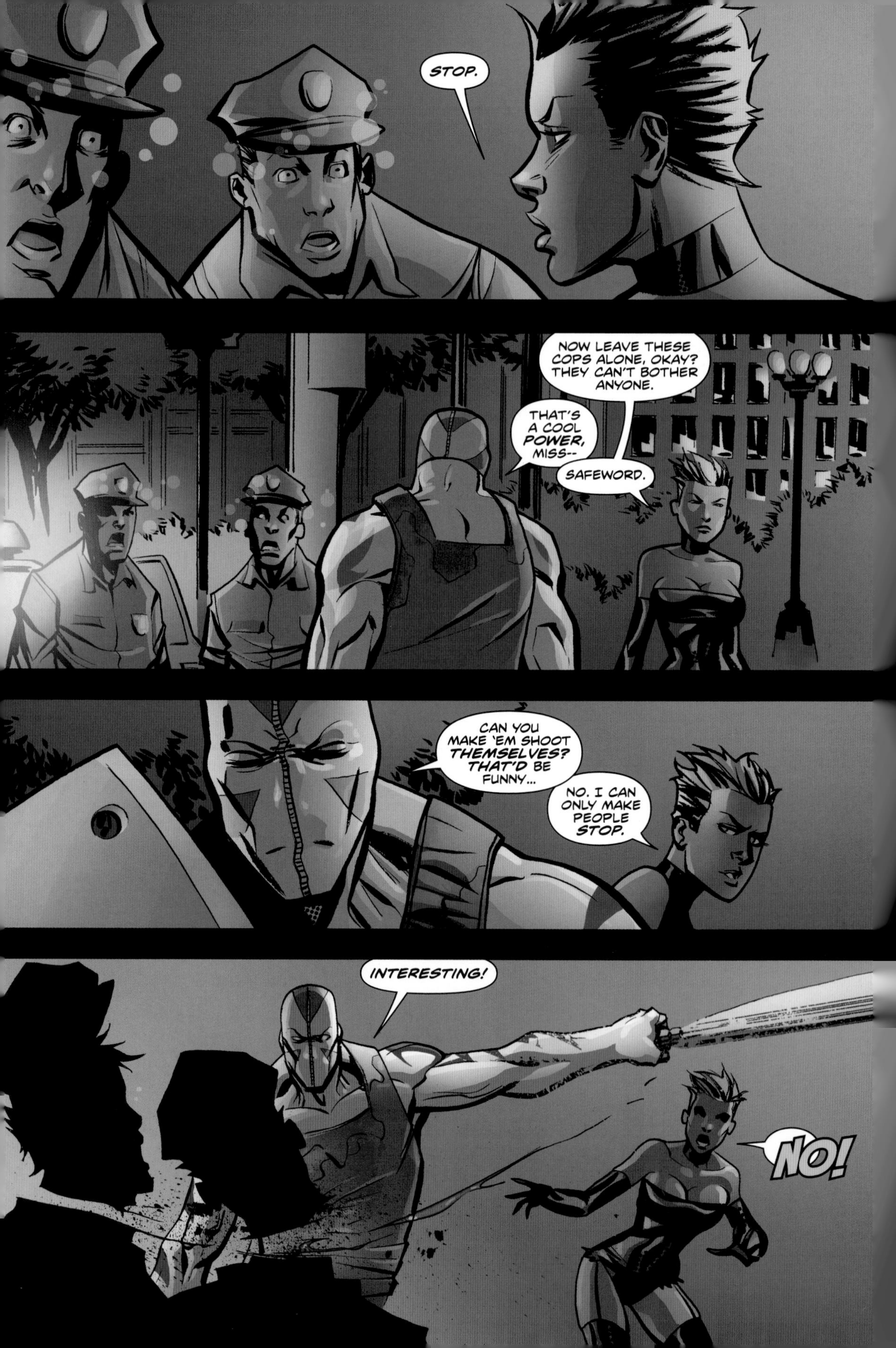
STOP.
NOW LEAVE THESE COPS ALONE, OKAY? THEY CAN'T BOTHER ANYONE.
THAT'S A COOL *POWER*, MISS--
SAFEWORD.
CAN YOU MAKE 'EM SHOOT *THEMSELVES? THAT'D* BE FUNNY...
NO. I CAN ONLY MAKE PEOPLE *STOP.*
*INTERESTING!*
NO!

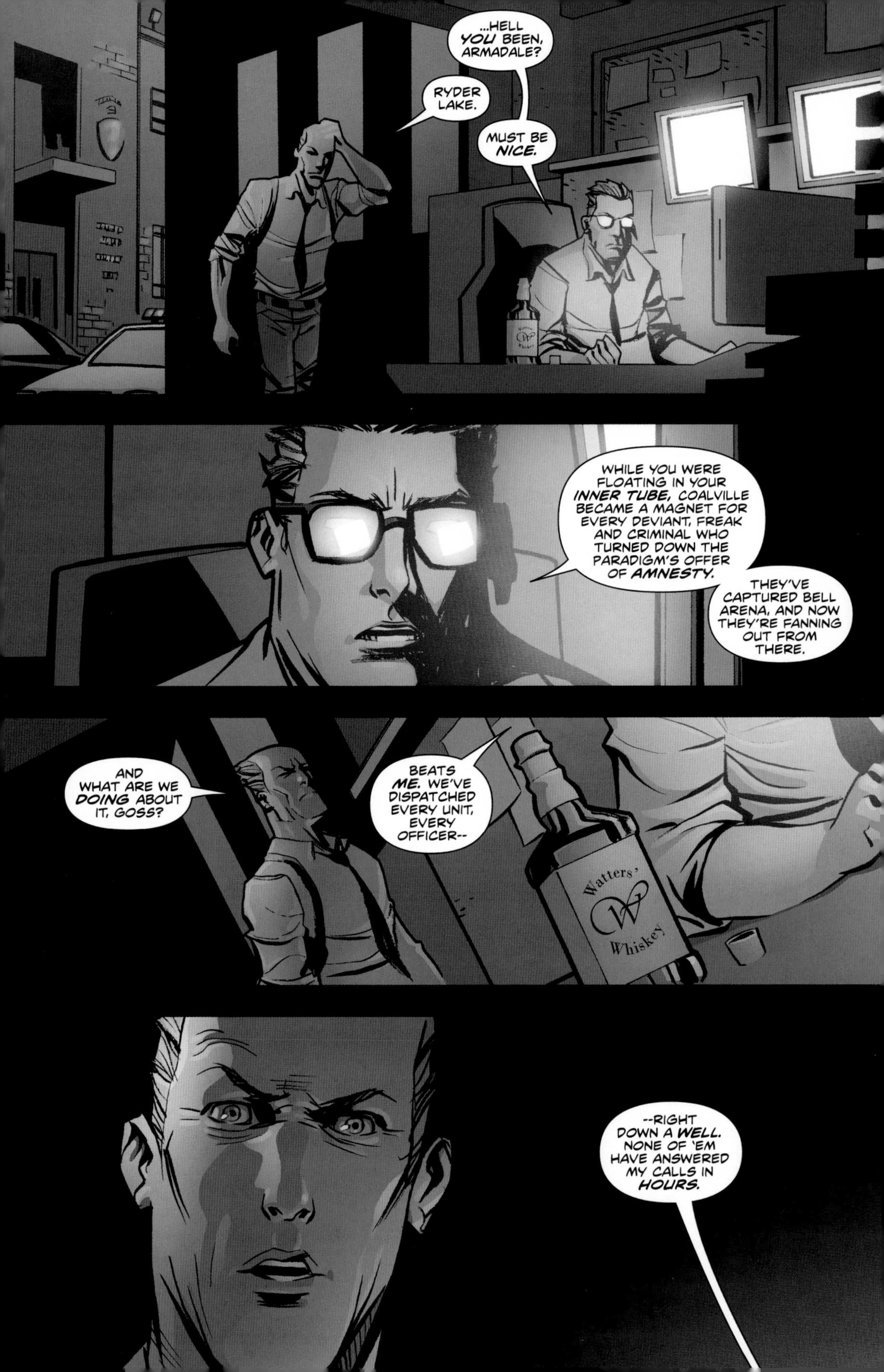

...HELL *YOU* BEEN, ARMADALE?
RYDER LAKE.
MUST BE *NICE.*
WHILE YOU WERE FLOATING IN YOUR *INNER TUBE,* COALVILLE BECAME A MAGNET FOR EVERY DEVIANT, FREAK AND CRIMINAL WHO TURNED DOWN THE PARADIGM'S OFFER OF *AMNESTY.*
THEY'VE CAPTURED BELL ARENA, AND NOW THEY'RE FANNING OUT FROM THERE.
AND WHAT ARE WE *DOING* ABOUT IT, GOSS?
BEATS *ME.* WE'VE DISPATCHED EVERY UNIT, EVERY OFFICER--
Watters' Whiskey
--RIGHT DOWN A *WELL.* NONE OF 'EM HAVE ANSWERED MY CALLS IN *HOURS.*

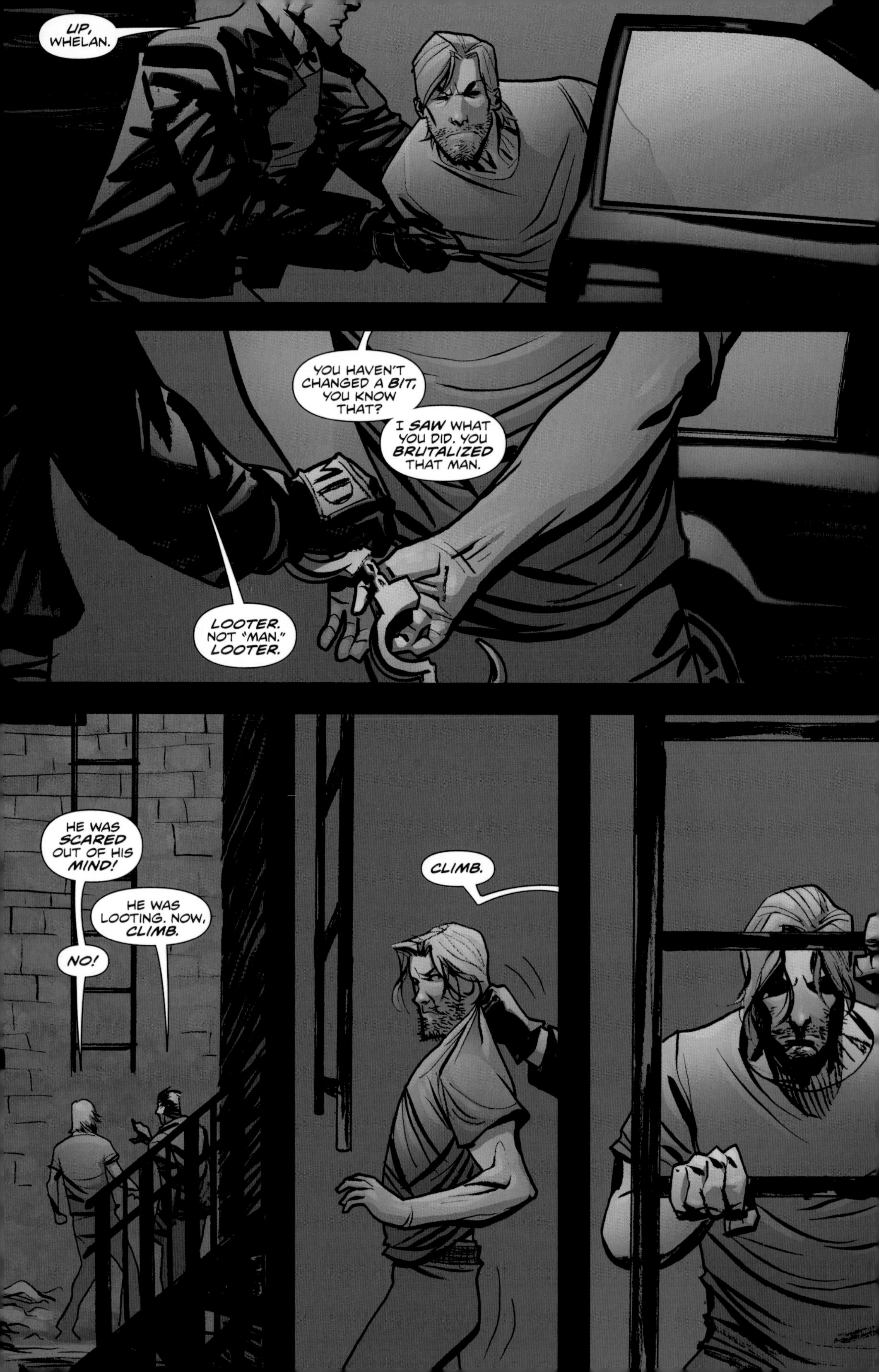
UP, WHELAN.
YOU HAVEN'T CHANGED A BIT, YOU KNOW THAT?
I SAW WHAT YOU DID. YOU BRUTALIZED THAT MAN.
LOOTER. NOT "MAN." LOOTER.
HE WAS SCARED OUT OF HIS MIND!
HE WAS LOOTING. NOW, CLIMB.
NO!
CLIMB.

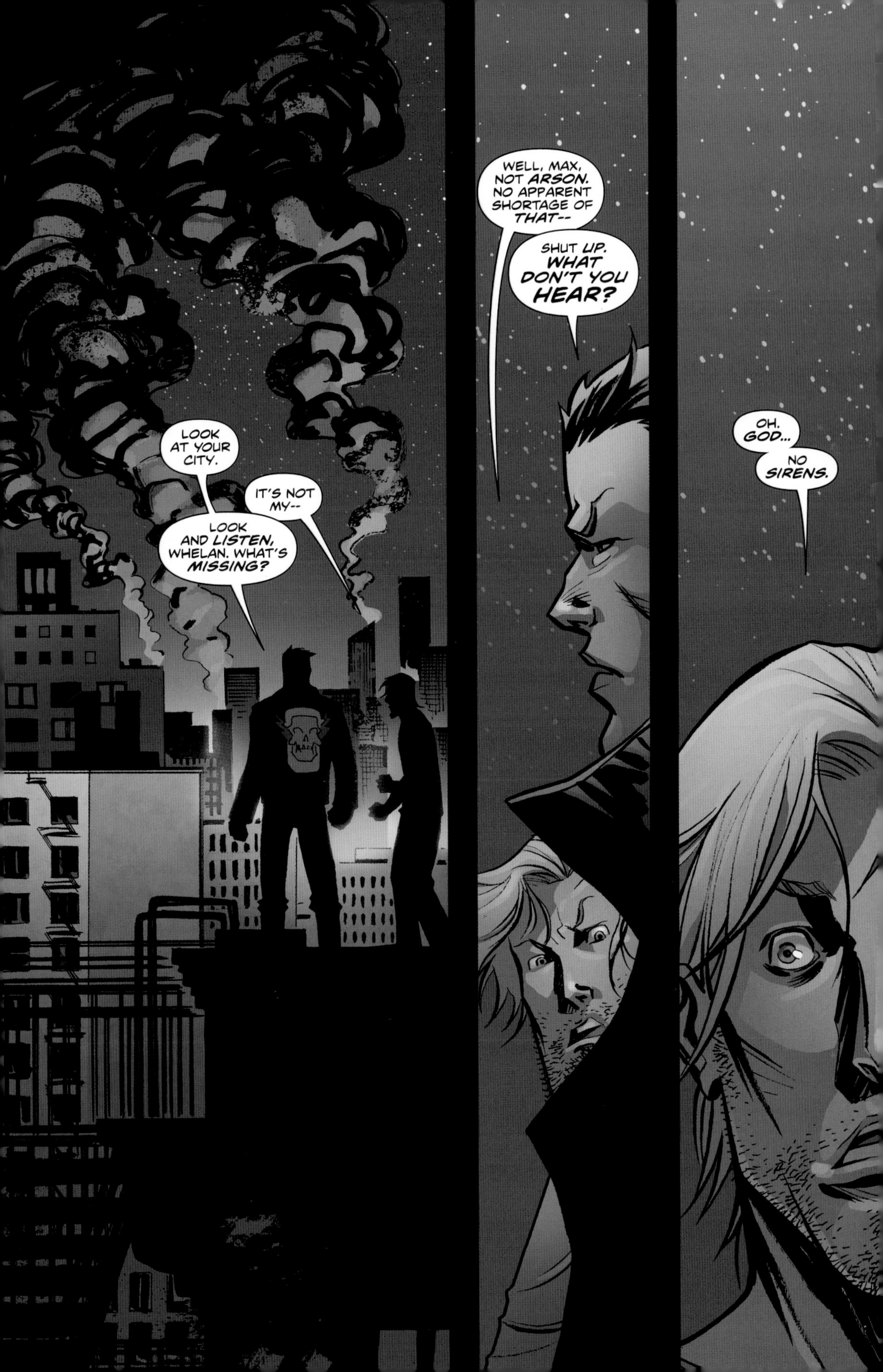
LOOK AT YOUR CITY.
IT'S NOT MY--
LOOK AND LISTEN, WHELAN. WHAT'S MISSING?
WELL, MAX, NOT ARSON. NO APPARENT SHORTAGE OF THAT--
SHUT UP. WHAT DON'T YOU HEAR?
OH. GOD...
NO SIRENS.

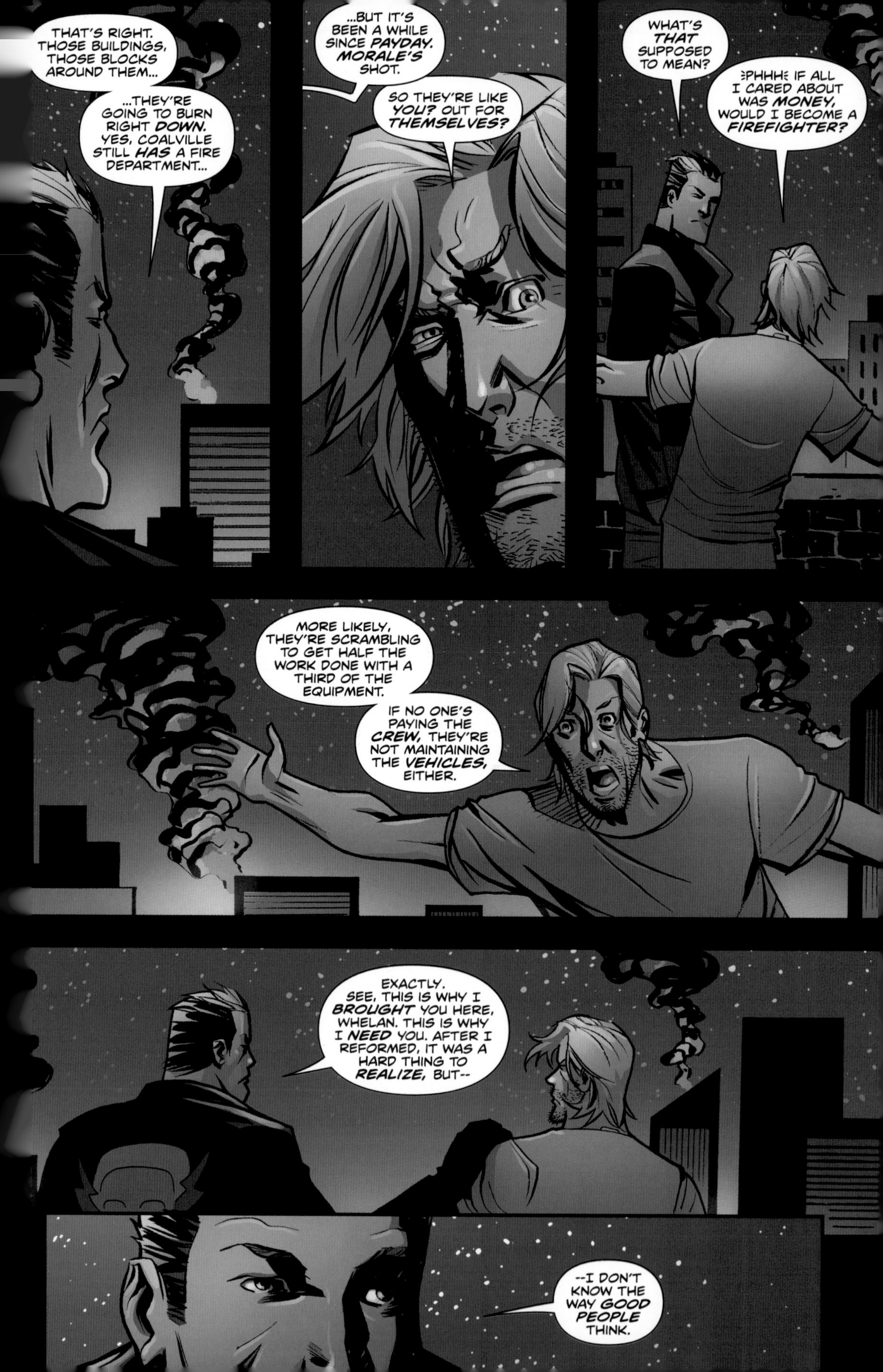
THAT'S RIGHT. THOSE BUILDINGS, THOSE BLOCKS AROUND THEM...
...THEY'RE GOING TO BURN RIGHT DOWN. YES, COALVILLE STILL HAS A FIRE DEPARTMENT...
...BUT IT'S BEEN A WHILE SINCE PAYDAY. MORALE'S SHOT.
SO THEY'RE LIKE YOU? OUT FOR THEMSELVES?
WHAT'S THAT SUPPOSED TO MEAN?
PHHH! IF ALL I CARED ABOUT WAS MONEY, WOULD I BECOME A FIREFIGHTER?
MORE LIKELY, THEY'RE SCRAMBLING TO GET HALF THE WORK DONE WITH A THIRD OF THE EQUIPMENT.
IF NO ONE'S PAYING THE CREW, THEY'RE NOT MAINTAINING THE VEHICLES, EITHER.
EXACTLY. SEE, THIS IS WHY I BROUGHT YOU HERE, WHELAN. THIS IS WHY I NEED YOU. AFTER I REFORMED, IT WAS A HARD THING TO REALIZE, BUT--
--I DON'T KNOW THE WAY GOOD PEOPLE THINK.

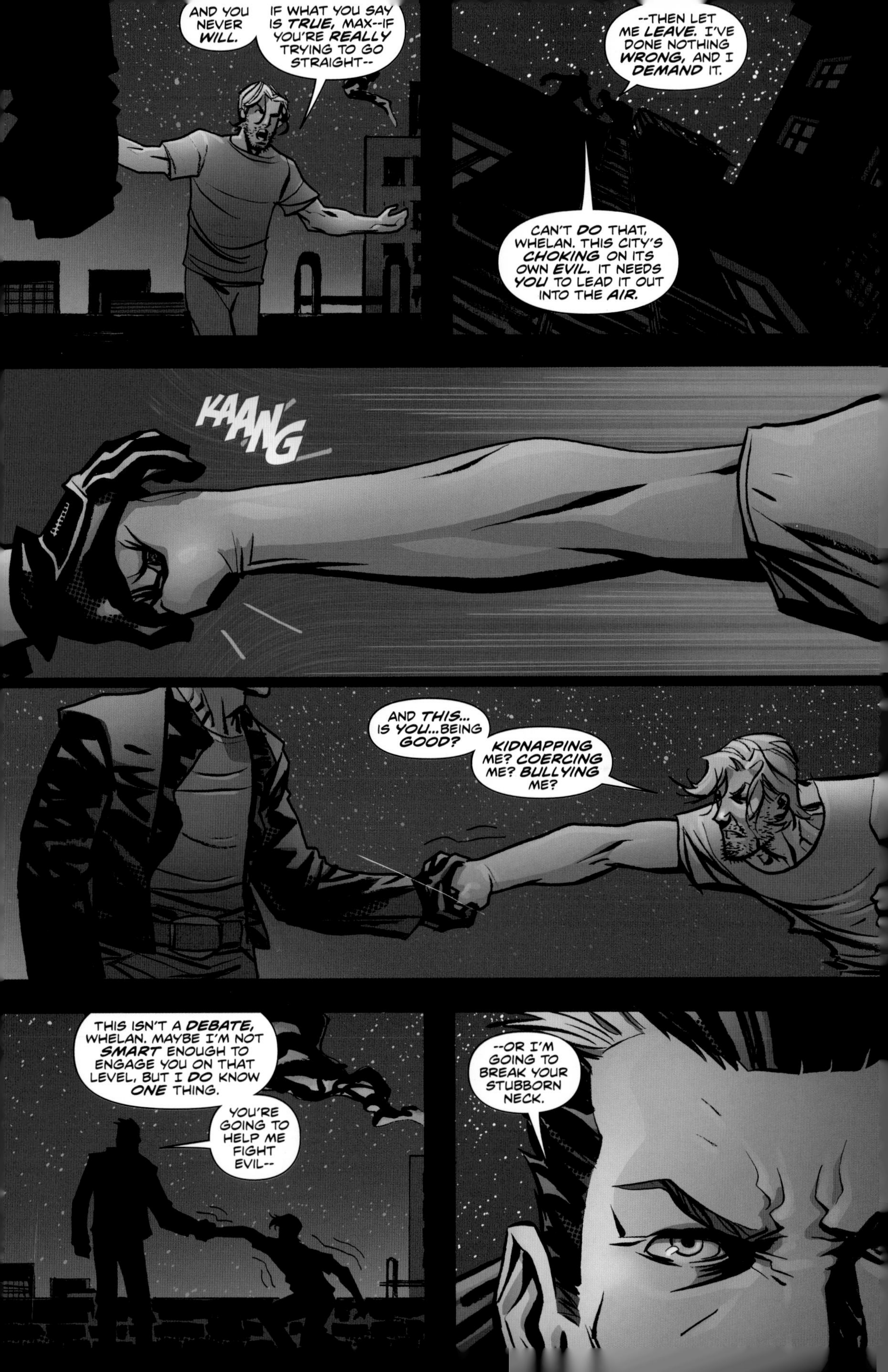
AND YOU NEVER WILL.
IF WHAT YOU SAY IS TRUE, MAX--IF YOU'RE REALLY TRYING TO GO STRAIGHT--
--THEN LET ME LEAVE. I'VE DONE NOTHING WRONG, AND I DEMAND IT.
CAN'T DO THAT, WHELAN. THIS CITY'S CHOKING ON ITS OWN EVIL. IT NEEDS YOU TO LEAD IT OUT INTO THE AIR.
KAANG
AND THIS... IS YOU...BEING GOOD?
KIDNAPPING ME? COERCING ME? BULLYING ME?
THIS ISN'T A DEBATE, WHELAN. MAYBE I'M NOT SMART ENOUGH TO ENGAGE YOU ON THAT LEVEL, BUT I DO KNOW ONE THING.
YOU'RE GOING TO HELP ME FIGHT EVIL--
--OR I'M GOING TO BREAK YOUR STUBBORN NECK.

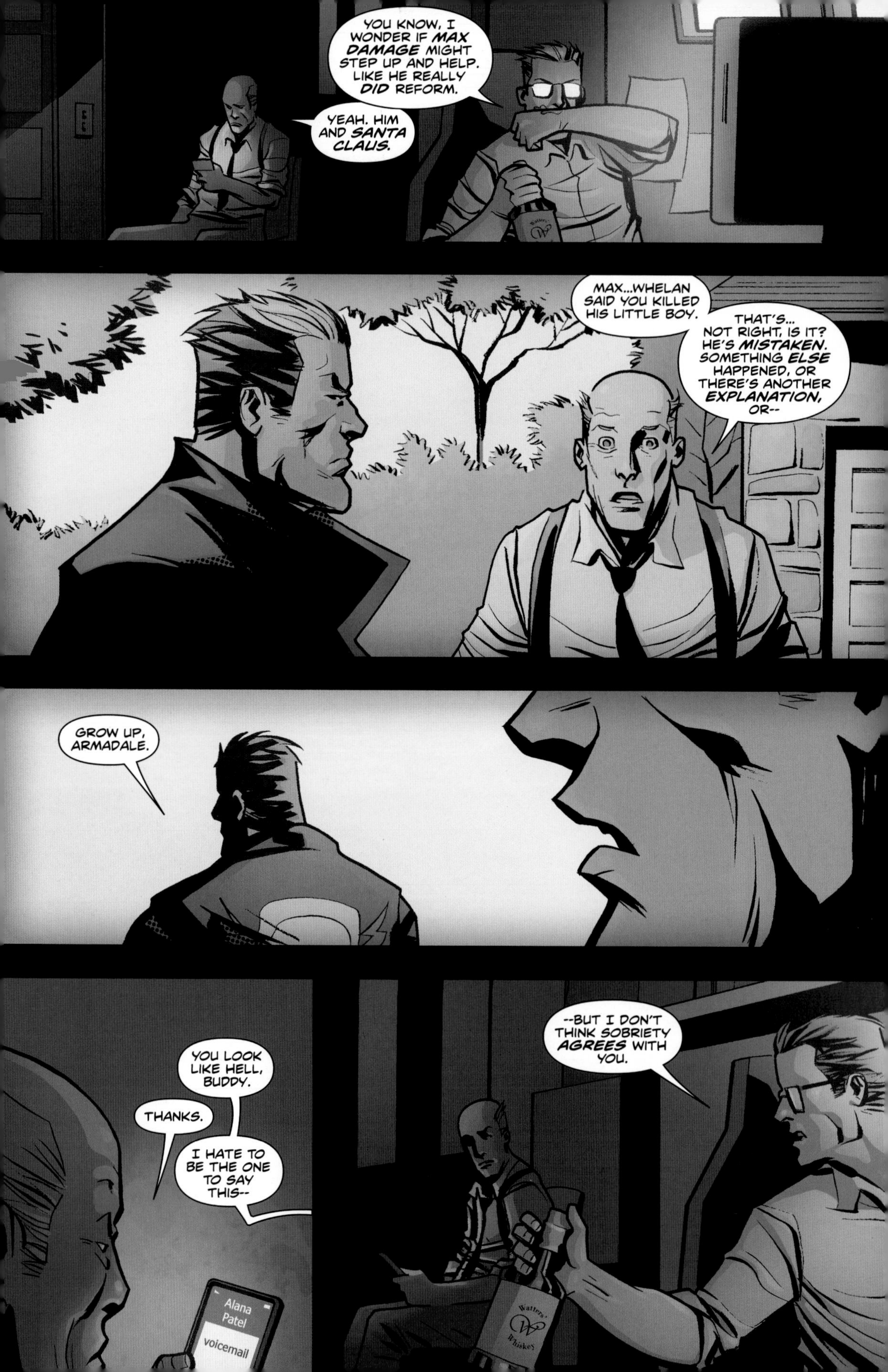
YOU KNOW, I WONDER IF MAX DAMAGE MIGHT STEP UP AND HELP. LIKE HE REALLY DID REFORM.
YEAH. HIM AND SANTA CLAUS.
Watters' W
MAX...WHELAN SAID YOU KILLED HIS LITTLE BOY.
THAT'S... NOT RIGHT, IS IT? HE'S MISTAKEN. SOMETHING ELSE HAPPENED, OR THERE'S ANOTHER EXPLANATION, OR--
GROW UP, ARMADALE.
YOU LOOK LIKE HELL, BUDDY.
THANKS.
I HATE TO BE THE ONE TO SAY THIS--
--BUT I DON'T THINK SOBRIETY AGREES WITH YOU.
Alana Patel
voicemail
Watters' W Whiskey

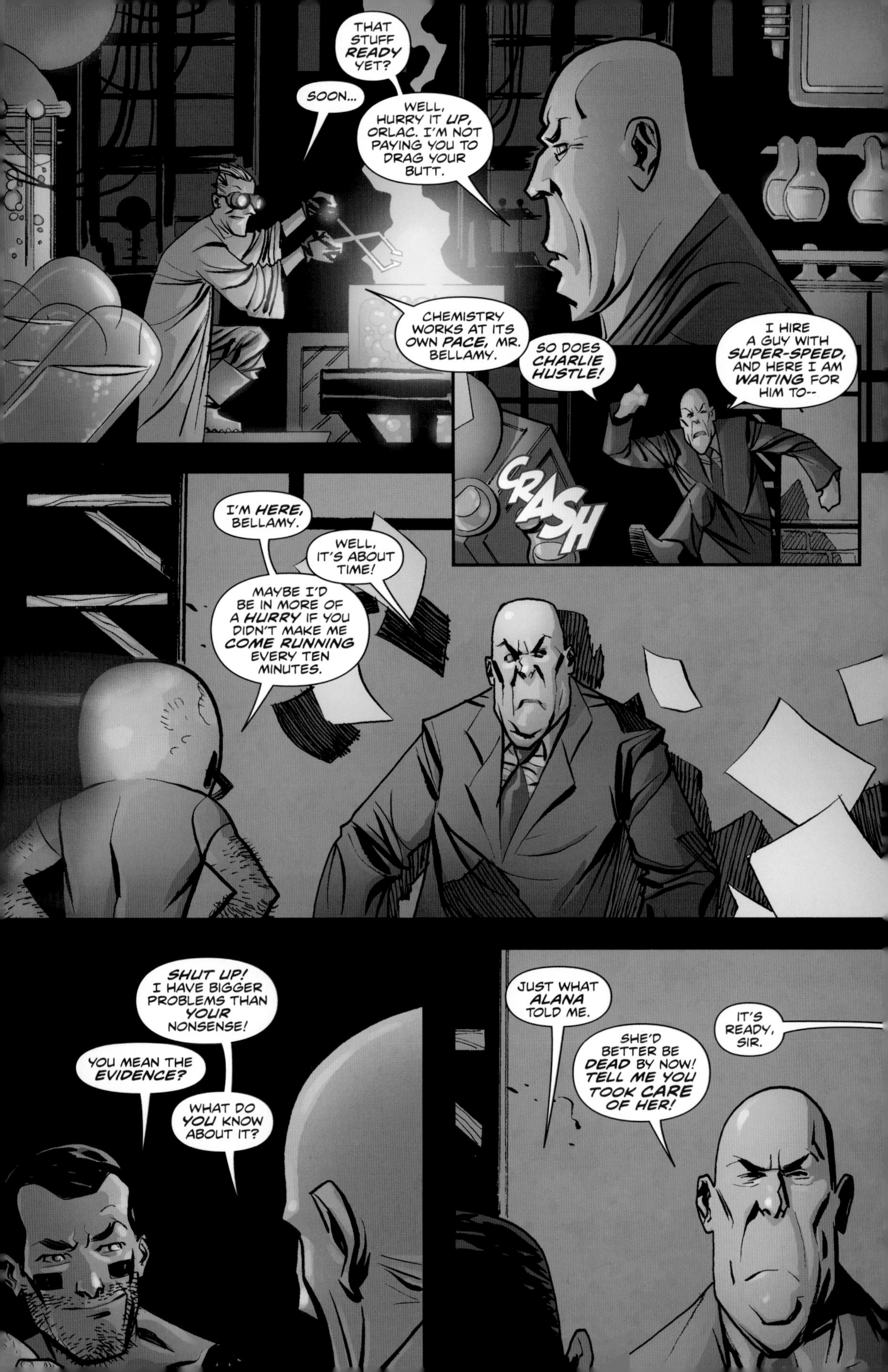
THAT STUFF READY YET?
SOON...
WELL, HURRY IT UP, ORLAC. I'M NOT PAYING YOU TO DRAG YOUR BUTT.
CHEMISTRY WORKS AT ITS OWN PACE, MR. BELLAMY.
SO DOES CHARLIE HUSTLE!
I HIRE A GUY WITH SUPER-SPEED, AND HERE I AM WAITING FOR HIM TO--
CRASH
I'M HERE, BELLAMY.
WELL, IT'S ABOUT TIME!
MAYBE I'D BE IN MORE OF A HURRY IF YOU DIDN'T MAKE ME COME RUNNING EVERY TEN MINUTES.
SHUT UP! I HAVE BIGGER PROBLEMS THAN YOUR NONSENSE!
YOU MEAN THE EVIDENCE?
WHAT DO YOU KNOW ABOUT IT?
JUST WHAT ALANA TOLD ME.
SHE'D BETTER BE DEAD BY NOW! TELL ME YOU TOOK CARE OF HER!
IT'S READY, SIR.

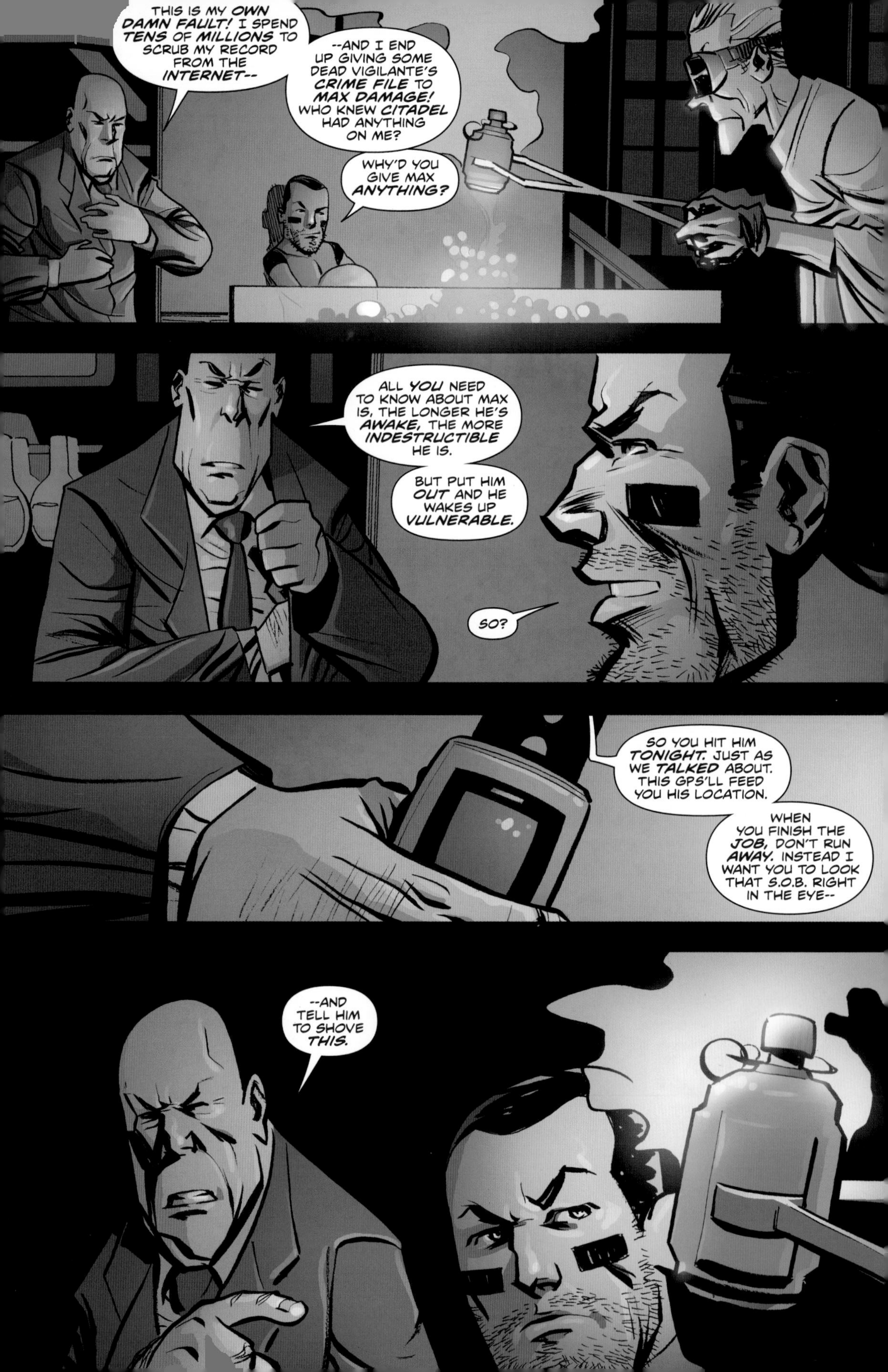
THIS IS MY OWN DAMN FAULT! I SPEND TENS OF MILLIONS TO SCRUB MY RECORD FROM THE INTERNET--
--AND I END UP GIVING SOME DEAD VIGILANTE'S CRIME FILE TO MAX DAMAGE! WHO KNEW CITADEL HAD ANYTHING ON ME?
WHY'D YOU GIVE MAX ANYTHING?
ALL YOU NEED TO KNOW ABOUT MAX IS, THE LONGER HE'S AWAKE, THE MORE INDESTRUCTIBLE HE IS.
BUT PUT HIM OUT AND HE WAKES UP VULNERABLE.
SO?
SO YOU HIT HIM TONIGHT. JUST AS WE TALKED ABOUT. THIS GPS'LL FEED YOU HIS LOCATION.
WHEN YOU FINISH THE JOB, DON'T RUN AWAY. INSTEAD I WANT YOU TO LOOK THAT S.O.B. RIGHT IN THE EYE--
--AND TELL HIM TO SHOVE THIS.

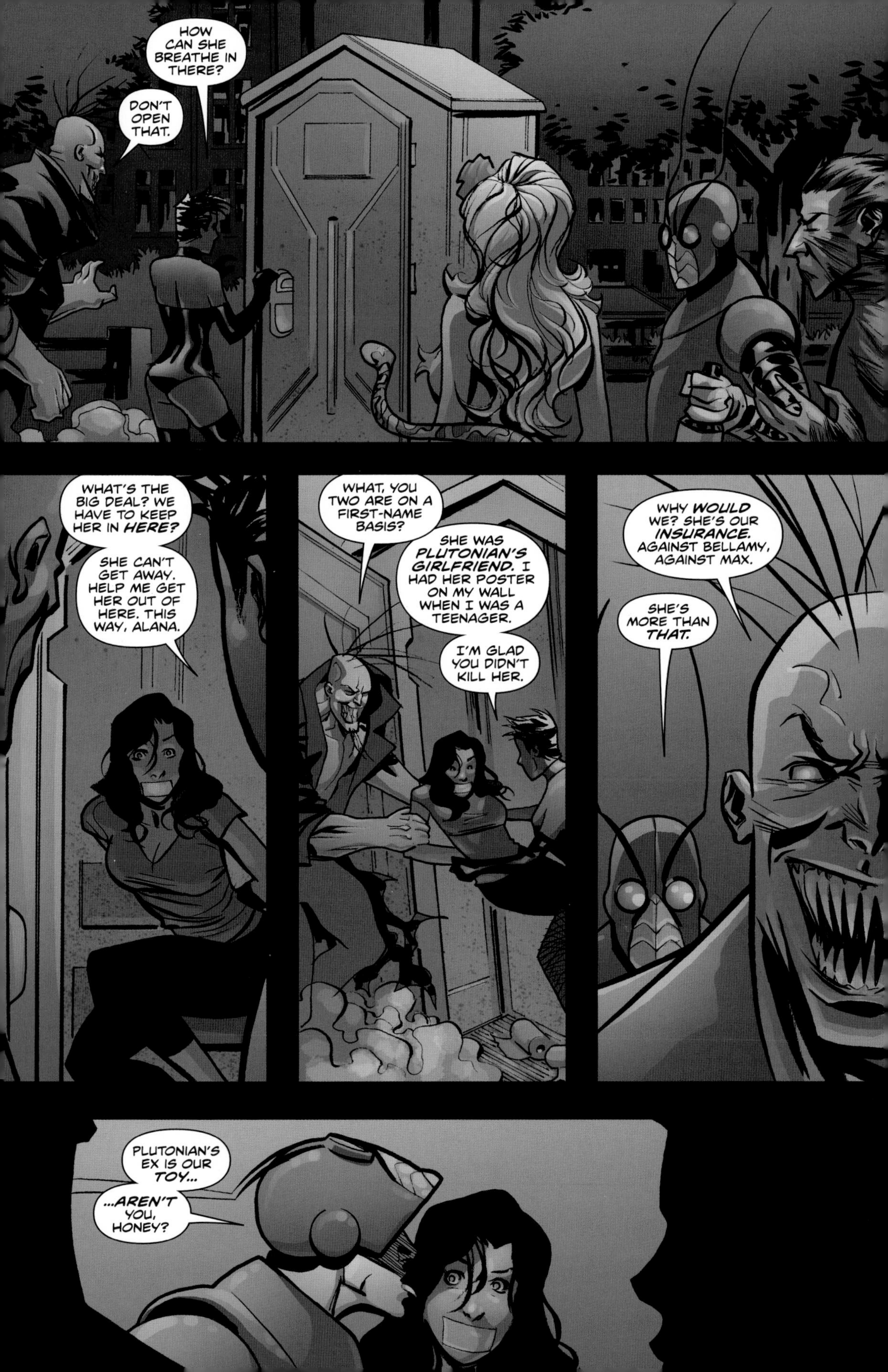
HOW CAN SHE BREATHE IN THERE?
DON'T OPEN THAT.
WHAT'S THE BIG DEAL? WE HAVE TO KEEP HER IN *HERE?*
SHE CAN'T GET AWAY. HELP ME GET HER OUT OF HERE. THIS WAY, ALANA.
WHAT, YOU TWO ARE ON A FIRST-NAME BASIS?
SHE WAS *PLUTONIAN'S GIRLFRIEND.* I HAD HER POSTER ON MY WALL WHEN I WAS A TEENAGER.
I'M GLAD YOU DIDN'T KILL HER.
WHY *WOULD* WE? SHE'S OUR *INSURANCE.* AGAINST BELLAMY, AGAINST MAX.
SHE'S MORE THAN *THAT.*
PLUTONIAN'S EX IS OUR *TOY...*
*...AREN'T* YOU, HONEY?

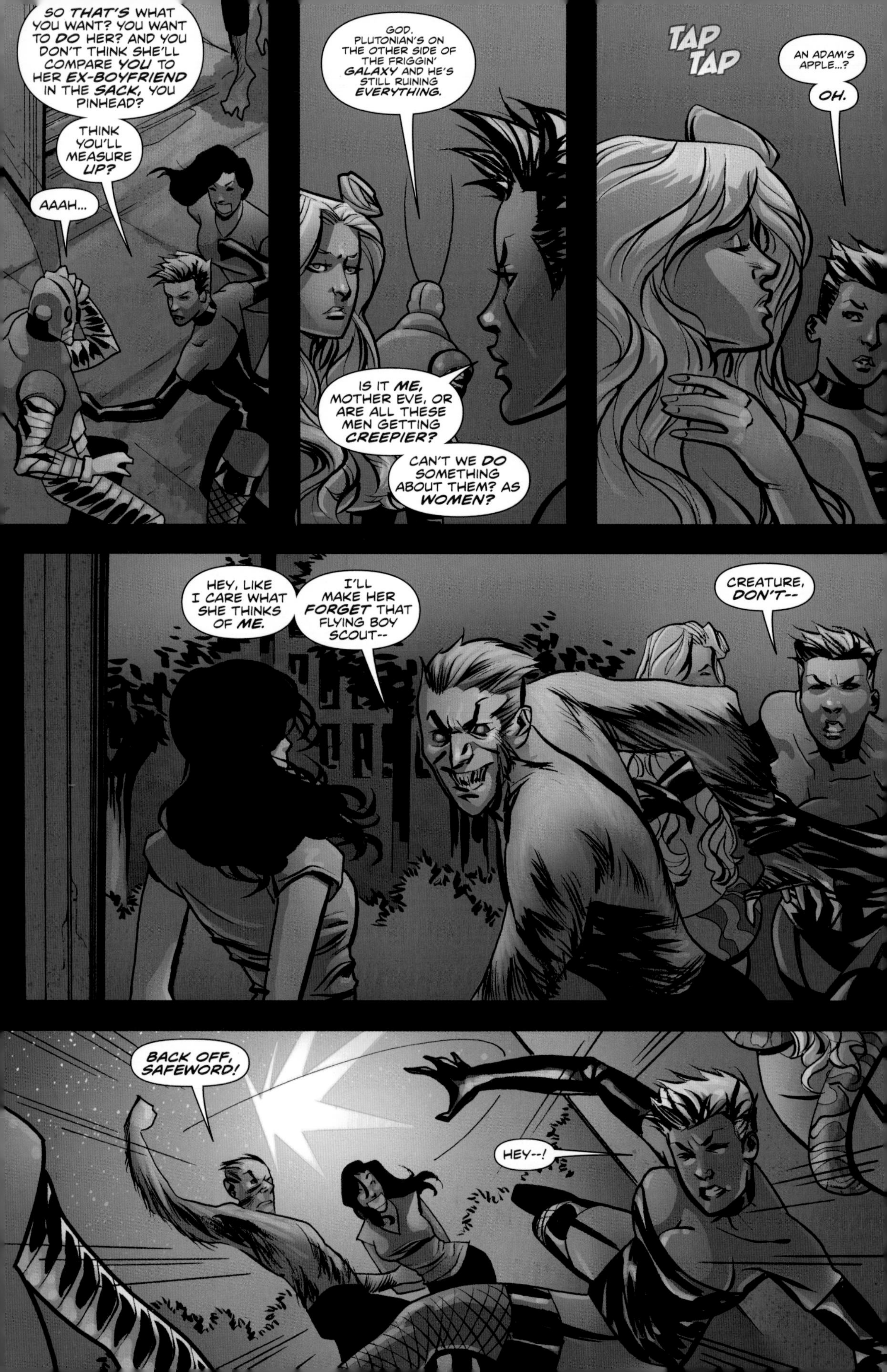

SO THAT'S WHAT YOU WANT? YOU WANT TO DO HER? AND YOU DON'T THINK SHE'LL COMPARE YOU TO HER EX-BOYFRIEND IN THE SACK, YOU PINHEAD?
THINK YOU'LL MEASURE UP?
AAAH...
GOD. PLUTONIAN'S ON THE OTHER SIDE OF THE FRIGGIN' GALAXY AND HE'S STILL RUINING EVERYTHING.
IS IT ME, MOTHER EVE, OR ARE ALL THESE MEN GETTING CREEPIER?
CAN'T WE DO SOMETHING ABOUT THEM? AS WOMEN?
TAP TAP
AN ADAM'S APPLE...?
OH.
HEY, LIKE I CARE WHAT SHE THINKS OF ME.
I'LL MAKE HER FORGET THAT FLYING BOY SCOUT--
CREATURE, DON'T--
BACK OFF, SAFEWORD!
HEY--!

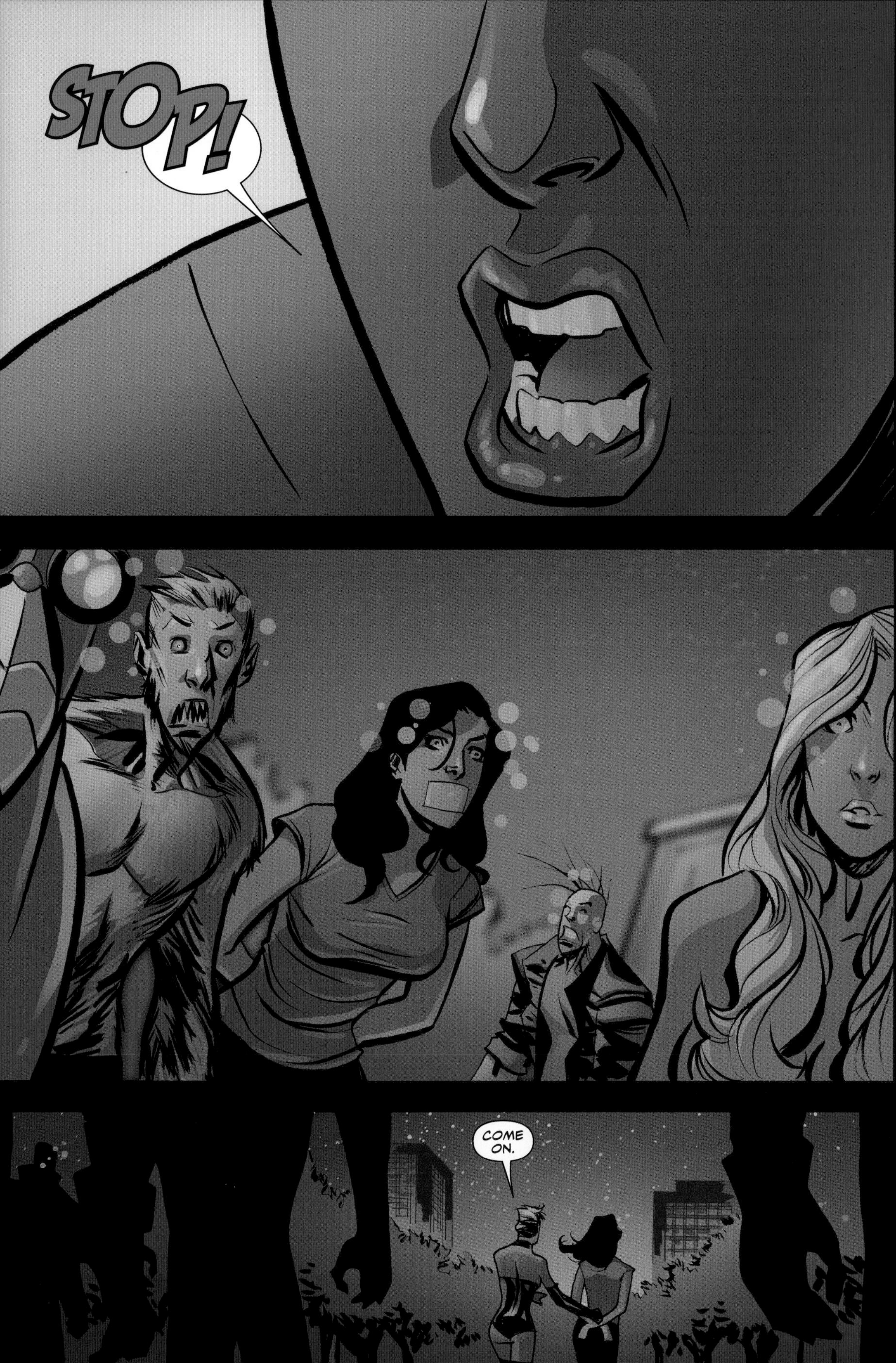
STOP!
COME ON.

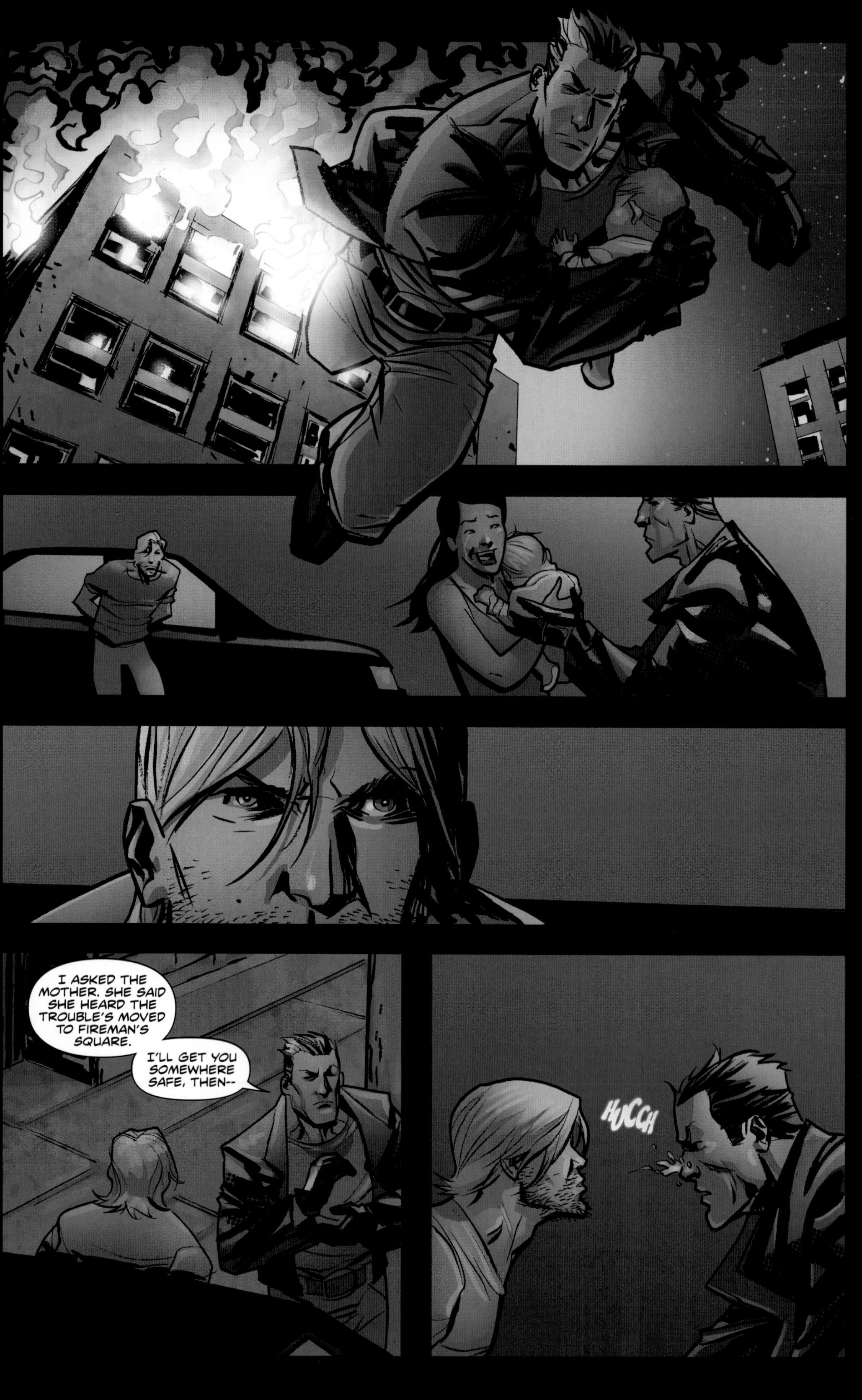
I ASKED THE MOTHER. SHE SAID SHE HEARD THE TROUBLE'S MOVED TO FIREMAN'S SQUARE.
I'LL GET YOU SOMEWHERE SAFE, THEN--
HUCCH

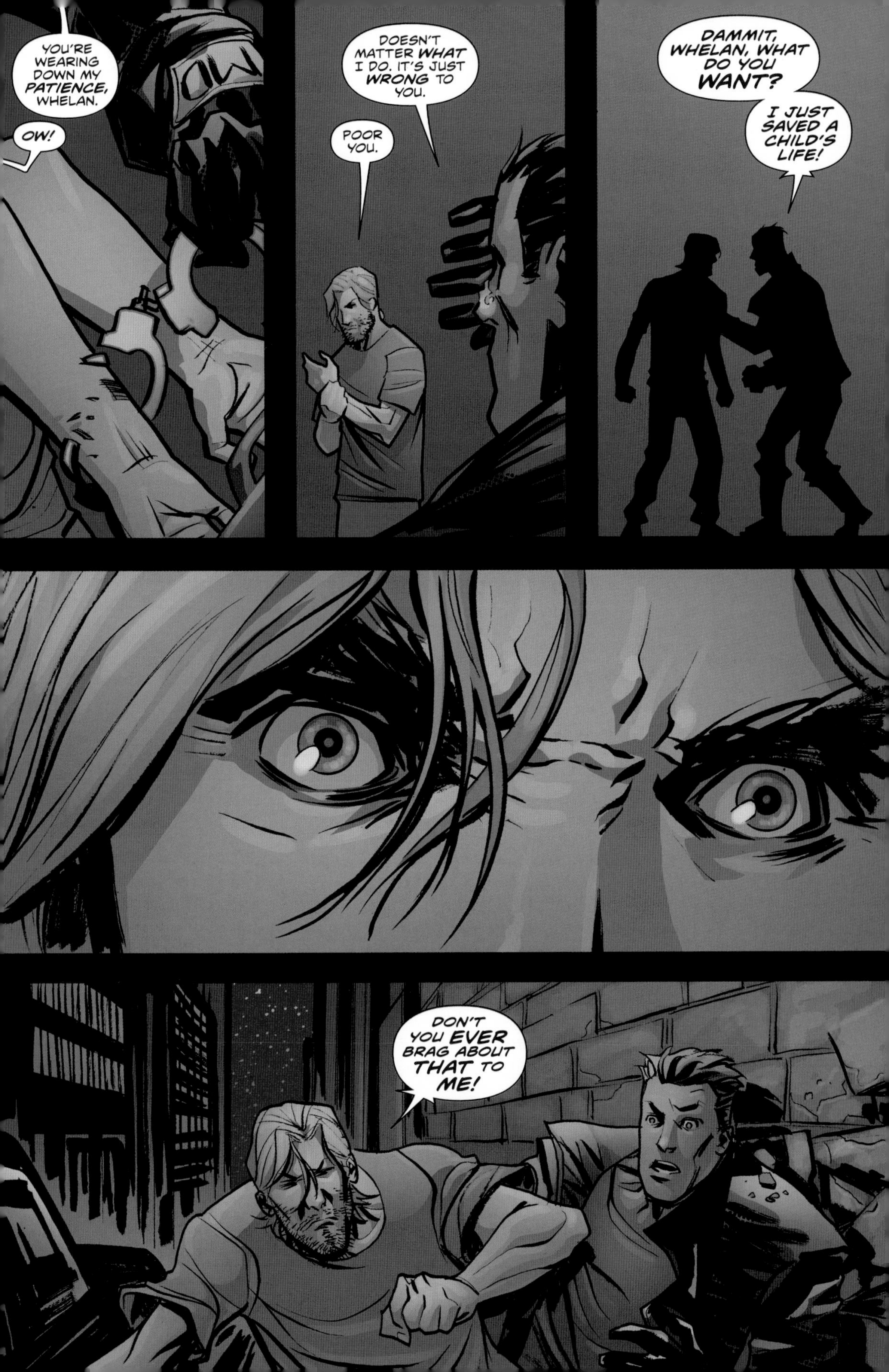
YOU'RE WEARING DOWN MY PATIENCE, WHELAN.
OW!
DOESN'T MATTER WHAT I DO. IT'S JUST WRONG TO YOU.
POOR YOU.
DAMMIT, WHELAN, WHAT DO YOU WANT?
I JUST SAVED A CHILD'S LIFE!
DON'T YOU EVER BRAG ABOUT THAT TO ME!

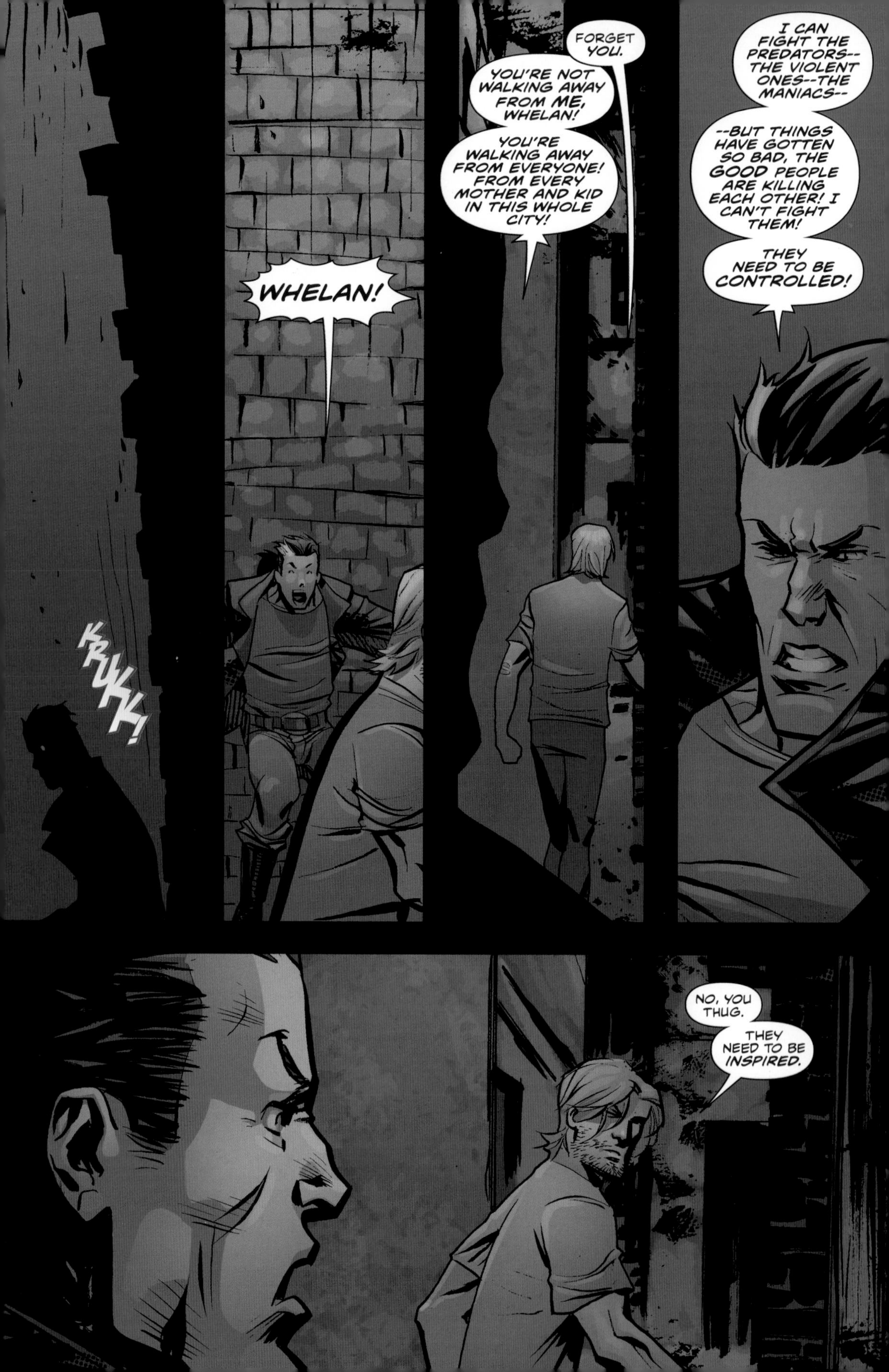
KRUKK!
WHELAN!
FORGET YOU.
YOU'RE NOT WALKING AWAY FROM ME, WHELAN!
YOU'RE WALKING AWAY FROM EVERYONE! FROM EVERY MOTHER AND KID IN THIS WHOLE CITY!
I CAN FIGHT THE PREDATORS-- THE VIOLENT ONES--THE MANIACS--
--BUT THINGS HAVE GOTTEN SO BAD, THE GOOD PEOPLE ARE KILLING EACH OTHER! I CAN'T FIGHT THEM!
THEY NEED TO BE CONTROLLED!
NO, YOU THUG.
THEY NEED TO BE INSPIRED.

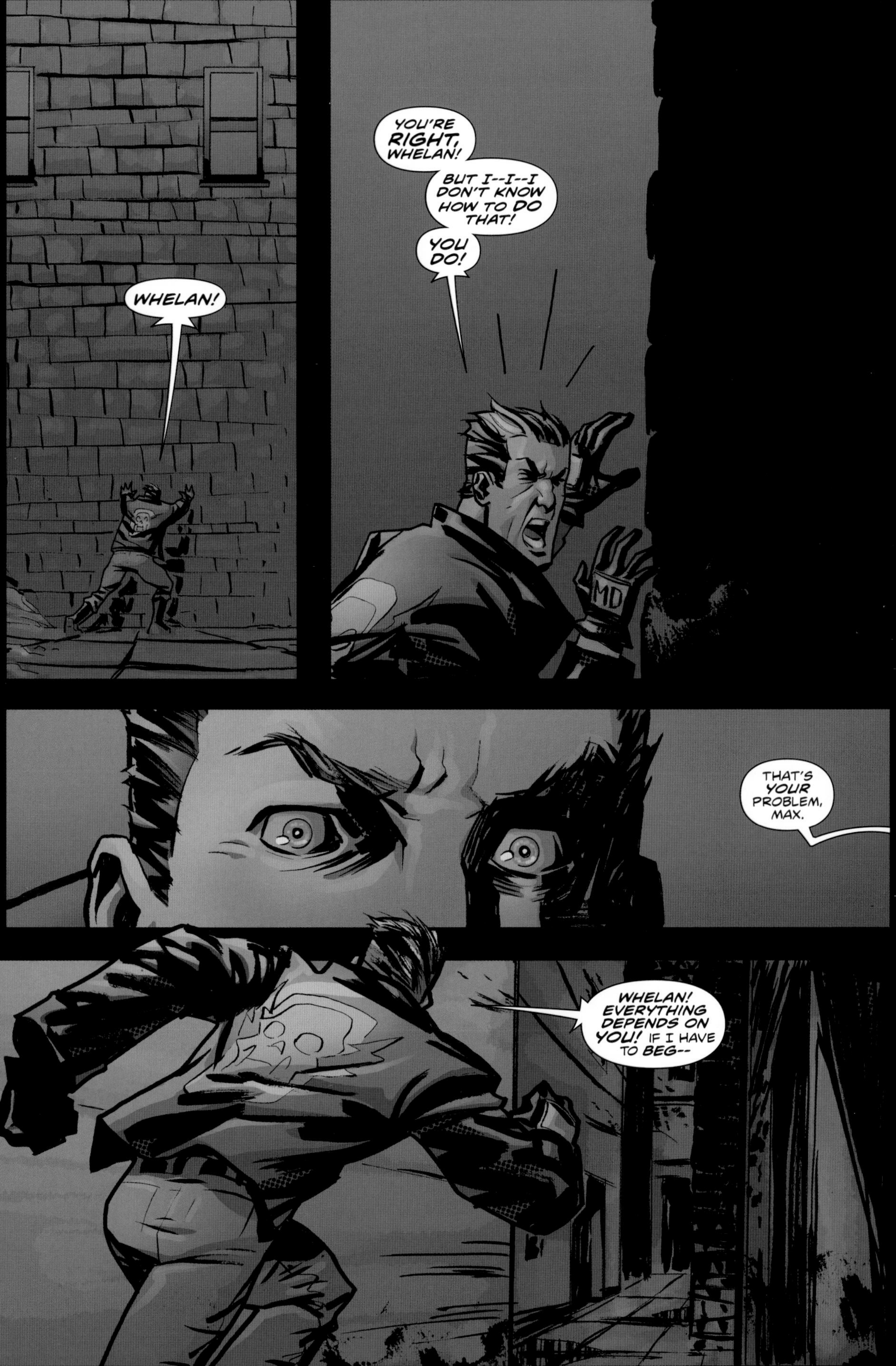
WHELAN!
YOU'RE RIGHT, WHELAN!
BUT I--I--I DON'T KNOW HOW TO DO THAT!
YOU DO!
MD
THAT'S YOUR PROBLEM, MAX.
WHELAN! EVERYTHING DEPENDS ON YOU! IF I HAVE TO BEG--

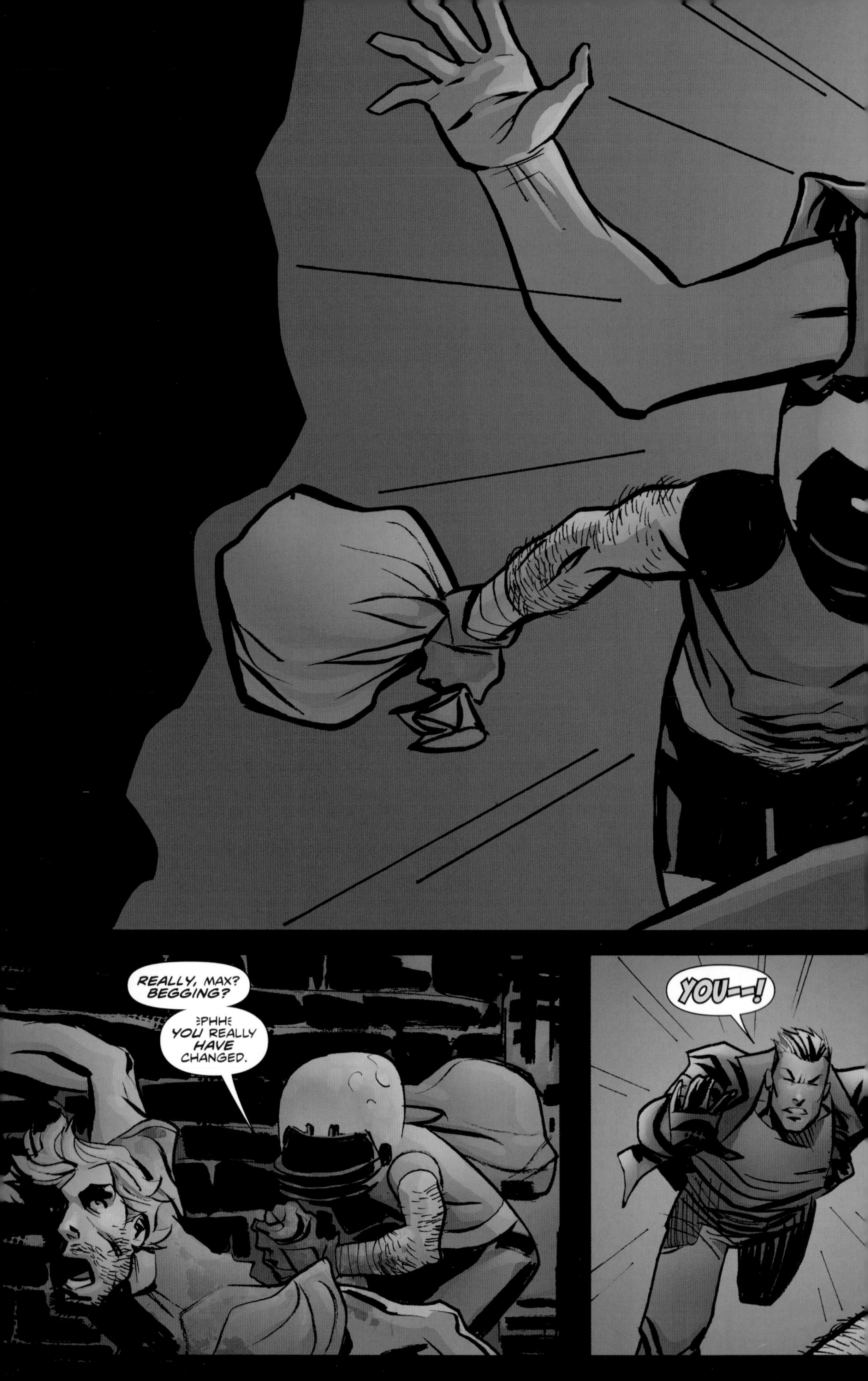
REALLY, MAX? BEGGING?
PHH YOU REALLY HAVE CHANGED.
YOU--!

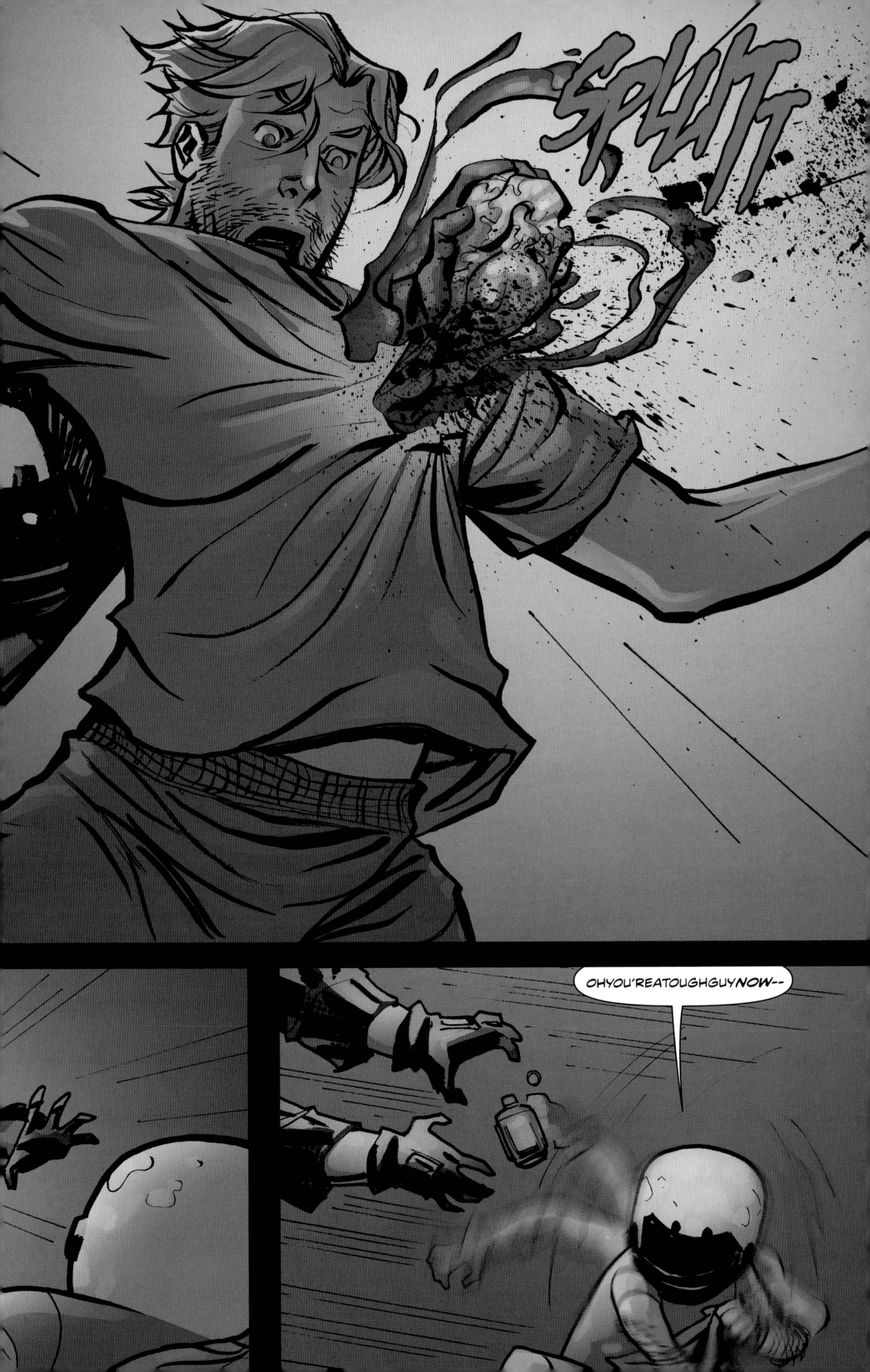
SPLUTT
OHYOU'REATOUGHGUY*NOW*--

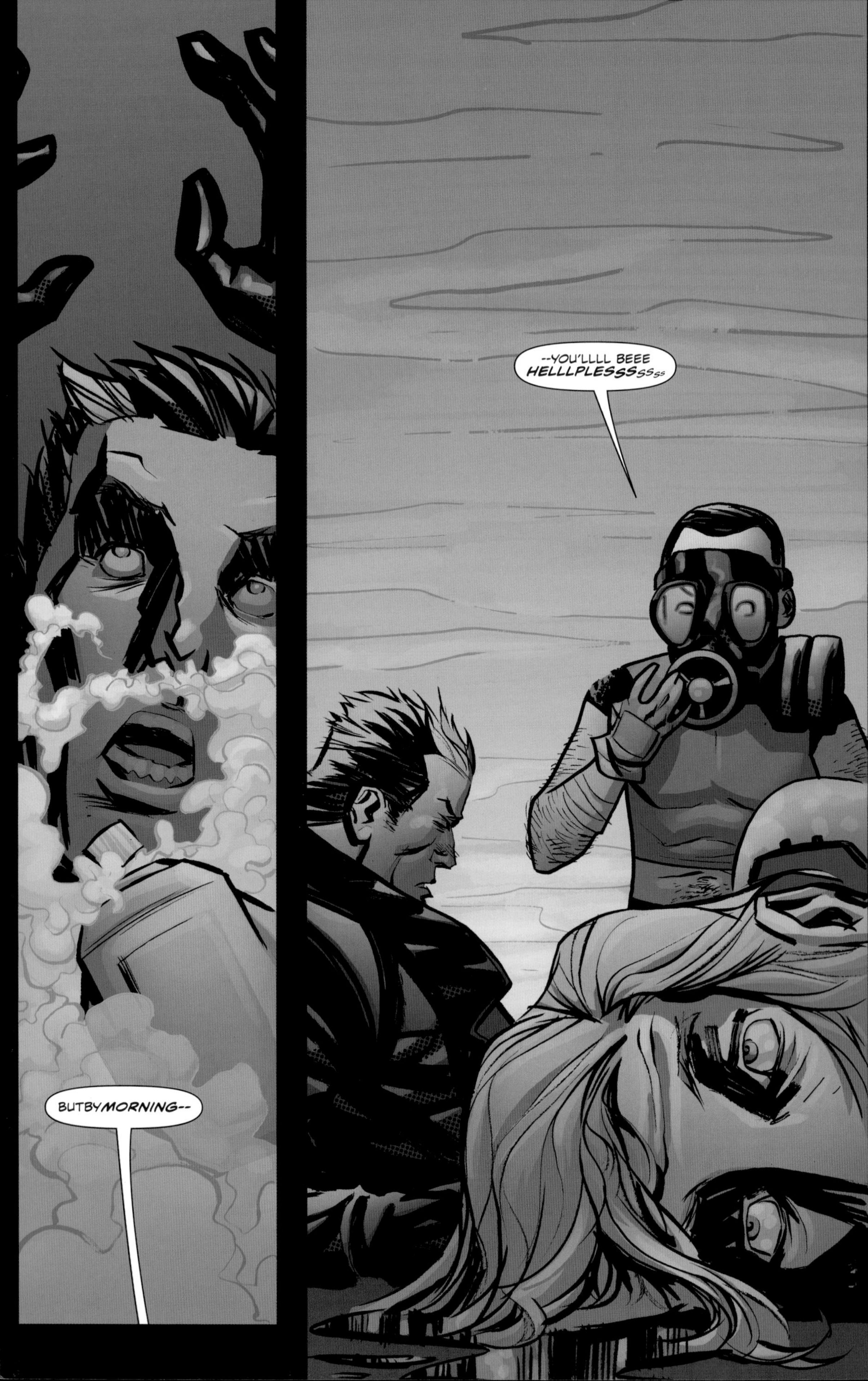
--YOU'LLLL BEEE HELLLPLESSSssss
BUTBYMORNING--

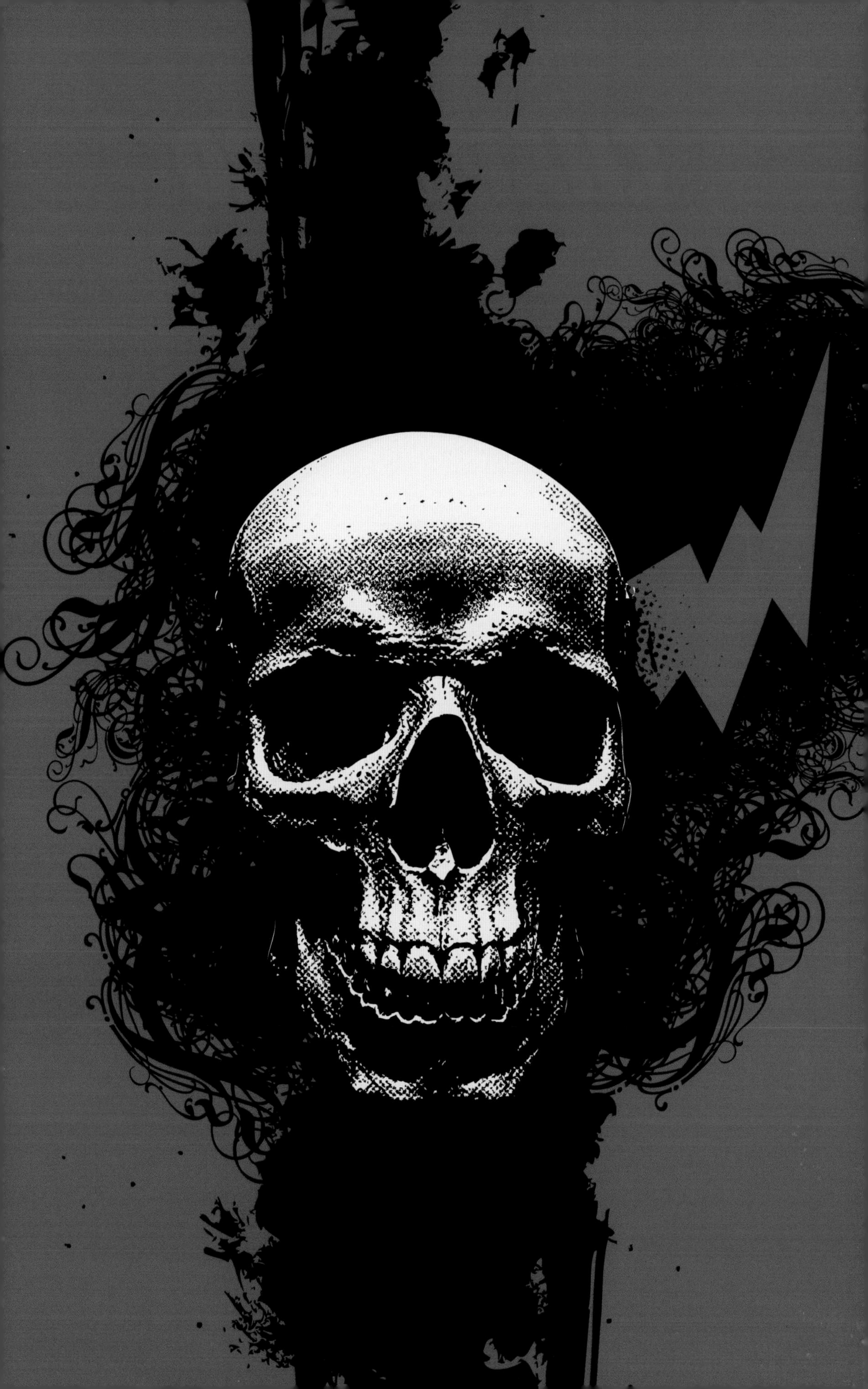

# CHAPTER 20

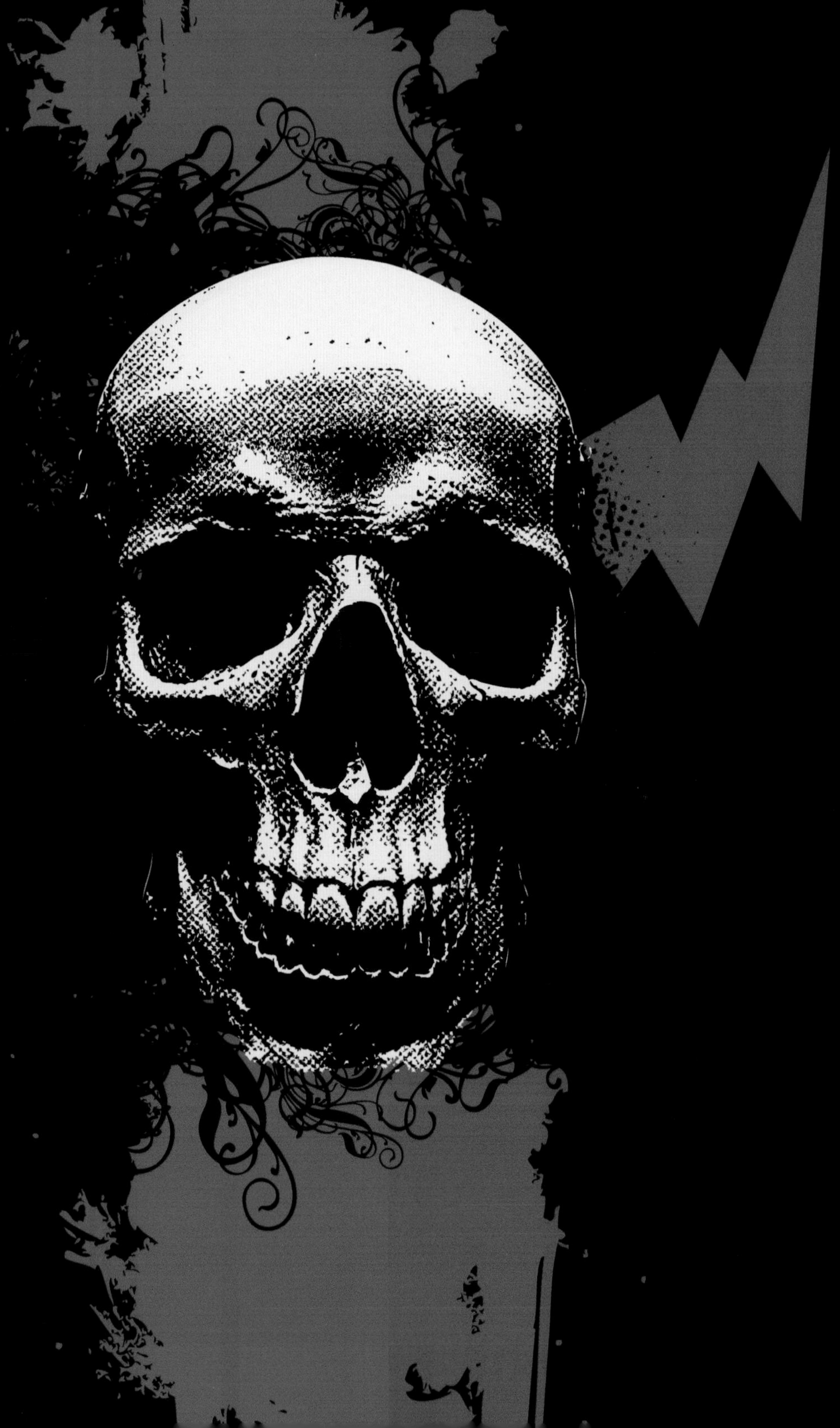

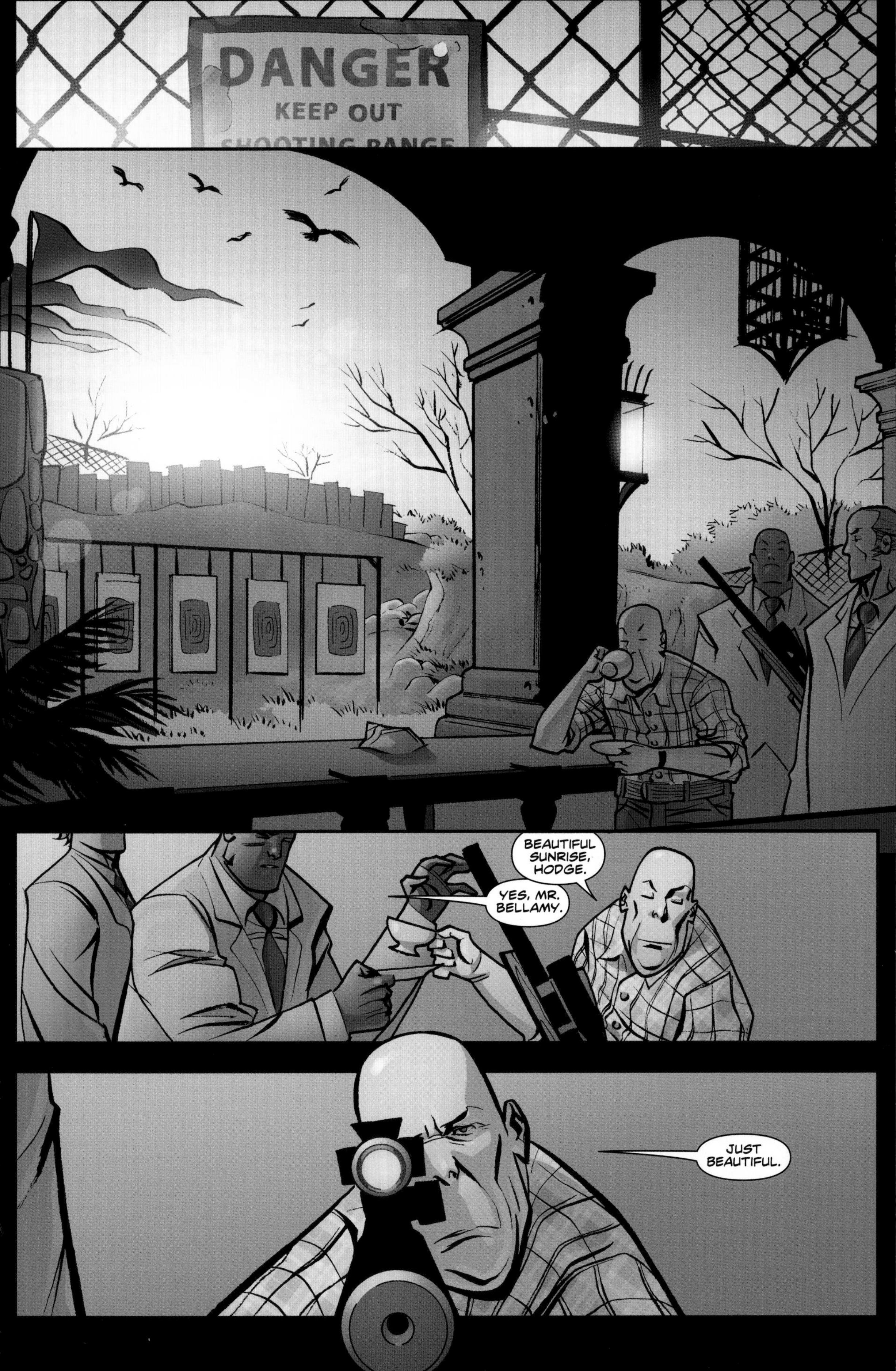
DANGER
KEEP OUT
BEAUTIFUL SUNRISE, HODGE.
YES, MR. BELLAMY.
JUST BEAUTIFUL.

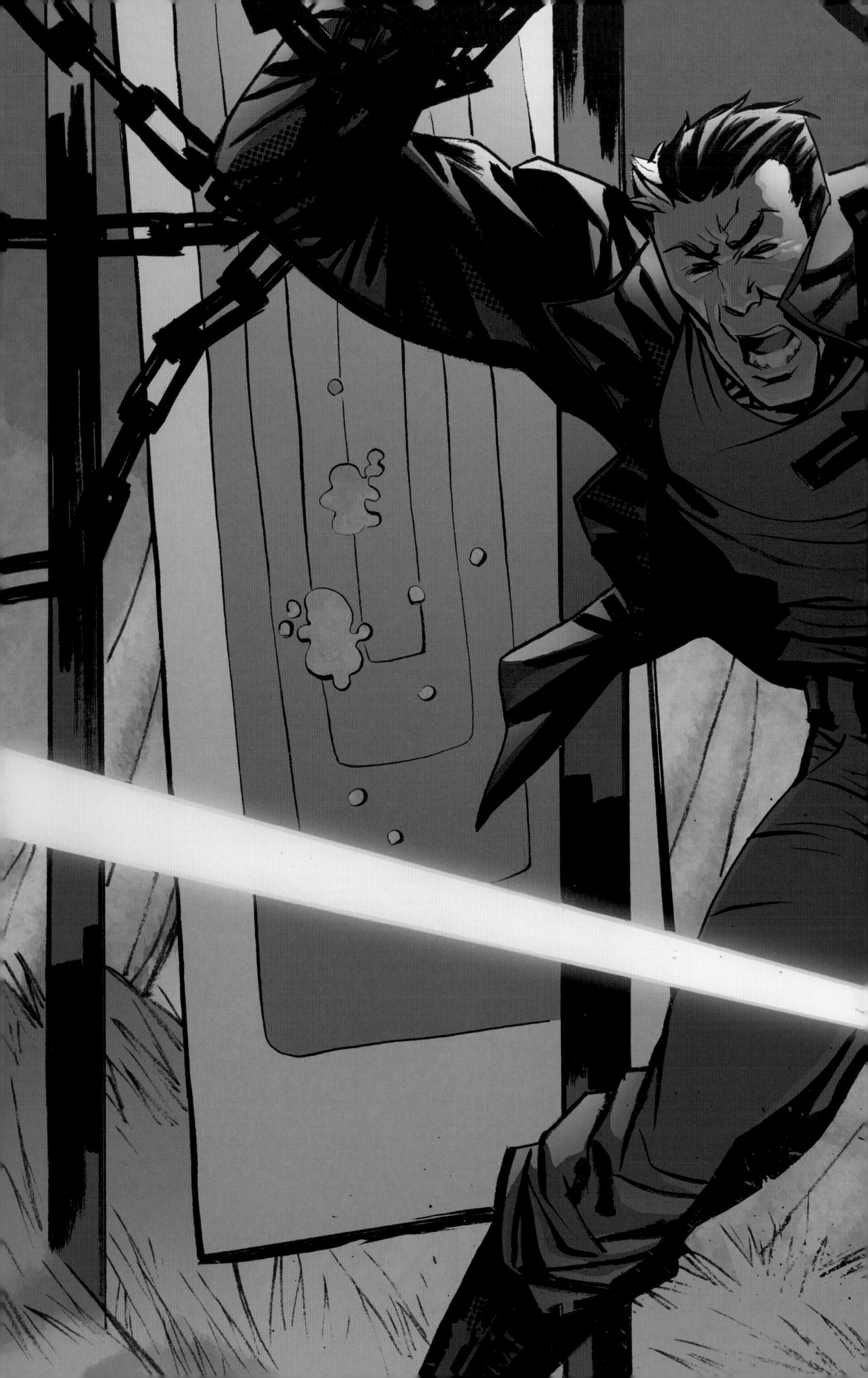

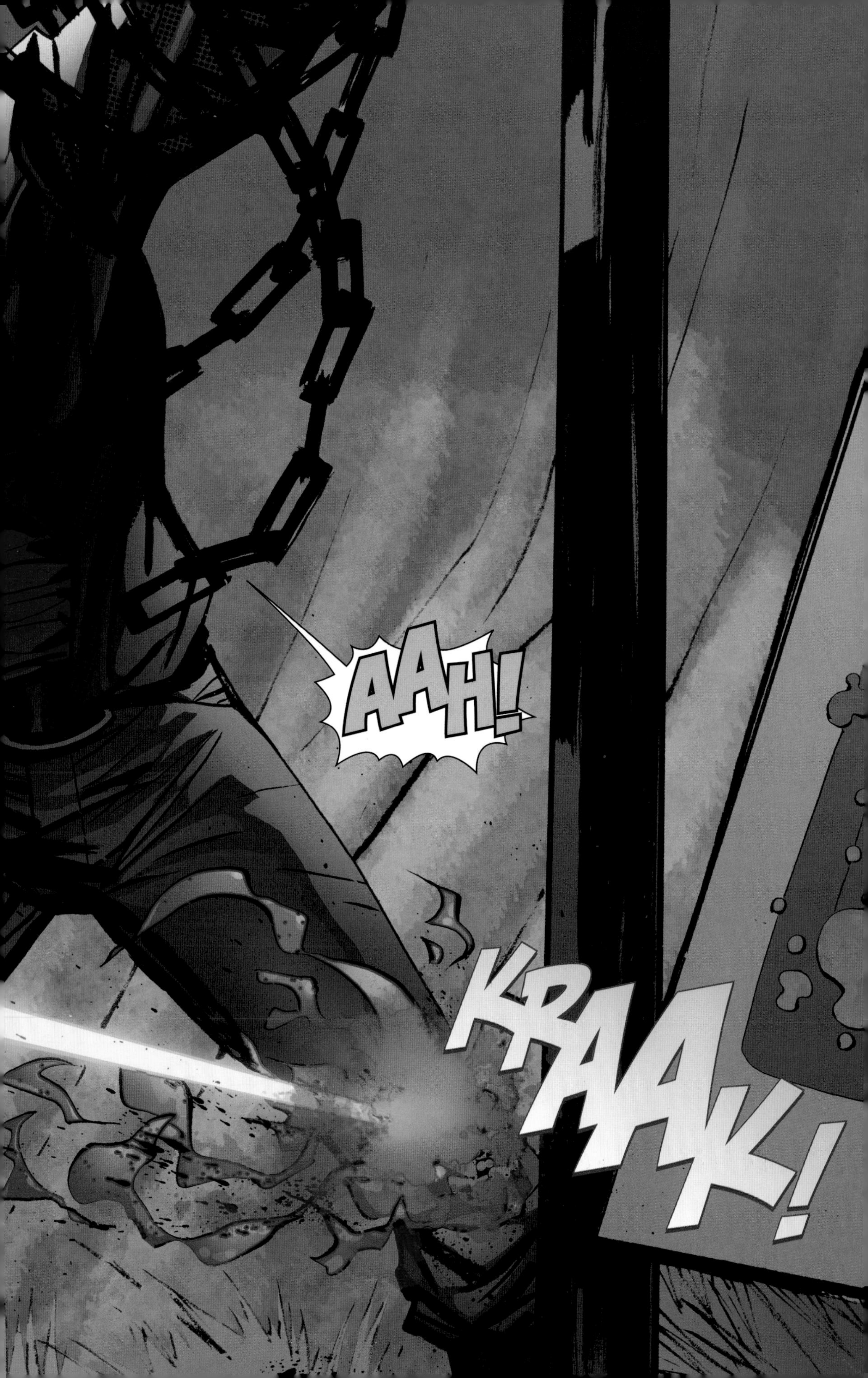
AAH!
KRAAAK!

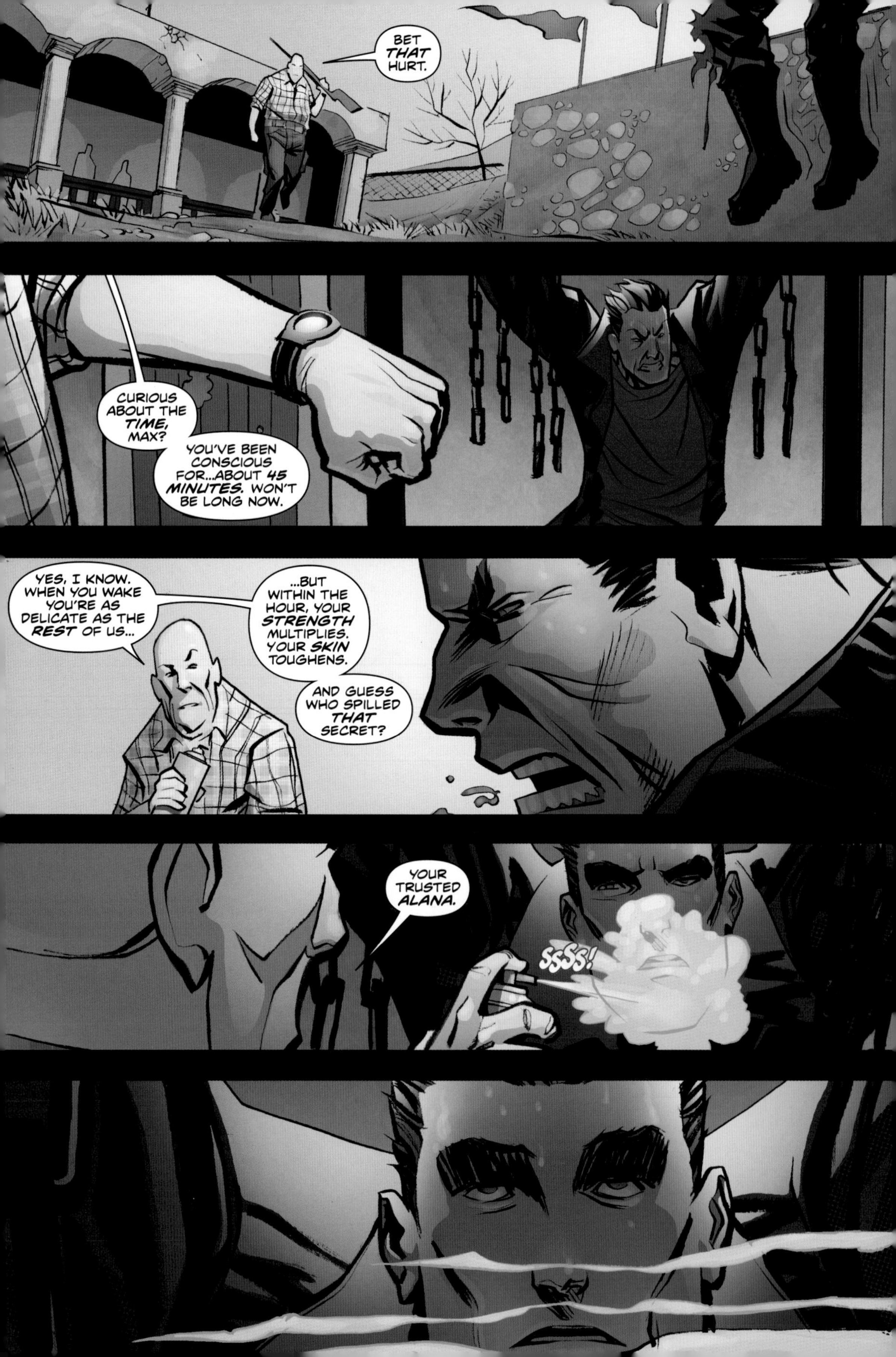
BET THAT HURT.
CURIOUS ABOUT THE TIME, MAX?
YOU'VE BEEN CONSCIOUS FOR...ABOUT 45 MINUTES. WON'T BE LONG NOW.
YES, I KNOW. WHEN YOU WAKE YOU'RE AS DELICATE AS THE REST OF US...
...BUT WITHIN THE HOUR, YOUR STRENGTH MULTIPLIES. YOUR SKIN TOUGHENS.
AND GUESS WHO SPILLED THAT SECRET?
YOUR TRUSTED ALANA.
SSSS!

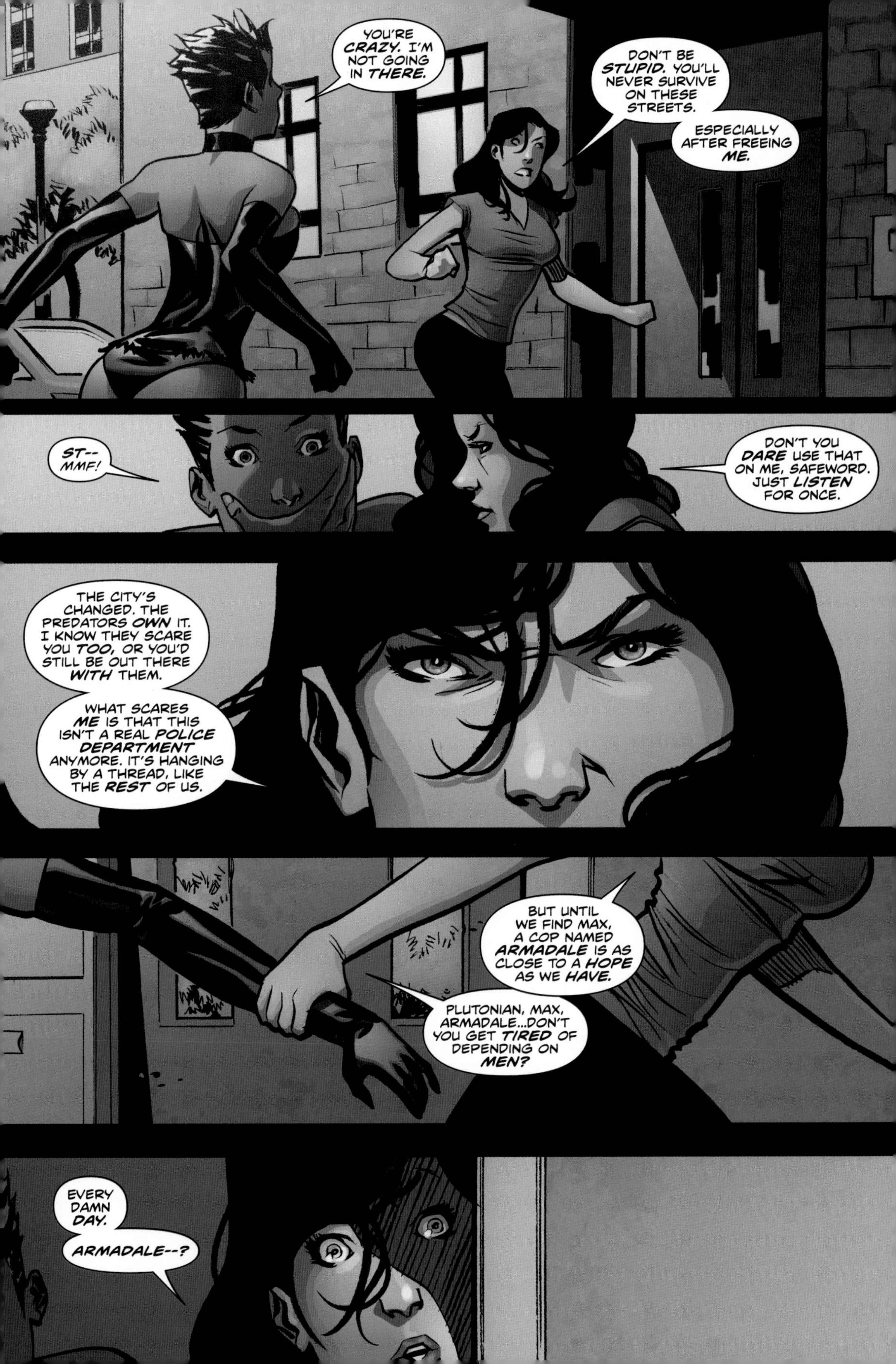
YOU'RE CRAZY. I'M NOT GOING IN THERE.
DON'T BE STUPID. YOU'LL NEVER SURVIVE ON THESE STREETS.
ESPECIALLY AFTER FREEING ME.
ST-- MMF!
DON'T YOU DARE USE THAT ON ME, SAFEWORD. JUST LISTEN FOR ONCE.
THE CITY'S CHANGED. THE PREDATORS OWN IT. I KNOW THEY SCARE YOU TOO, OR YOU'D STILL BE OUT THERE WITH THEM.
WHAT SCARES ME IS THAT THIS ISN'T A REAL POLICE DEPARTMENT ANYMORE. IT'S HANGING BY A THREAD, LIKE THE REST OF US.
BUT UNTIL WE FIND MAX, A COP NAMED ARMADALE IS AS CLOSE TO A HOPE AS WE HAVE.
PLUTONIAN, MAX, ARMADALE...DON'T YOU GET TIRED OF DEPENDING ON MEN?
EVERY DAMN DAY.
ARMADALE--?

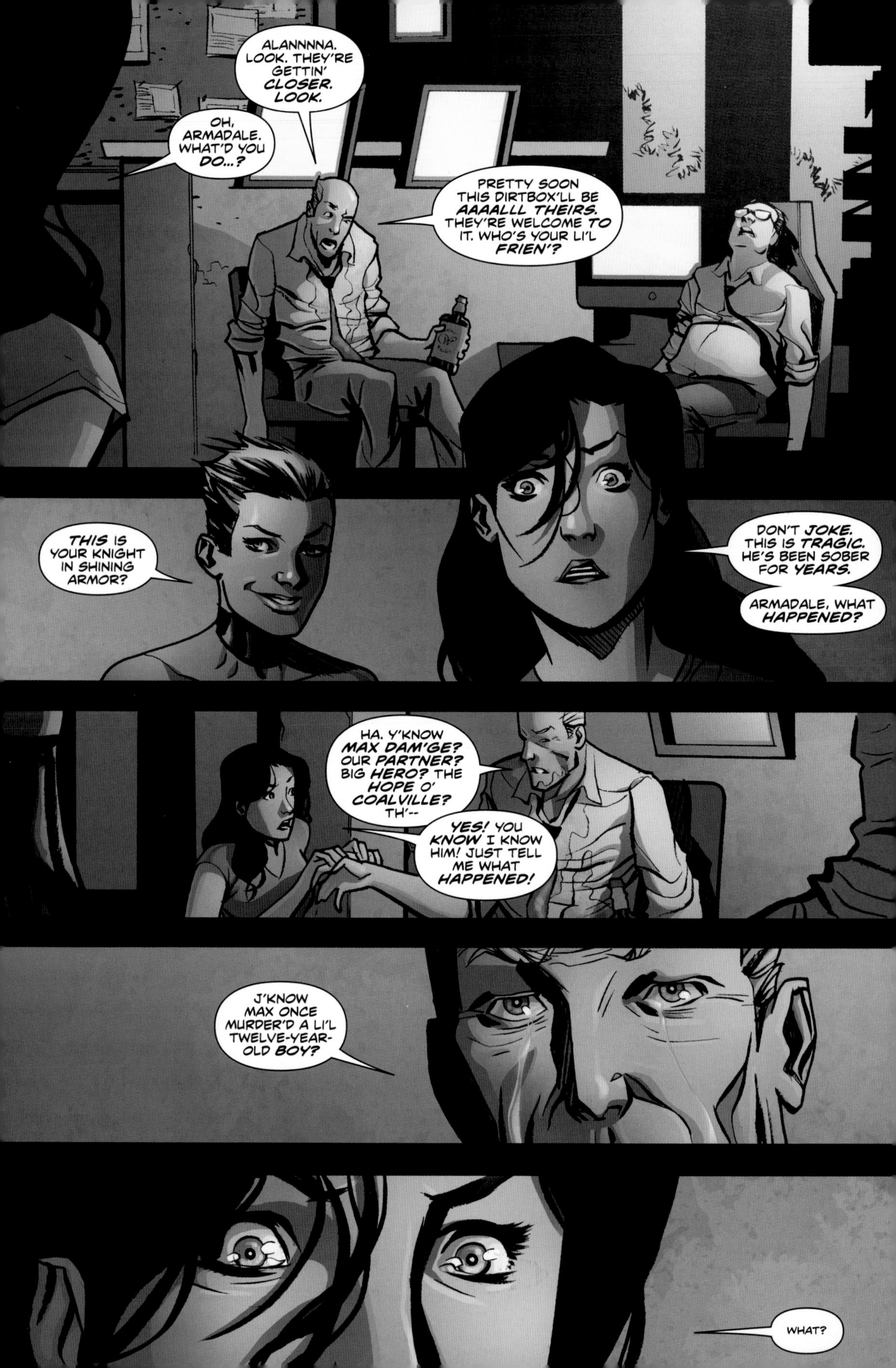
ALANNNNA. LOOK. THEY'RE GETTIN' CLOSER. LOOK.
OH, ARMADALE. WHAT'D YOU DO...?
PRETTY SOON THIS DIRTBOX'LL BE AAAALLL THEIRS. THEY'RE WELCOME TO IT. WHO'S YOUR LI'L FRIEN'?
THIS IS YOUR KNIGHT IN SHINING ARMOR?
DON'T JOKE. THIS IS TRAGIC. HE'S BEEN SOBER FOR YEARS.
ARMADALE, WHAT HAPPENED?
HA. Y'KNOW MAX DAM'GE? OUR PARTNER? BIG HERO? THE HOPE O' COALVILLE? TH'--
YES! YOU KNOW I KNOW HIM! JUST TELL ME WHAT HAPPENED!
J'KNOW MAX ONCE MURDER'D A LI'L TWELVE-YEAR-OLD BOY?
WHAT?

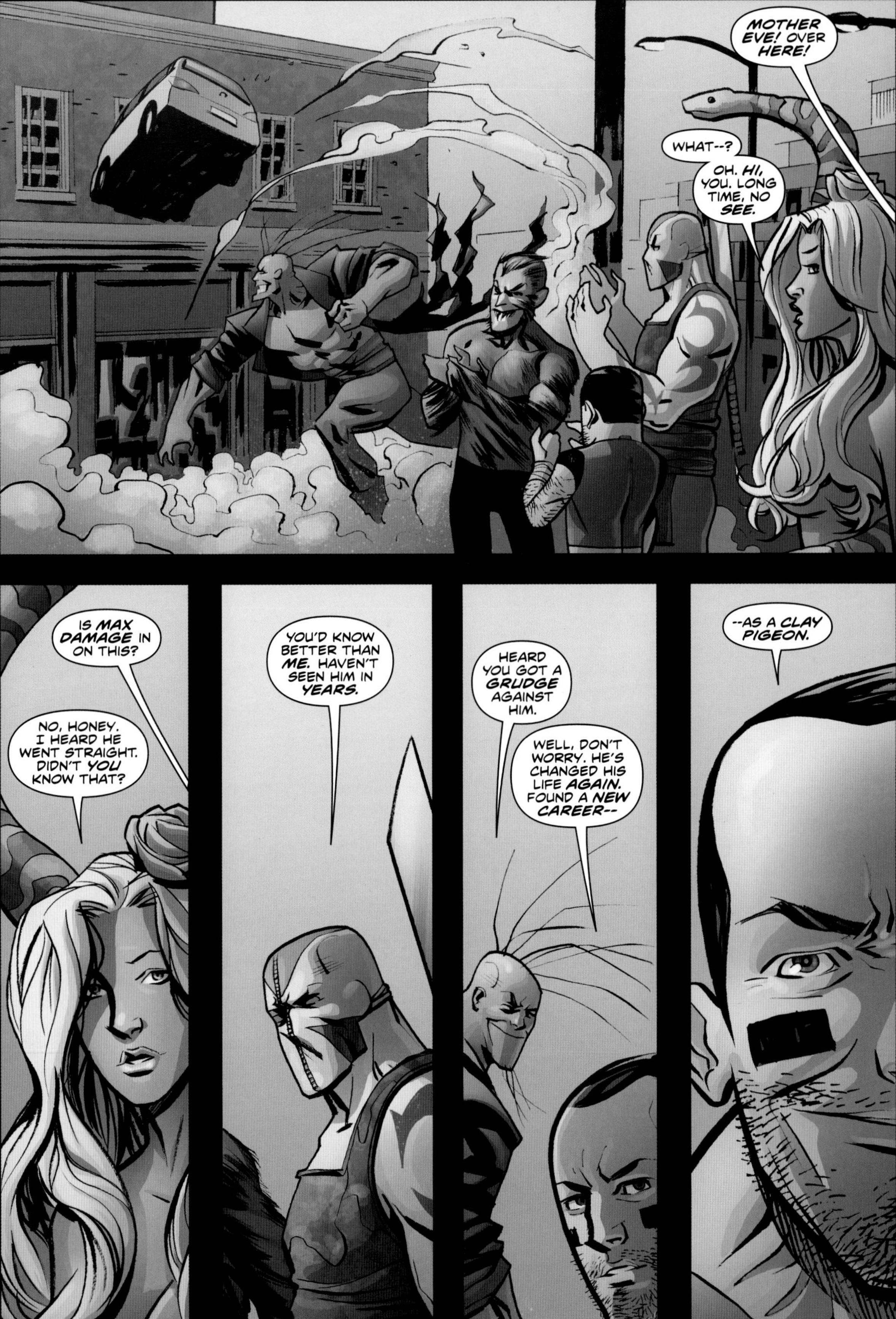
MOTHER EVE! OVER HERE!
WHAT--?
OH. HI, YOU. LONG TIME, NO SEE.
IS MAX DAMAGE IN ON THIS?
NO, HONEY. I HEARD HE WENT STRAIGHT. DIDN'T YOU KNOW THAT?
YOU'D KNOW BETTER THAN ME. HAVEN'T SEEN HIM IN YEARS.
HEARD YOU GOT A GRUDGE AGAINST HIM.
WELL, DON'T WORRY. HE'S CHANGED HIS LIFE AGAIN. FOUND A NEW CAREER--
--AS A CLAY PIGEON.

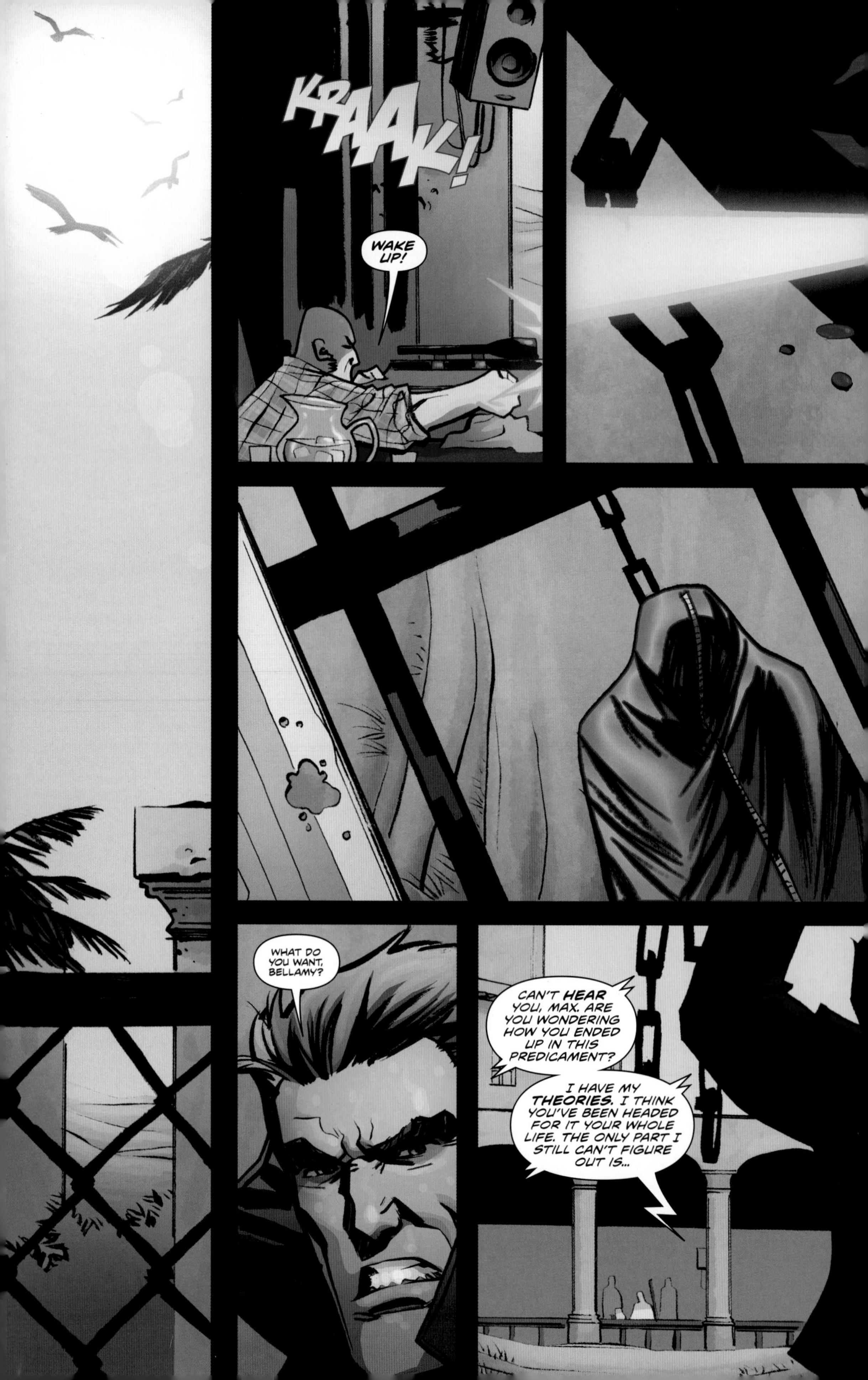
KRAAK!
WAKE UP!
WHAT DO YOU WANT, BELLAMY?
CAN'T HEAR YOU, MAX. ARE YOU WONDERING HOW YOU ENDED UP IN THIS PREDICAMENT?
I HAVE MY THEORIES. I THINK YOU'VE BEEN HEADED FOR IT YOUR WHOLE LIFE. THE ONLY PART I STILL CAN'T FIGURE OUT IS...

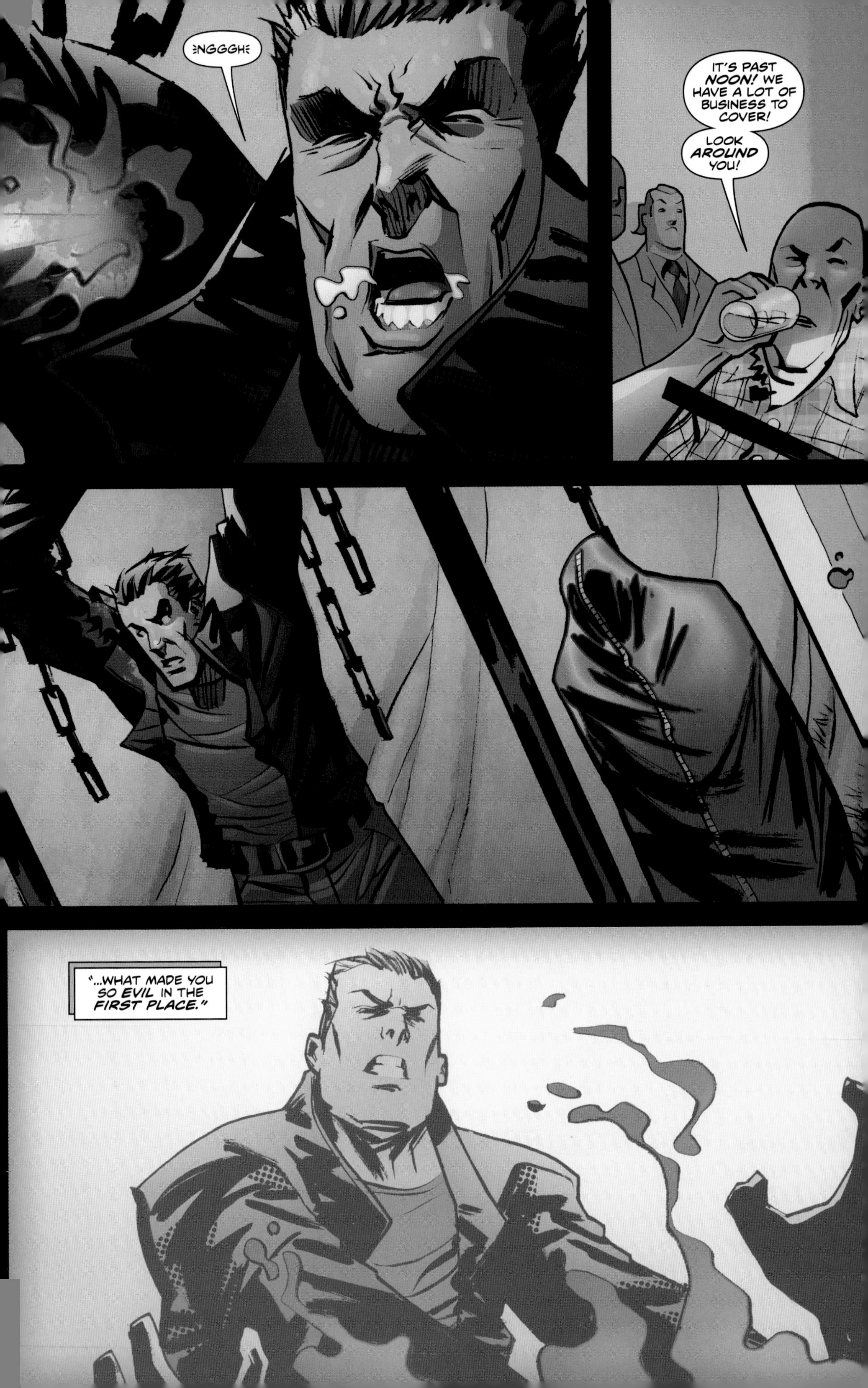

ENGGGH
IT'S PAST NOON! WE HAVE A LOT OF BUSINESS TO COVER!
LOOK AROUND YOU!
"...WHAT MADE YOU SO EVIL IN THE FIRST PLACE."

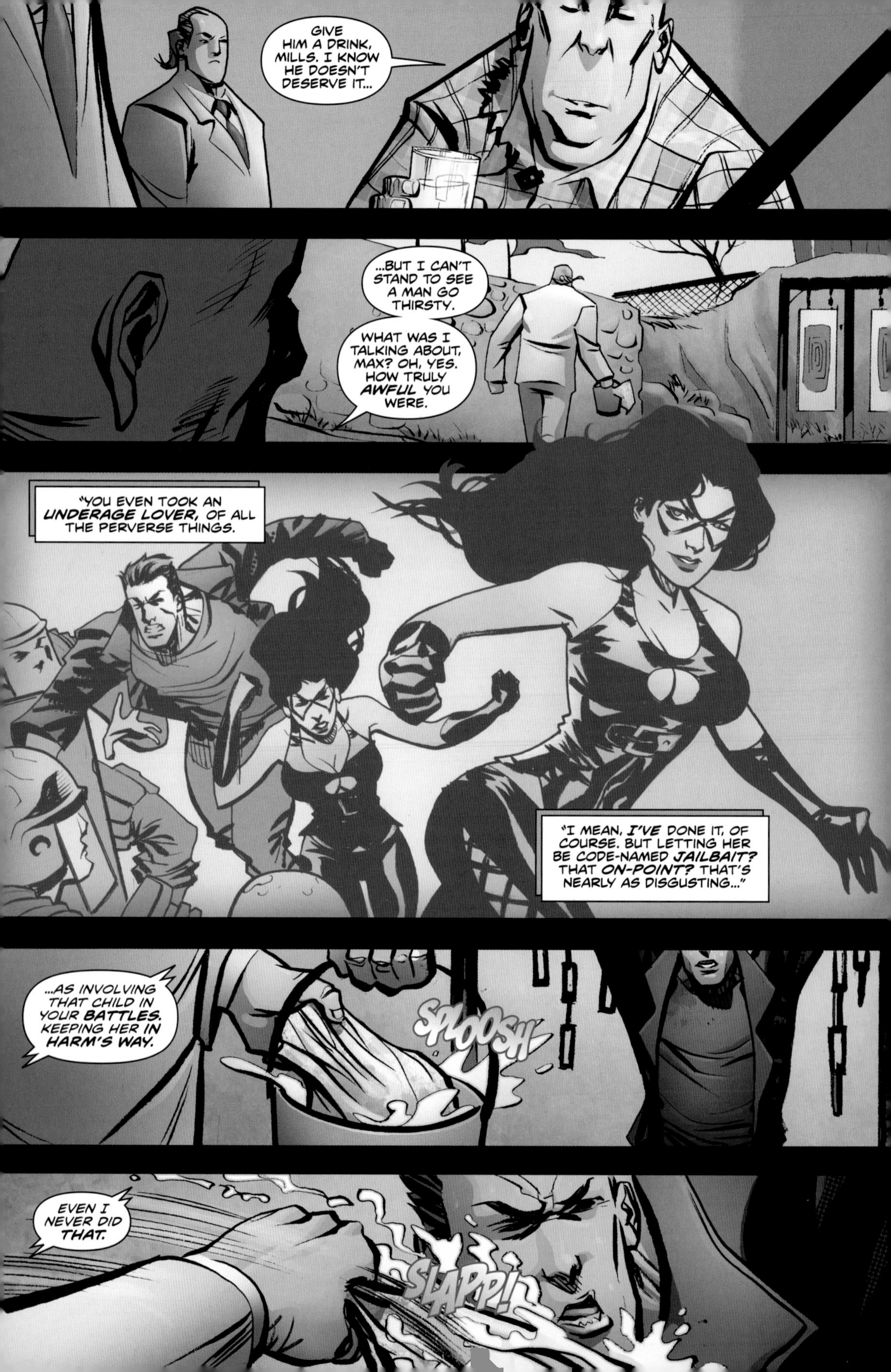
GIVE HIM A DRINK, MILLS. I KNOW HE DOESN'T DESERVE IT...
...BUT I CAN'T STAND TO SEE A MAN GO THIRSTY.
WHAT WAS I TALKING ABOUT, MAX? OH, YES. HOW TRULY AWFUL YOU WERE.
"YOU EVEN TOOK AN UNDERAGE LOVER, OF ALL THE PERVERSE THINGS.
"I MEAN, I'VE DONE IT, OF COURSE. BUT LETTING HER BE CODE-NAMED JAILBAIT? THAT ON-POINT? THAT'S NEARLY AS DISGUSTING..."
...AS INVOLVING THAT CHILD IN YOUR BATTLES. KEEPING HER IN HARM'S WAY.
SPLOOSH
EVEN I NEVER DID THAT.
SLAPP!

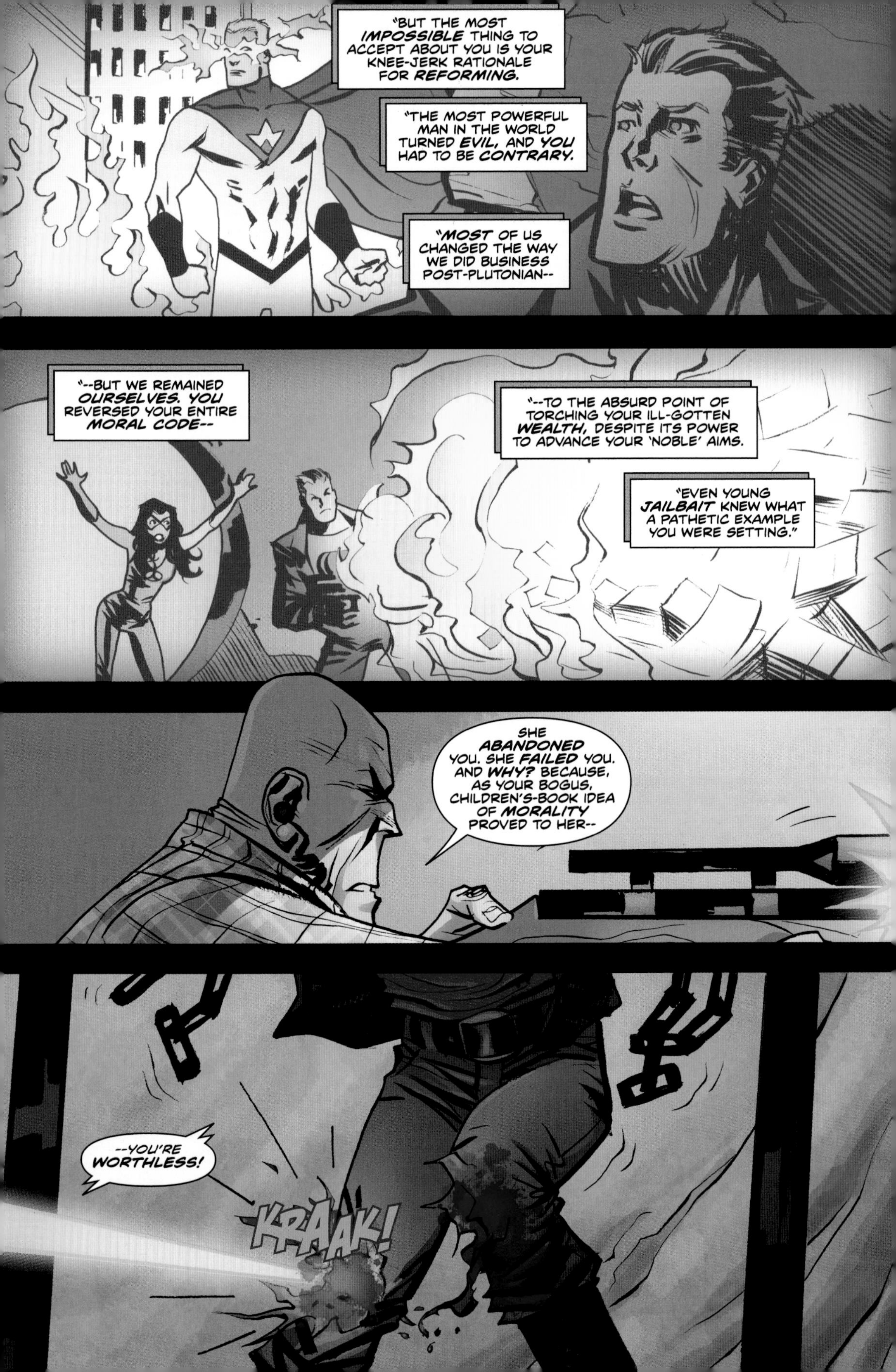
"BUT THE MOST IMPOSSIBLE THING TO ACCEPT ABOUT YOU IS YOUR KNEE-JERK RATIONALE FOR REFORMING.
"THE MOST POWERFUL MAN IN THE WORLD TURNED EVIL, AND YOU HAD TO BE CONTRARY.
"MOST OF US CHANGED THE WAY WE DID BUSINESS POST-PLUTONIAN--
"--BUT WE REMAINED OURSELVES. YOU REVERSED YOUR ENTIRE MORAL CODE--
"--TO THE ABSURD POINT OF TORCHING YOUR ILL-GOTTEN WEALTH, DESPITE ITS POWER TO ADVANCE YOUR 'NOBLE' AIMS.
"EVEN YOUNG JAILBAIT KNEW WHAT A PATHETIC EXAMPLE YOU WERE SETTING."
SHE ABANDONED YOU. SHE FAILED YOU. AND WHY? BECAUSE, AS YOUR BOGUS, CHILDREN'S-BOOK IDEA OF MORALITY PROVED TO HER--
--YOU'RE WORTHLESS!
KRAAK!

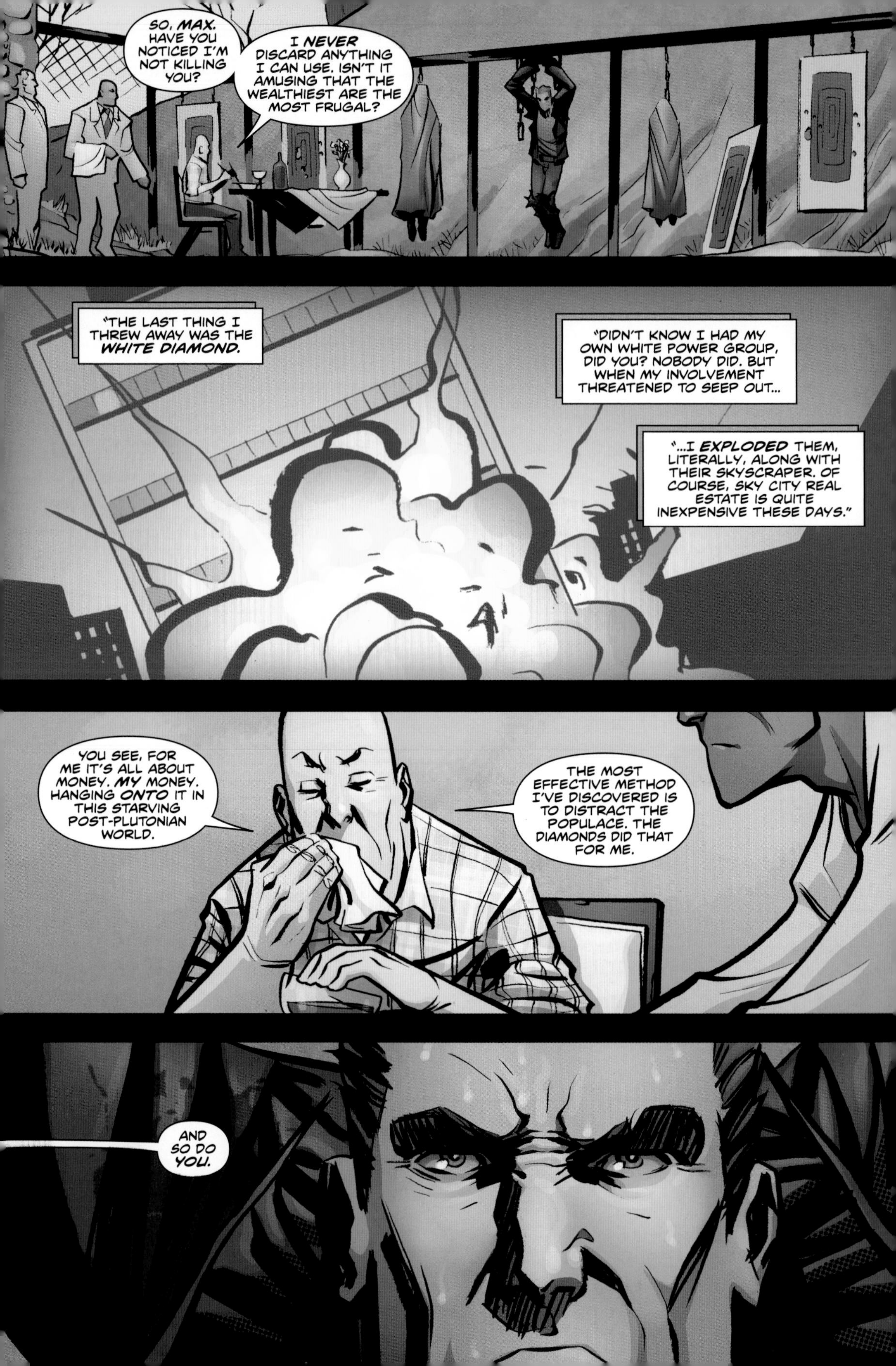
SO, MAX. HAVE YOU NOTICED I'M NOT KILLING YOU?
I NEVER DISCARD ANYTHING I CAN USE. ISN'T IT AMUSING THAT THE WEALTHIEST ARE THE MOST FRUGAL?
"THE LAST THING I THREW AWAY WAS THE WHITE DIAMOND.
"DIDN'T KNOW I HAD MY OWN WHITE POWER GROUP, DID YOU? NOBODY DID. BUT WHEN MY INVOLVEMENT THREATENED TO SEEP OUT...
"...I EXPLODED THEM, LITERALLY, ALONG WITH THEIR SKYSCRAPER. OF COURSE, SKY CITY REAL ESTATE IS QUITE INEXPENSIVE THESE DAYS."
YOU SEE, FOR ME IT'S ALL ABOUT MONEY. MY MONEY. HANGING ONTO IT IN THIS STARVING POST-PLUTONIAN WORLD.
THE MOST EFFECTIVE METHOD I'VE DISCOVERED IS TO DISTRACT THE POPULACE. THE DIAMONDS DID THAT FOR ME.
AND SO DO YOU.

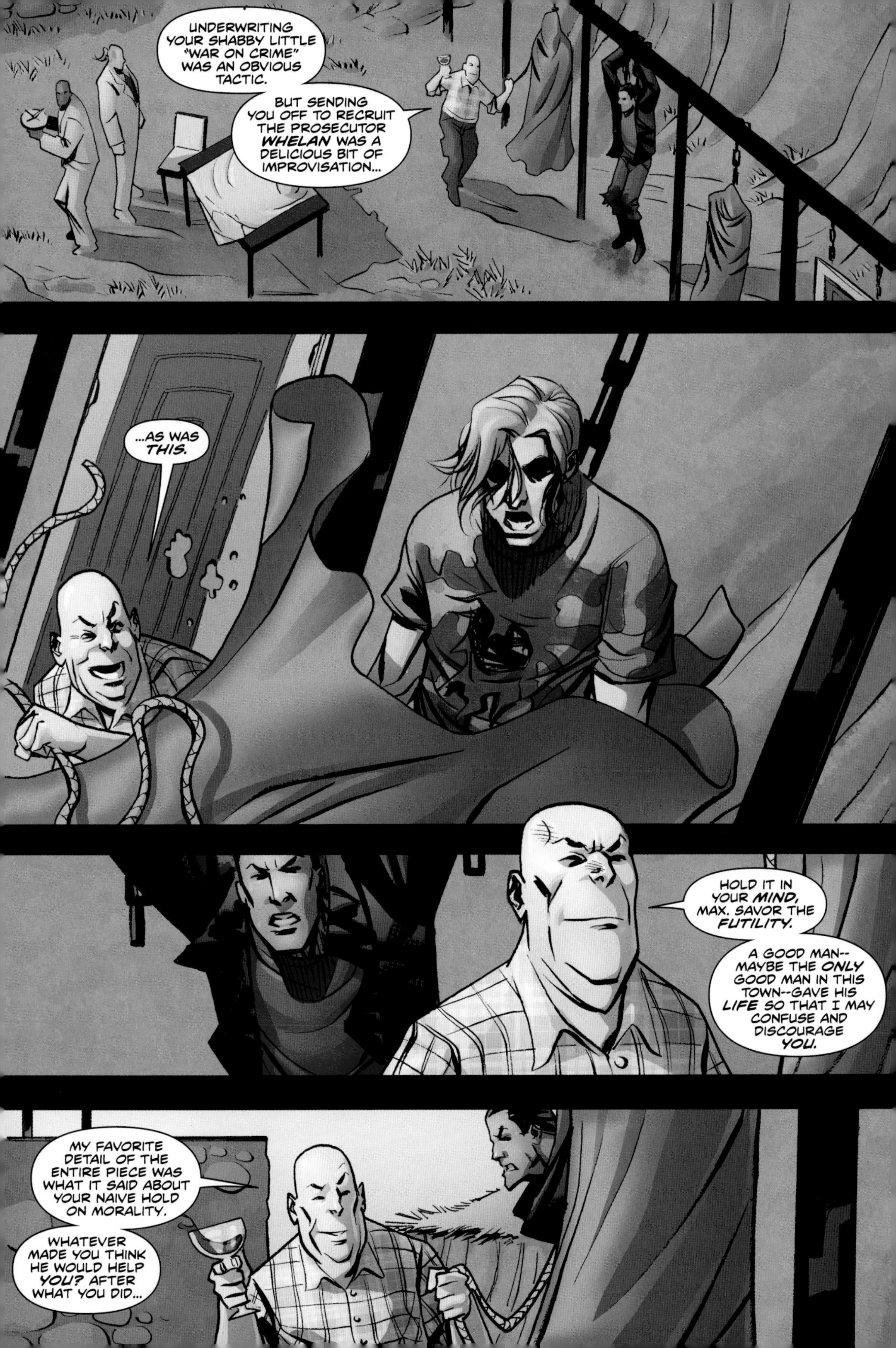
UNDERWRITING YOUR SHABBY LITTLE "WAR ON CRIME" WAS AN OBVIOUS TACTIC.
BUT SENDING YOU OFF TO RECRUIT THE PROSECUTOR *WHELAN* WAS A DELICIOUS BIT OF IMPROVISATION...
...AS WAS *THIS.*
HOLD IT IN YOUR *MIND,* MAX. SAVOR THE *FUTILITY.*
A GOOD MAN--MAYBE THE *ONLY* GOOD MAN IN THIS TOWN--GAVE HIS *LIFE* SO THAT I MAY CONFUSE AND DISCOURAGE *YOU.*
MY FAVORITE DETAIL OF THE ENTIRE PIECE WAS WHAT IT SAID ABOUT YOUR NAIVE HOLD ON MORALITY.
WHATEVER MADE YOU THINK HE WOULD HELP *YOU?* AFTER WHAT YOU DID...

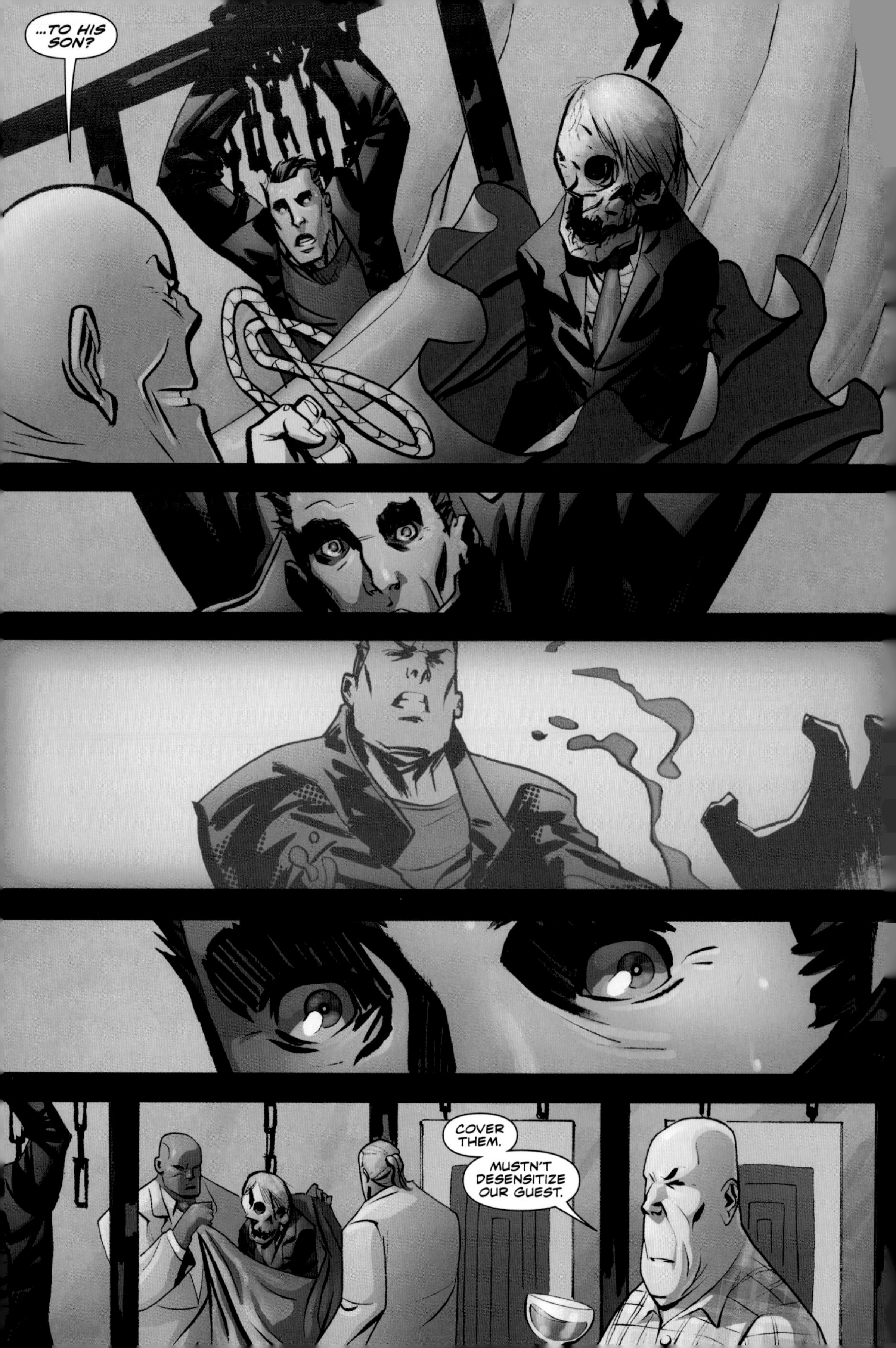
...TO HIS SON?
COVER THEM.
MUSTN'T DESENSITIZE OUR GUEST.

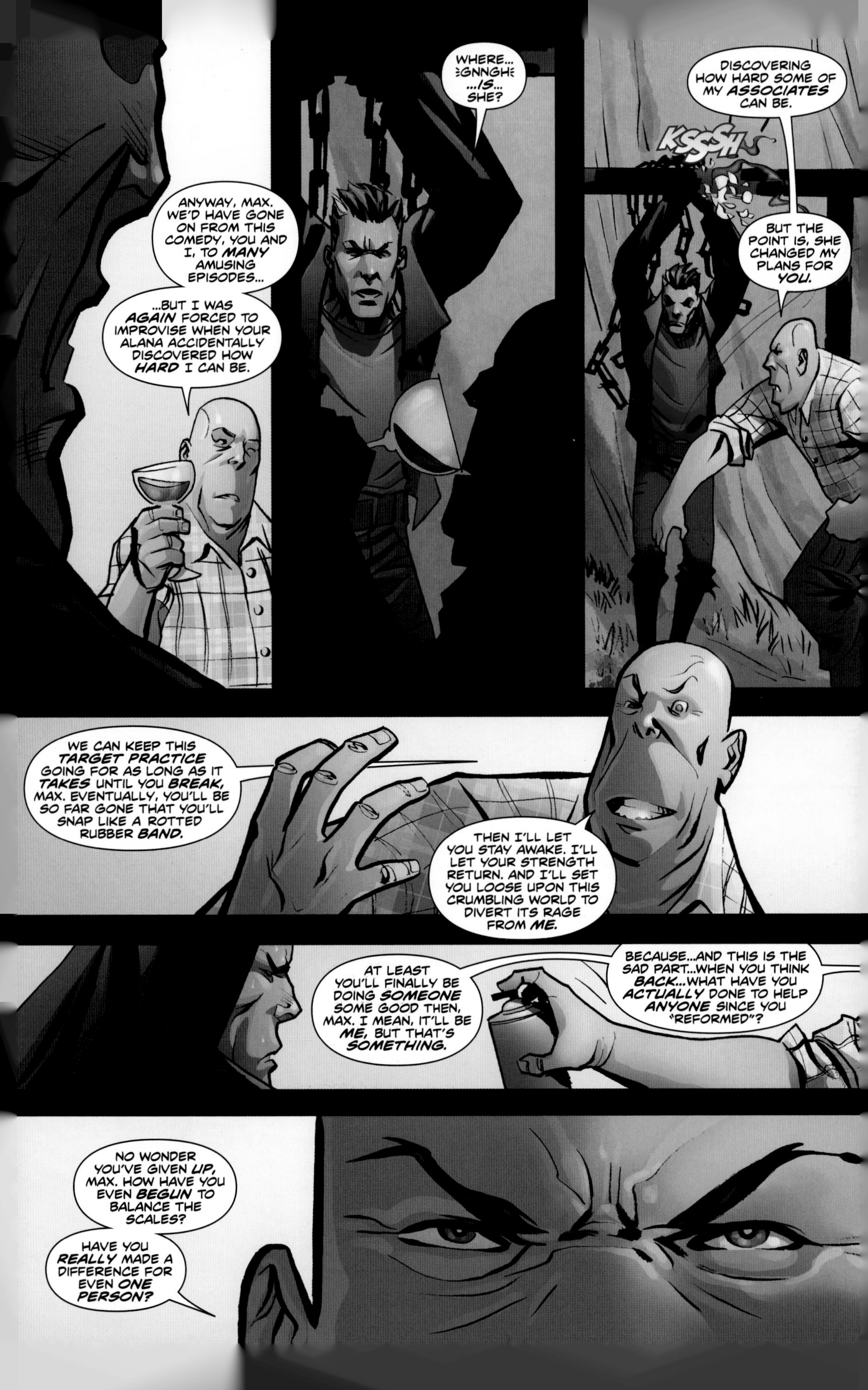
ANYWAY, MAX. WE'D HAVE GONE ON FROM THIS COMEDY, YOU AND I, TO MANY AMUSING EPISODES...
...BUT I WAS AGAIN FORCED TO IMPROVISE WHEN YOUR ALANA ACCIDENTALLY DISCOVERED HOW HARD I CAN BE.
WHERE... GNNGH ...IS... SHE?
DISCOVERING HOW HARD SOME OF MY ASSOCIATES CAN BE.
KSSSH
BUT THE POINT IS, SHE CHANGED MY PLANS FOR YOU.
WE CAN KEEP THIS TARGET PRACTICE GOING FOR AS LONG AS IT TAKES UNTIL YOU BREAK, MAX. EVENTUALLY, YOU'LL BE SO FAR GONE THAT YOU'LL SNAP LIKE A ROTTED RUBBER BAND.
THEN I'LL LET YOU STAY AWAKE. I'LL LET YOUR STRENGTH RETURN. AND I'LL SET YOU LOOSE UPON THIS CRUMBLING WORLD TO DIVERT ITS RAGE FROM ME.
AT LEAST YOU'LL FINALLY BE DOING SOMEONE SOME GOOD THEN, MAX. I MEAN, IT'LL BE ME, BUT THAT'S SOMETHING.
BECAUSE...AND THIS IS THE SAD PART...WHEN YOU THINK BACK...WHAT HAVE YOU ACTUALLY DONE TO HELP ANYONE SINCE YOU "REFORMED"?
NO WONDER YOU'VE GIVEN UP, MAX. HOW HAVE YOU EVEN BEGUN TO BALANCE THE SCALES?
HAVE YOU REALLY MADE A DIFFERENCE FOR EVEN ONE PERSON?

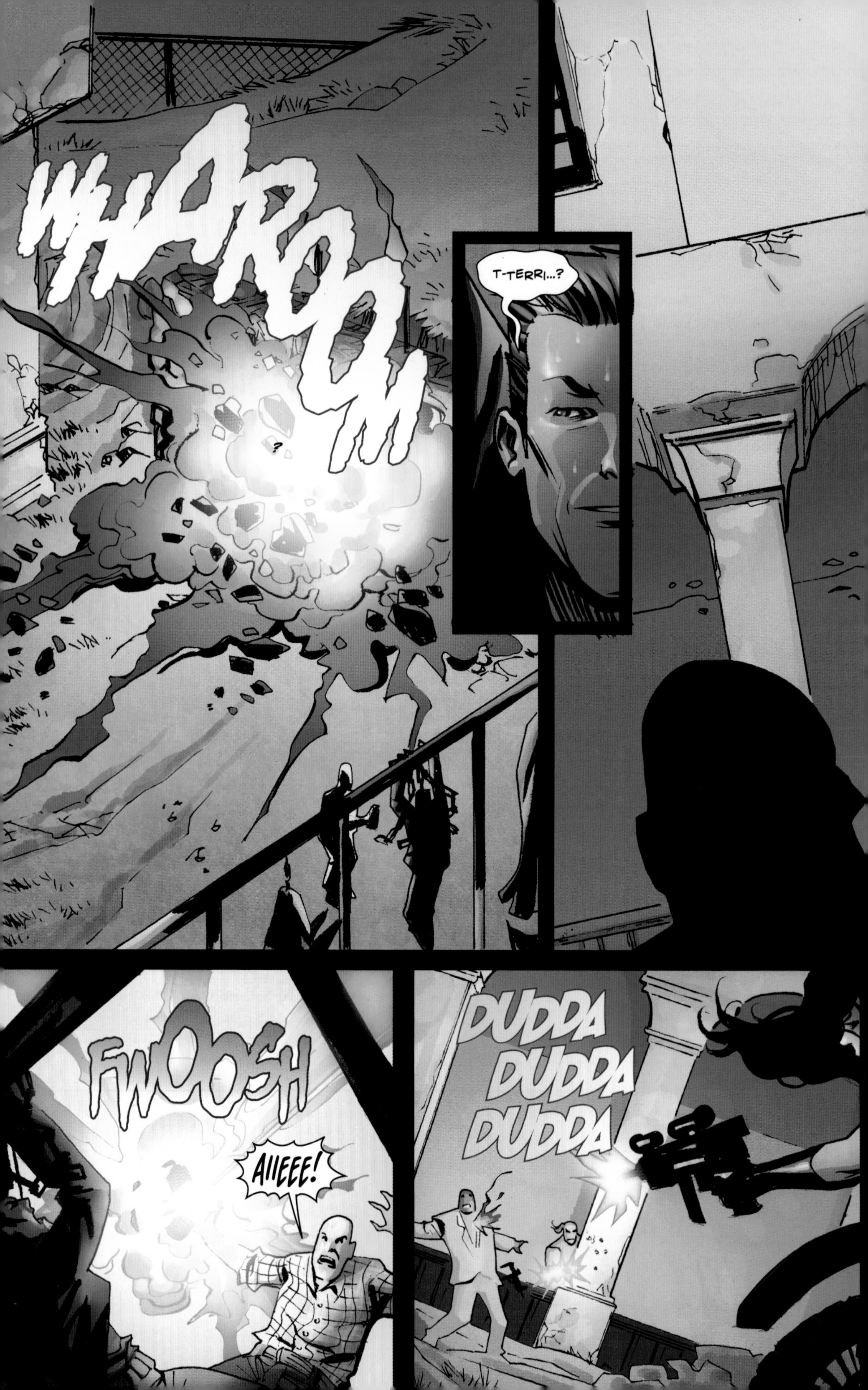
WHAROOM
T-TERRI...?
FWOOSH
AIIEEE!
DUDDA
DUDDA
DUDDA

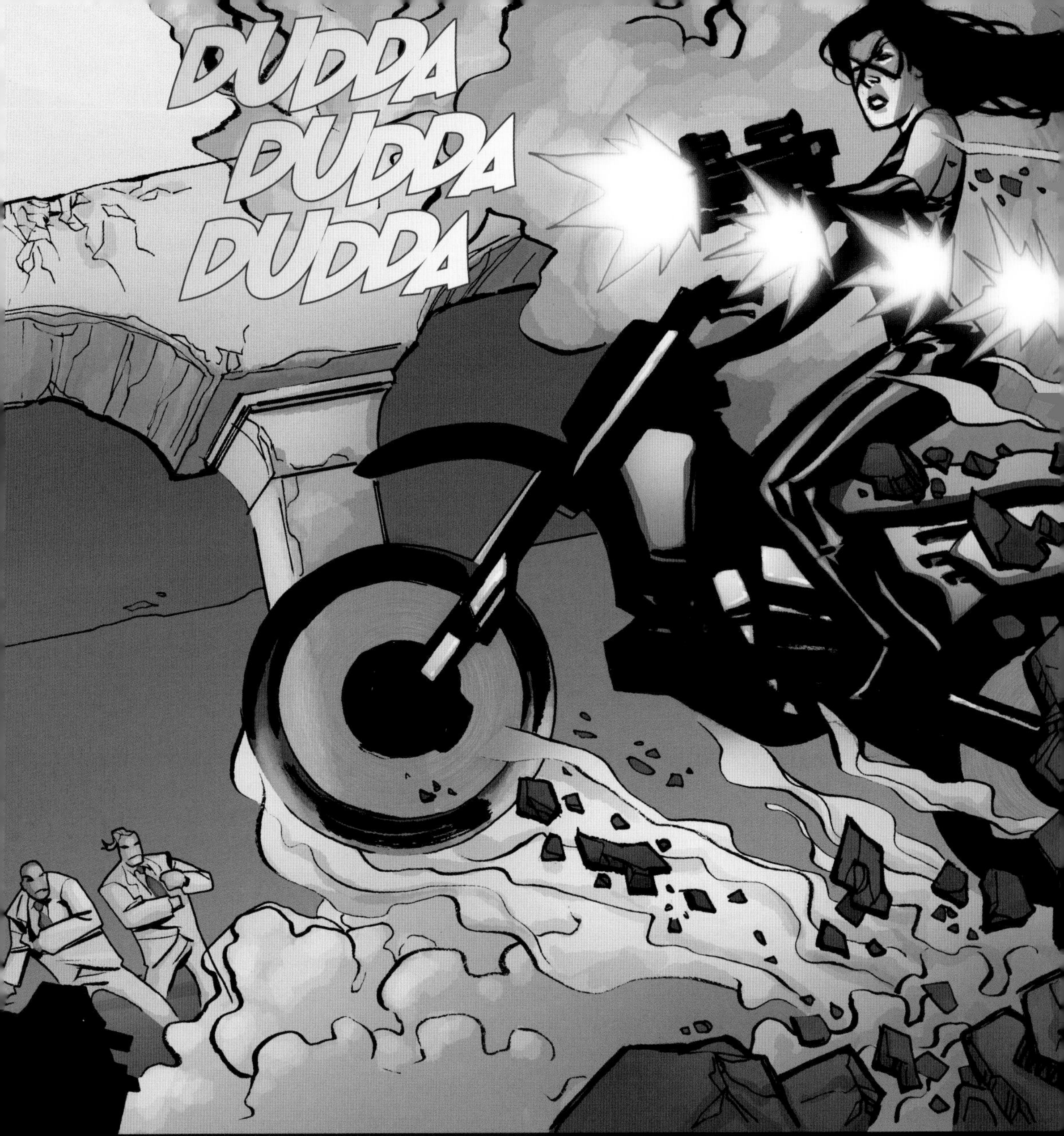
DUDDA
DUDDA
DUDDA
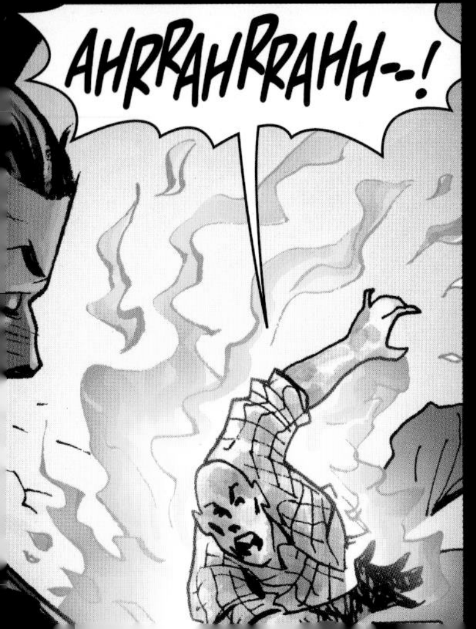
AHRRAHRRAHH--!
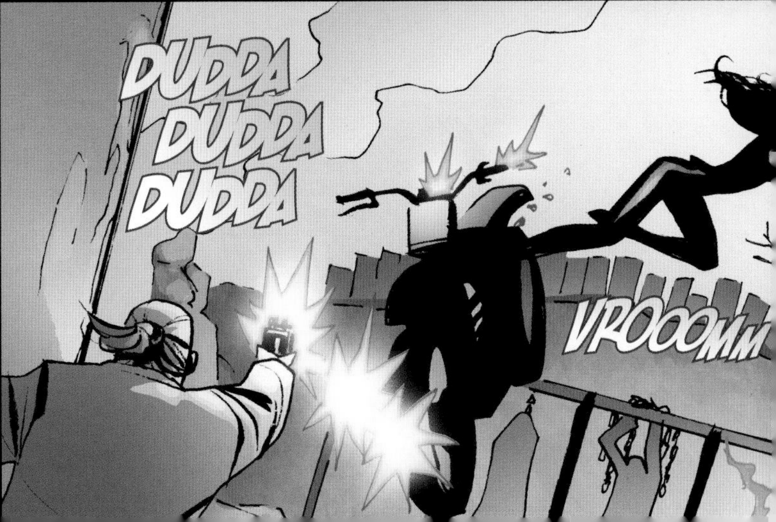
DUDDA
DUDDA
DUDDA
VROOOMM

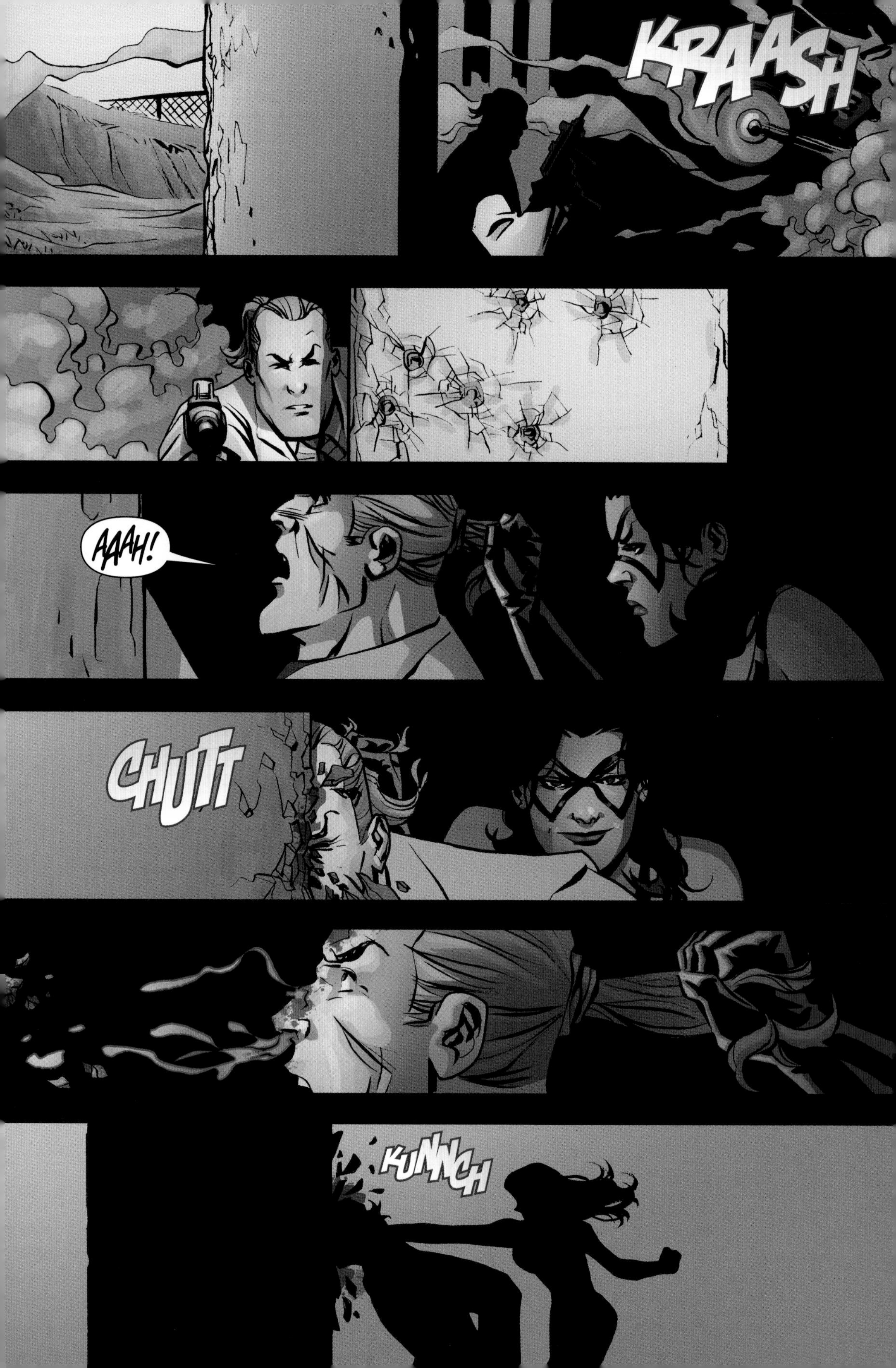
KRAASH
AAAH!
CHUTT
KUNNCH

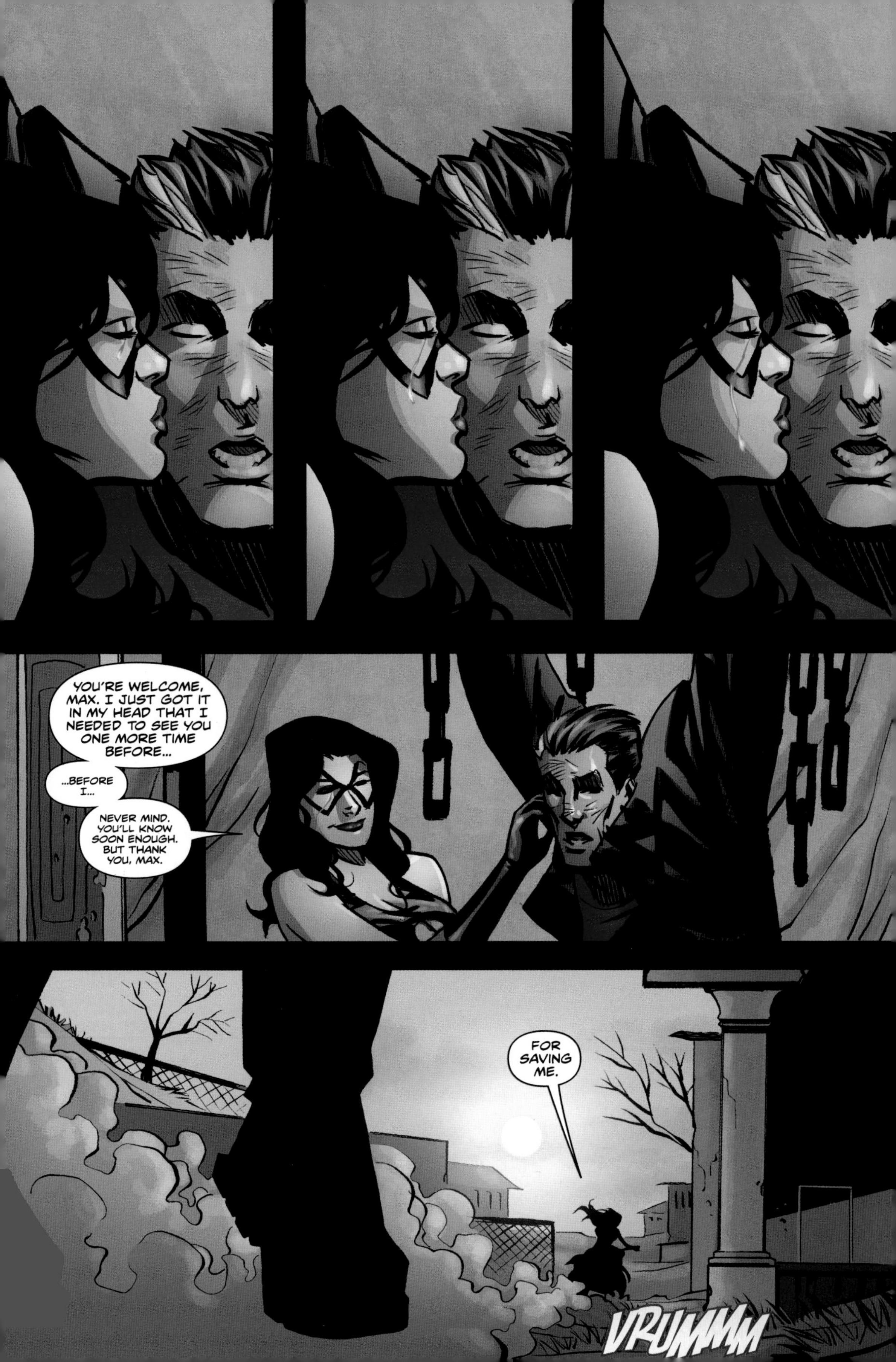
YOU'RE WELCOME, MAX. I JUST GOT IT IN MY HEAD THAT I NEEDED TO SEE YOU ONE MORE TIME BEFORE...
...BEFORE I...
NEVER MIND. YOU'LL KNOW SOON ENOUGH. BUT THANK YOU, MAX.
FOR SAVING ME.
VRUMMM

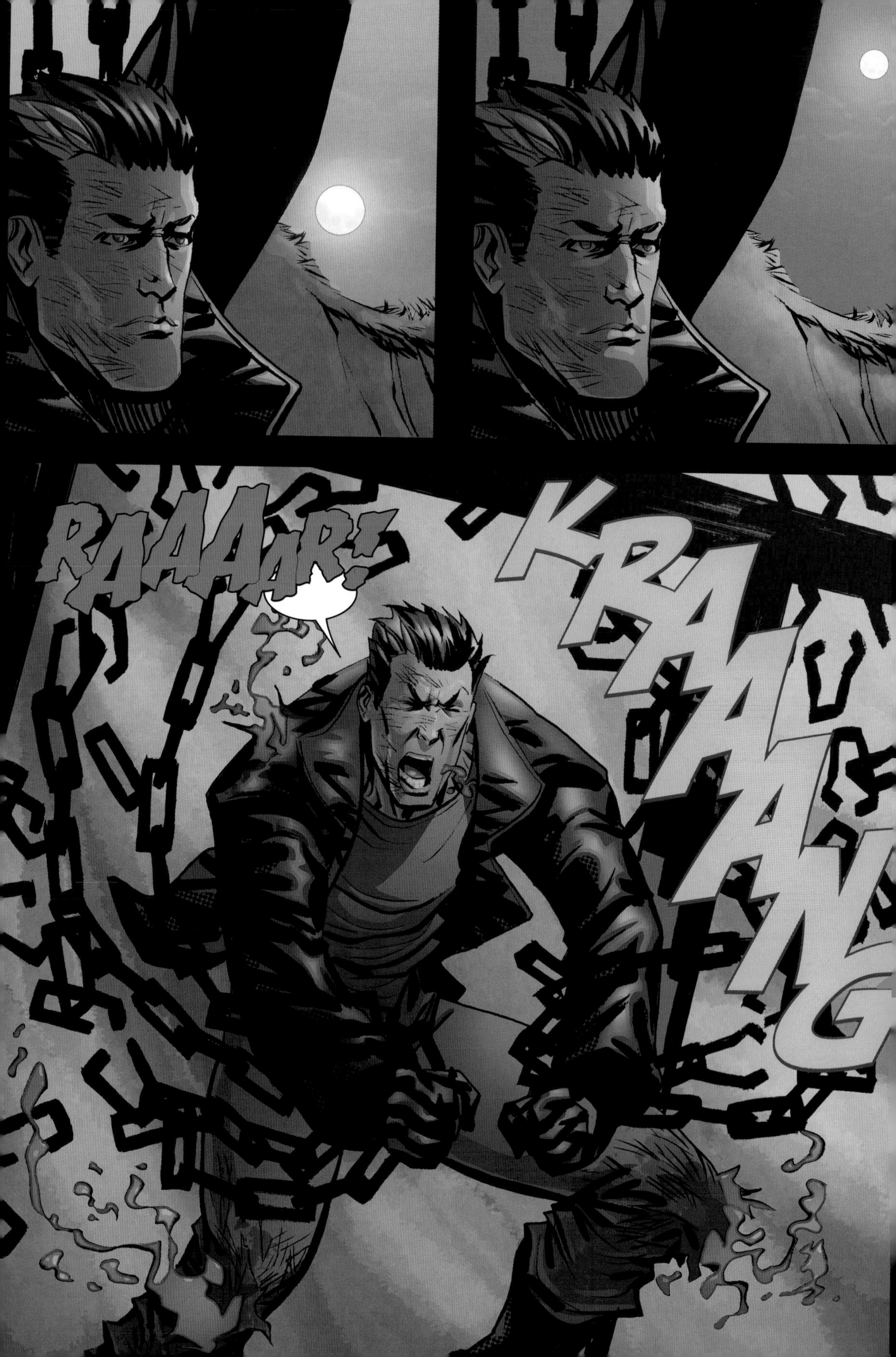
RAAAAR!
KRAAANG

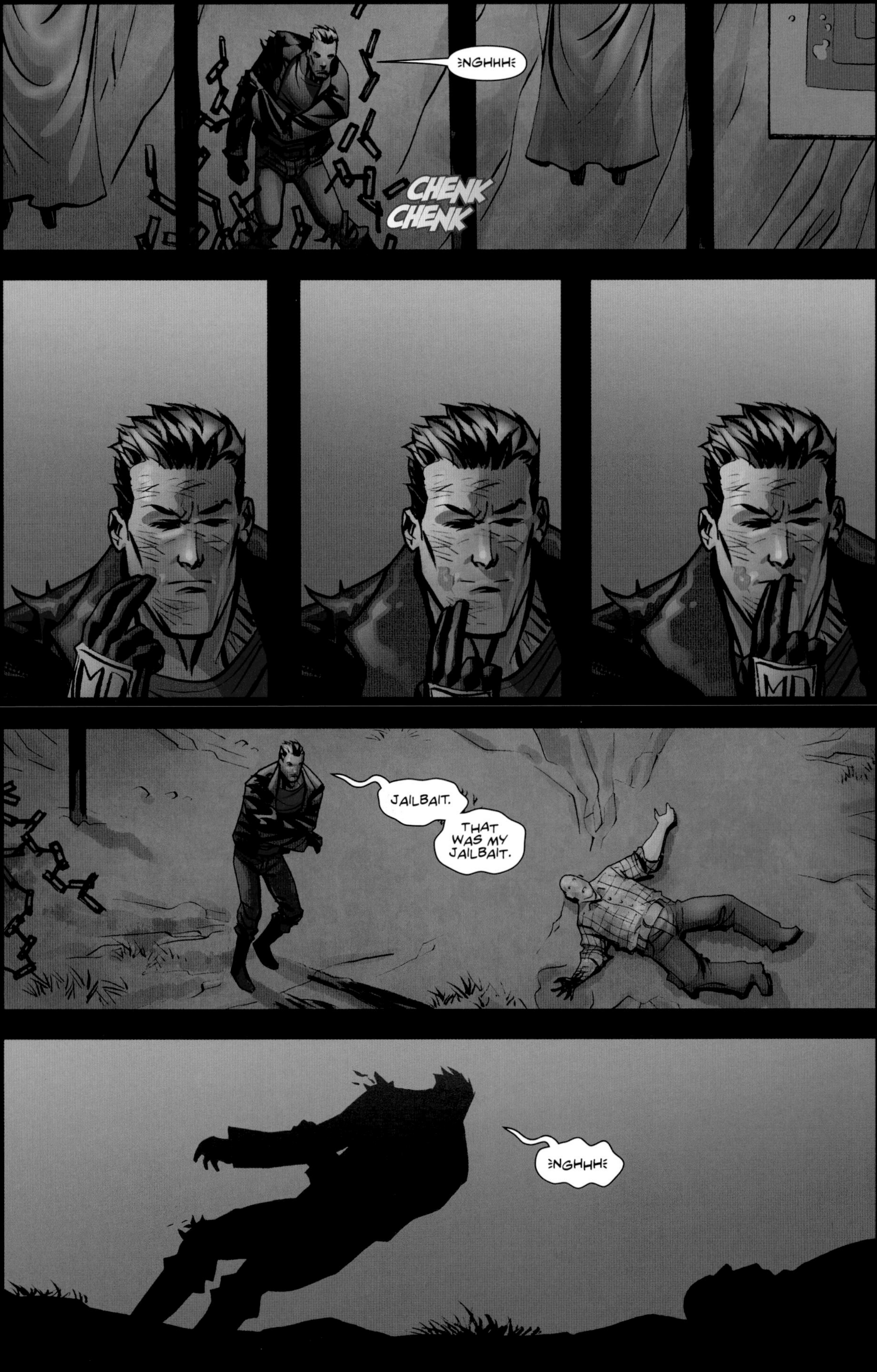
NGHHH
CHENK
CHENK
JAILBAIT.
THAT WAS MY JAILBAIT.
NGHHH

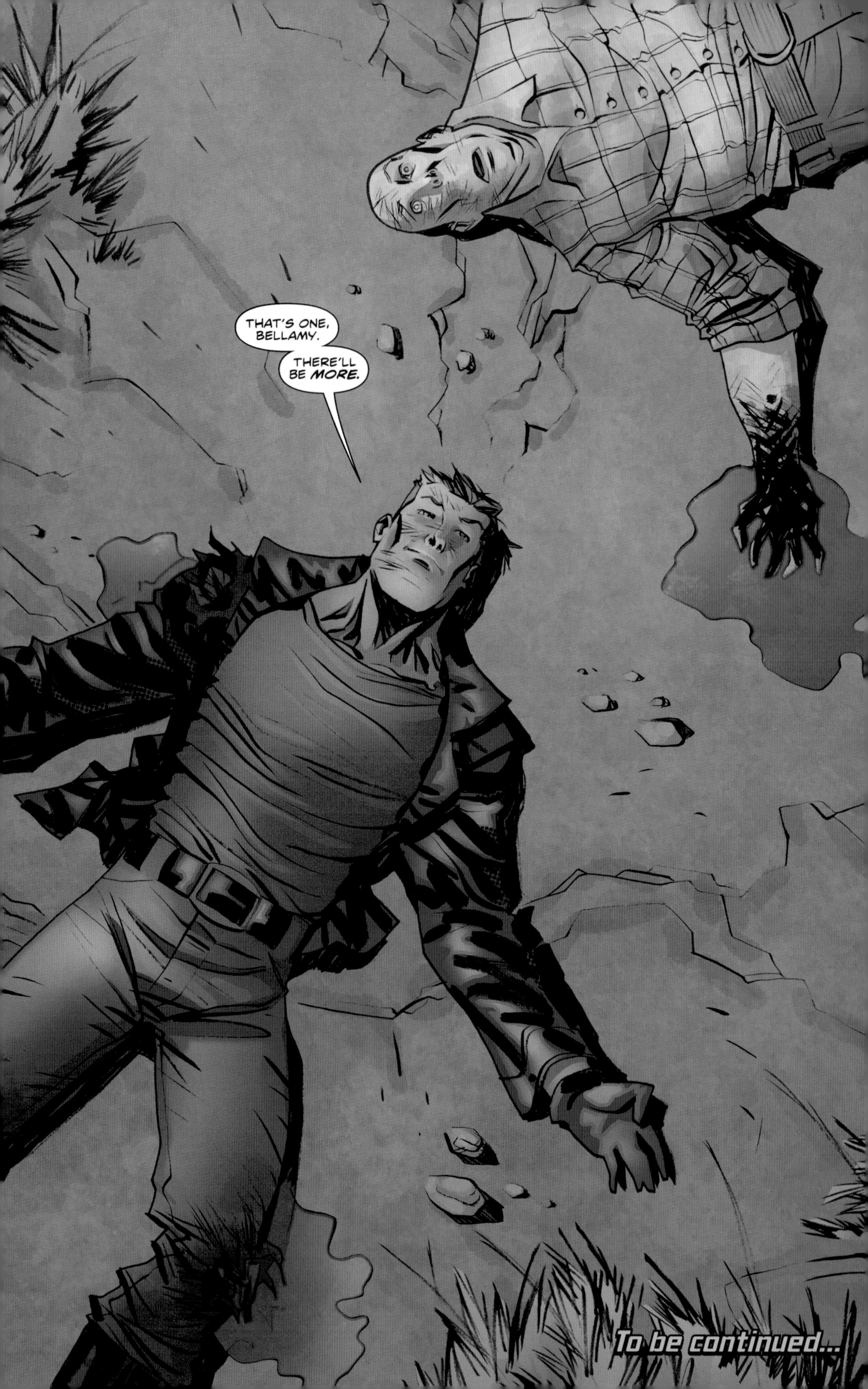
THAT'S ONE, BELLAMY.
THERE'LL BE *MORE.*
To be continued...

# COVER GALLERY

MD

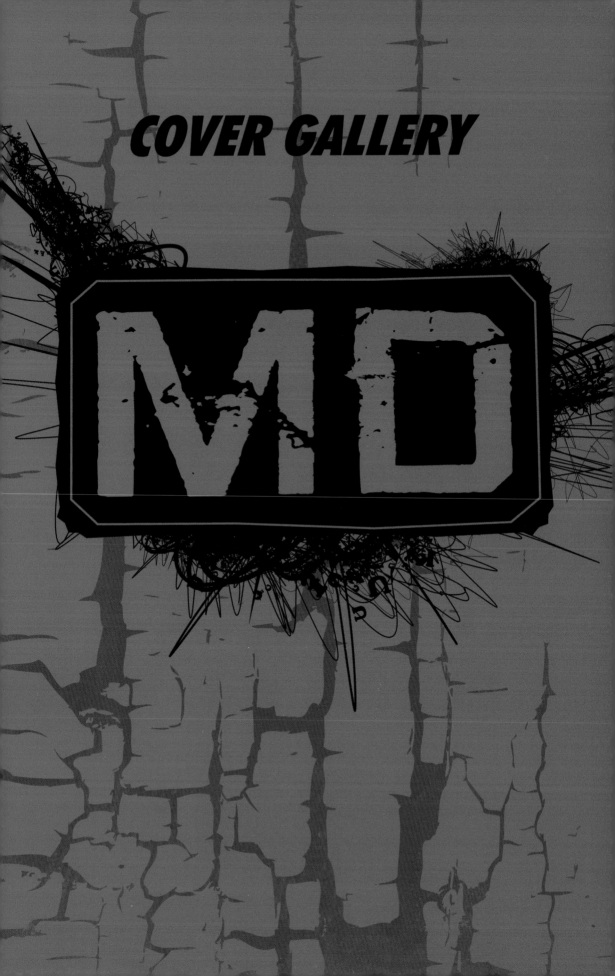

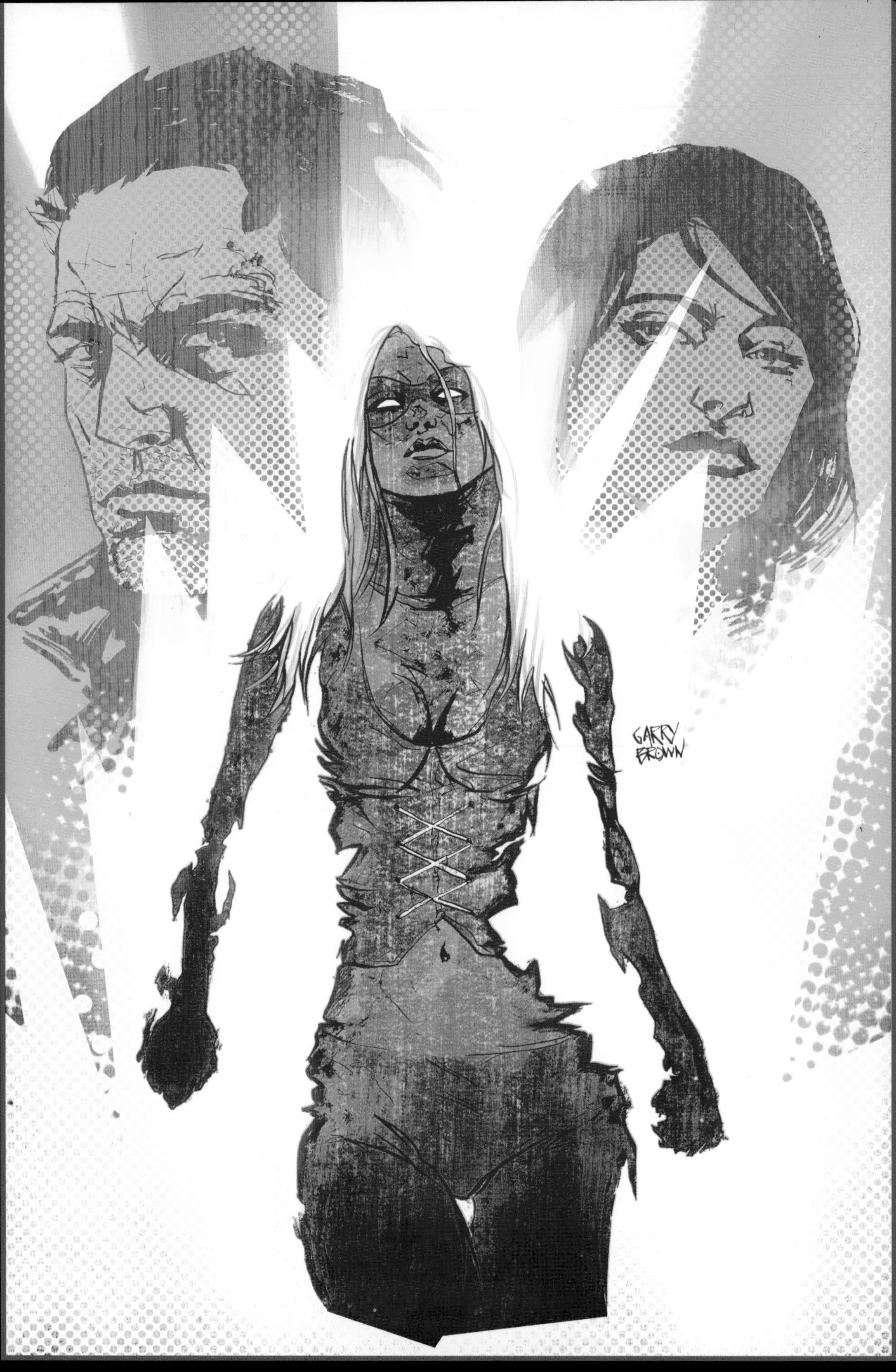
GARRY
BROWN

**COVER 17A: GARRY BROWN**

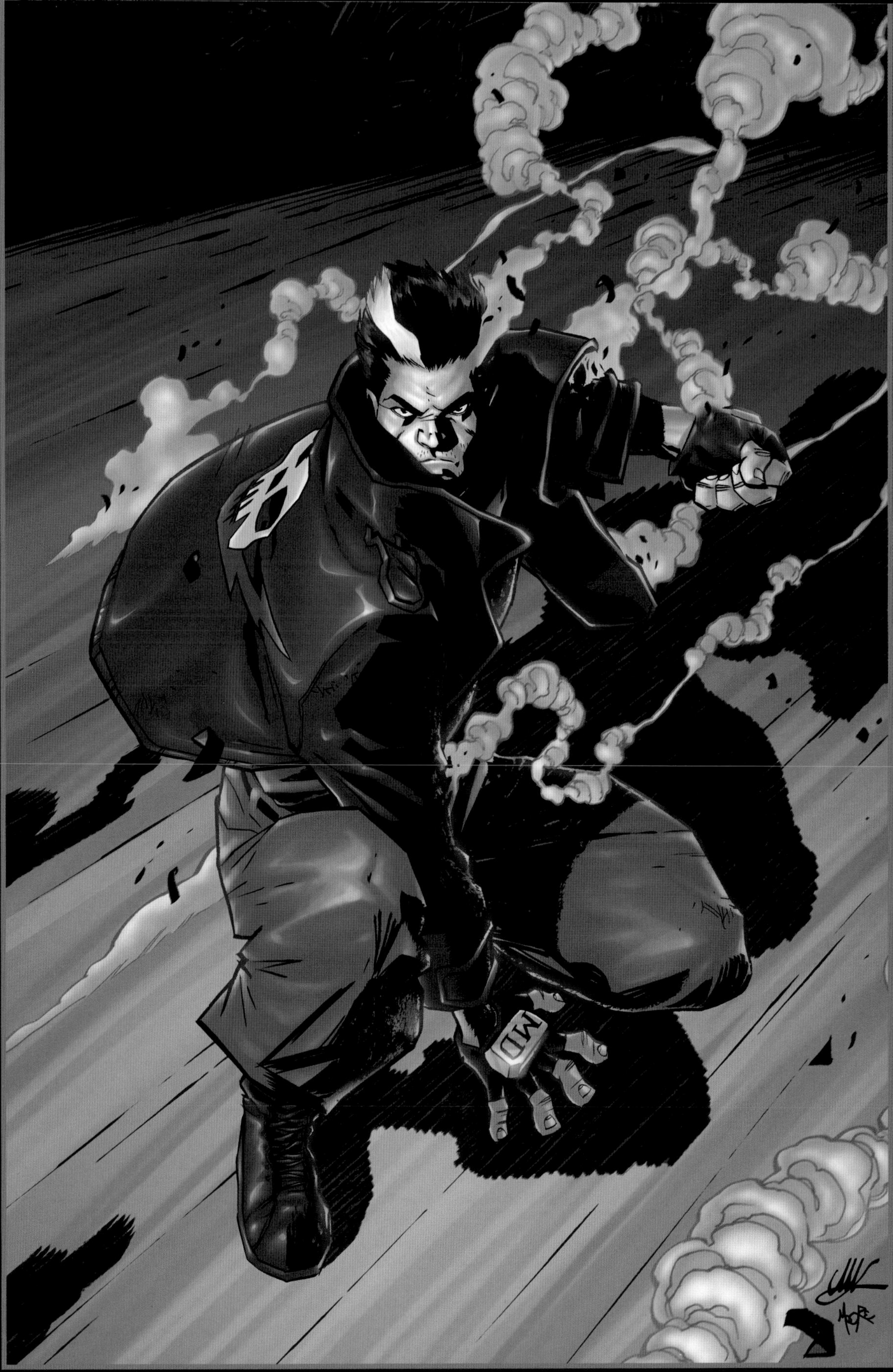

**COVER 17B: MATTEO SCALERA**
**COLORIST: DARRIN MOORE**

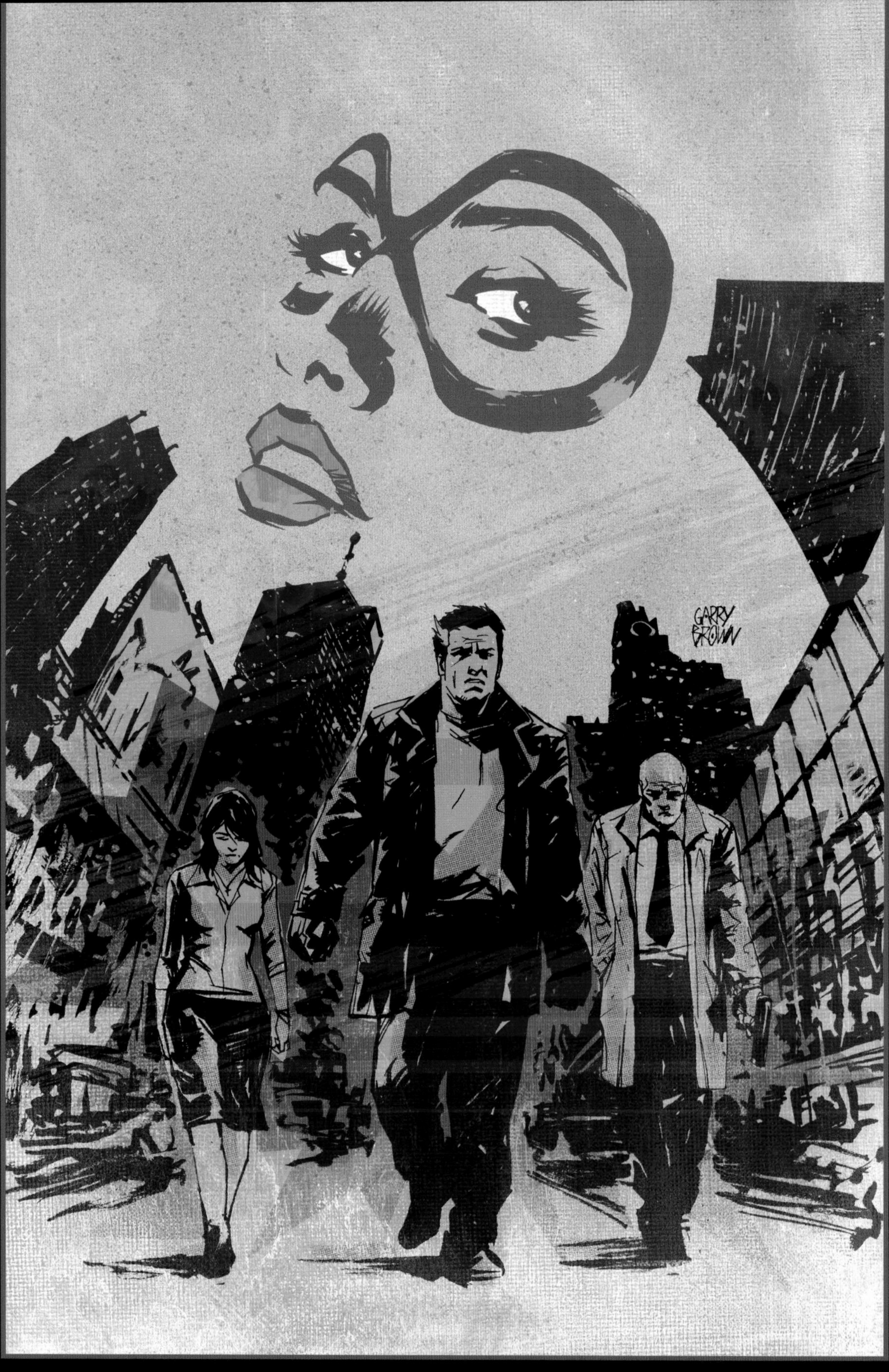
GARRY BROWN
COVER 18A: **GARRY BROWN**

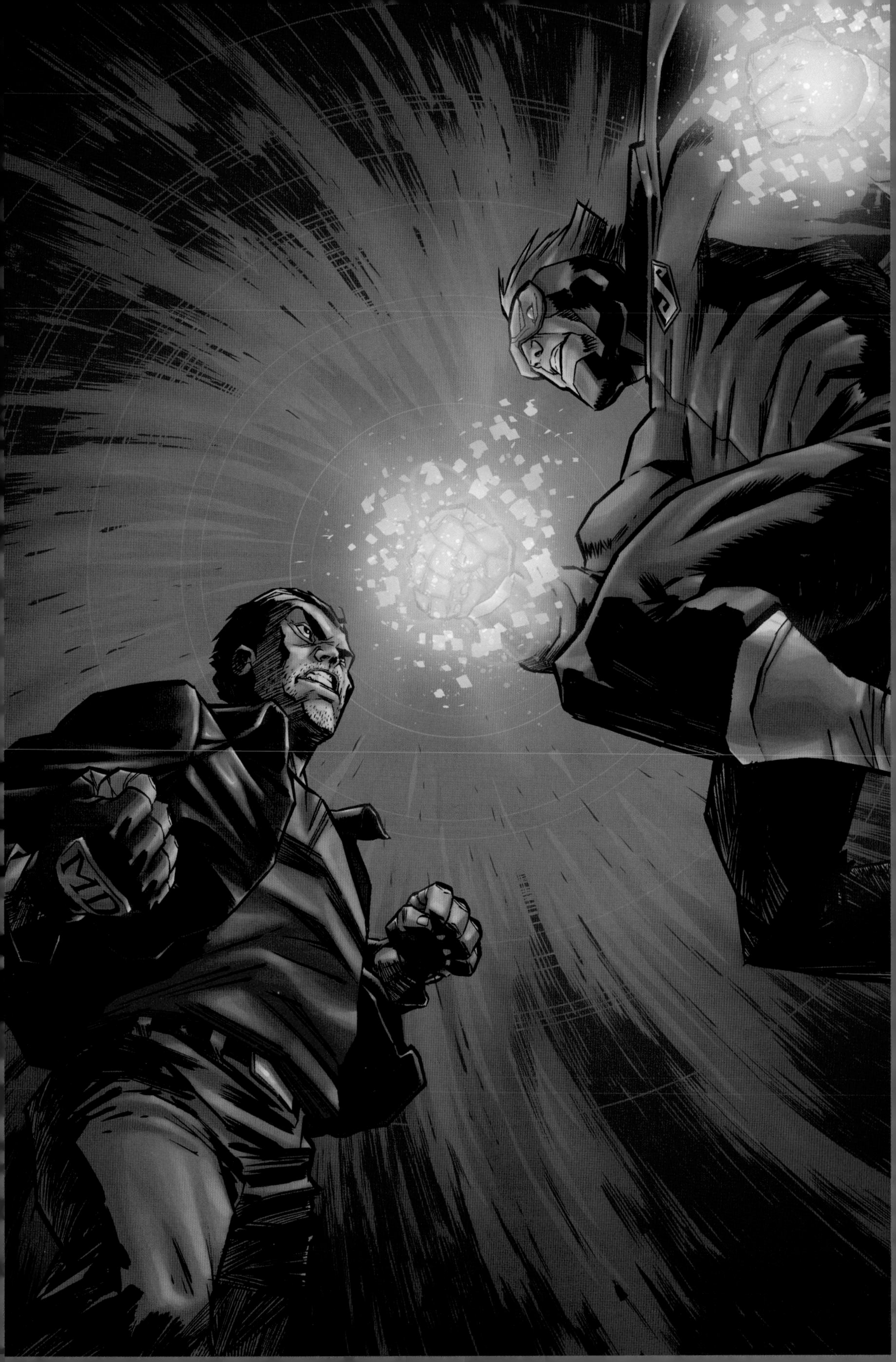

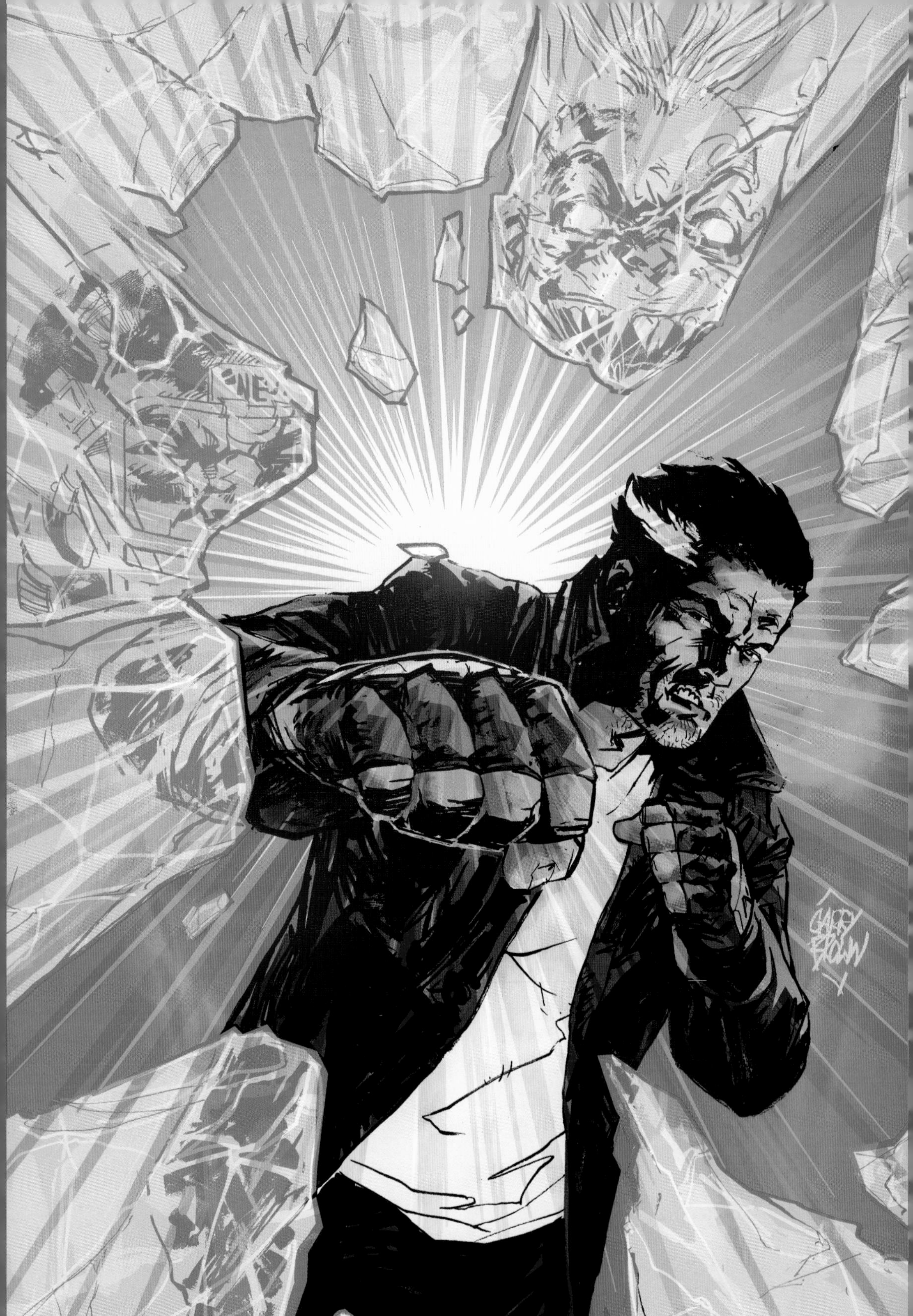

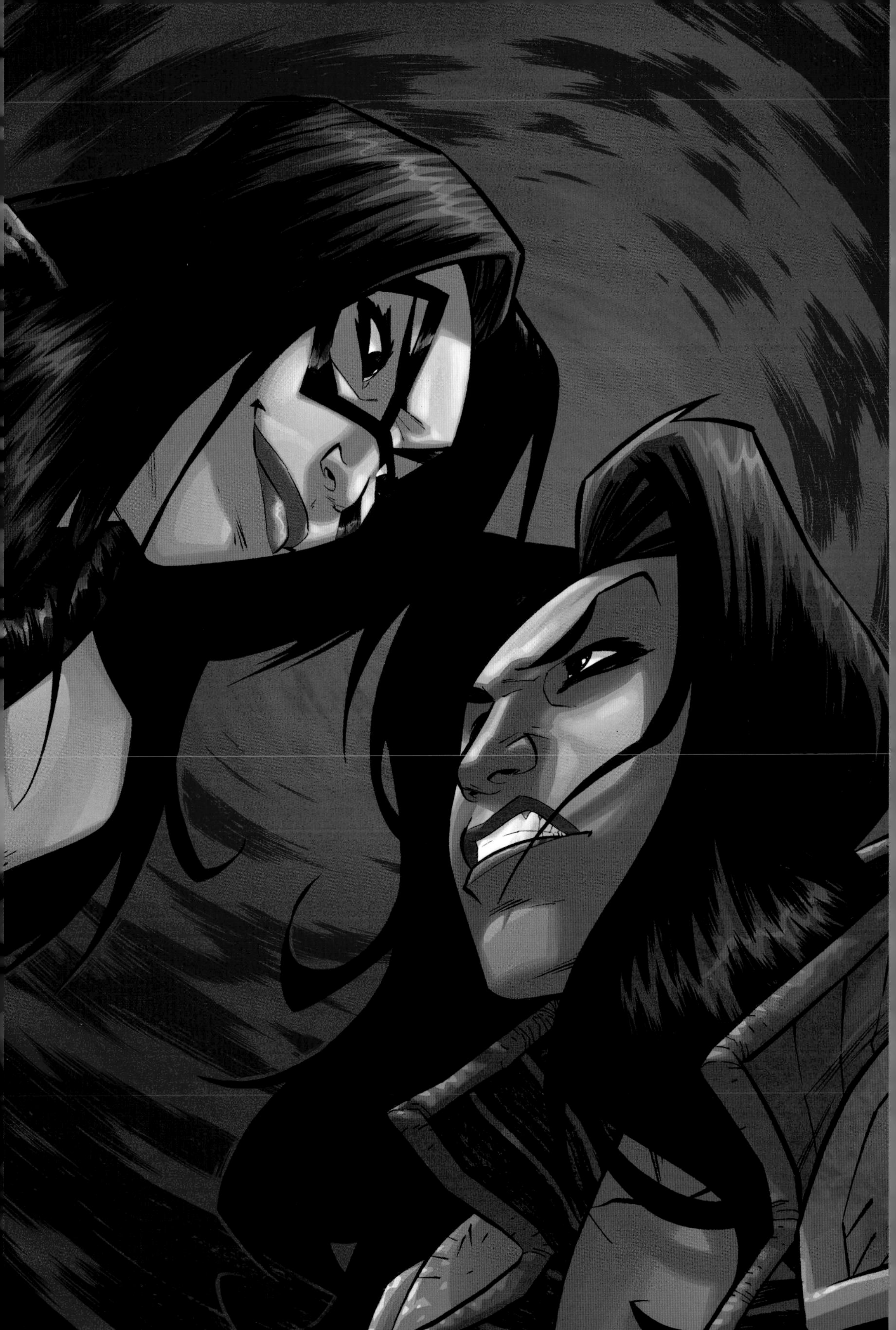

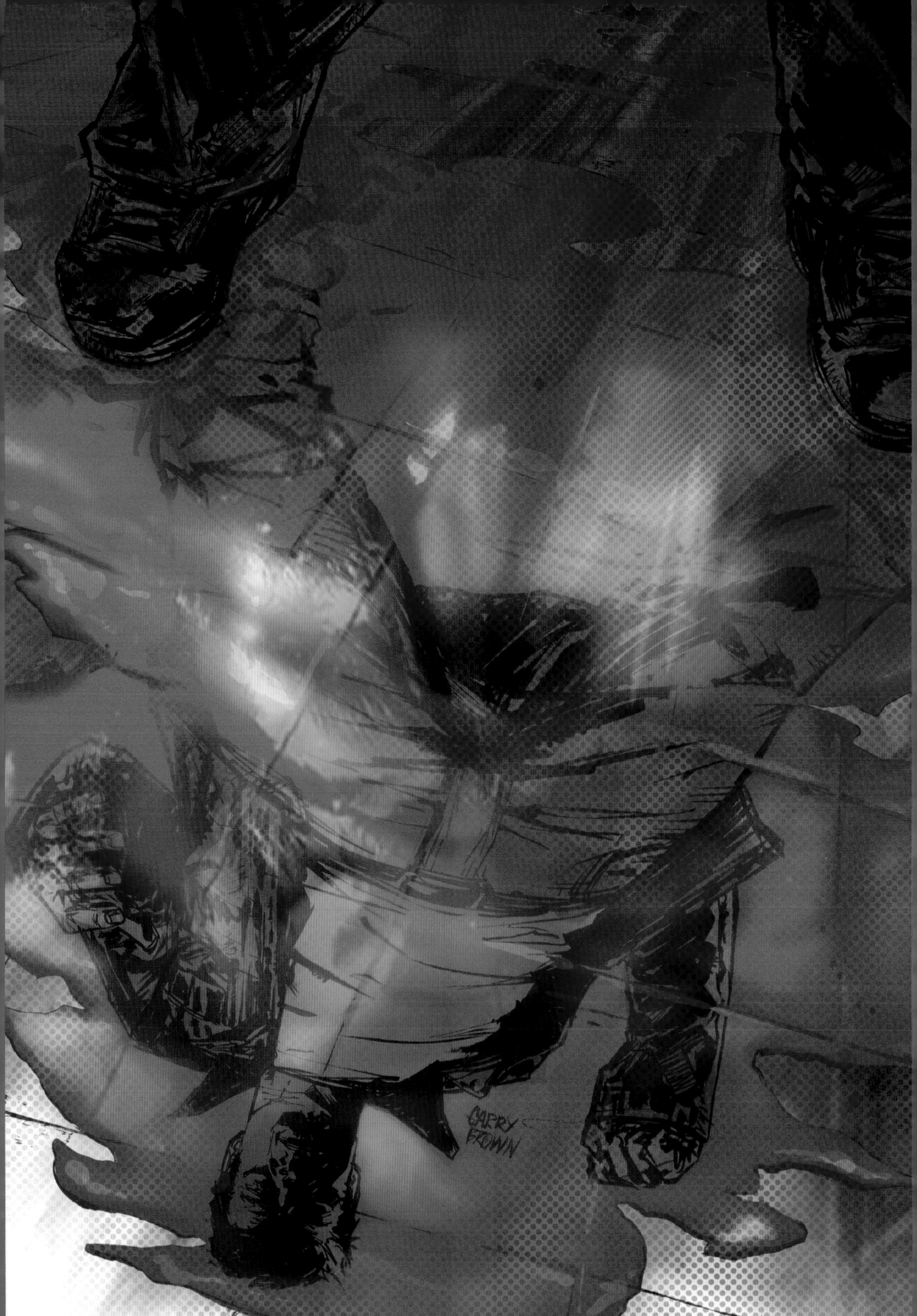
GARRY
BROWN

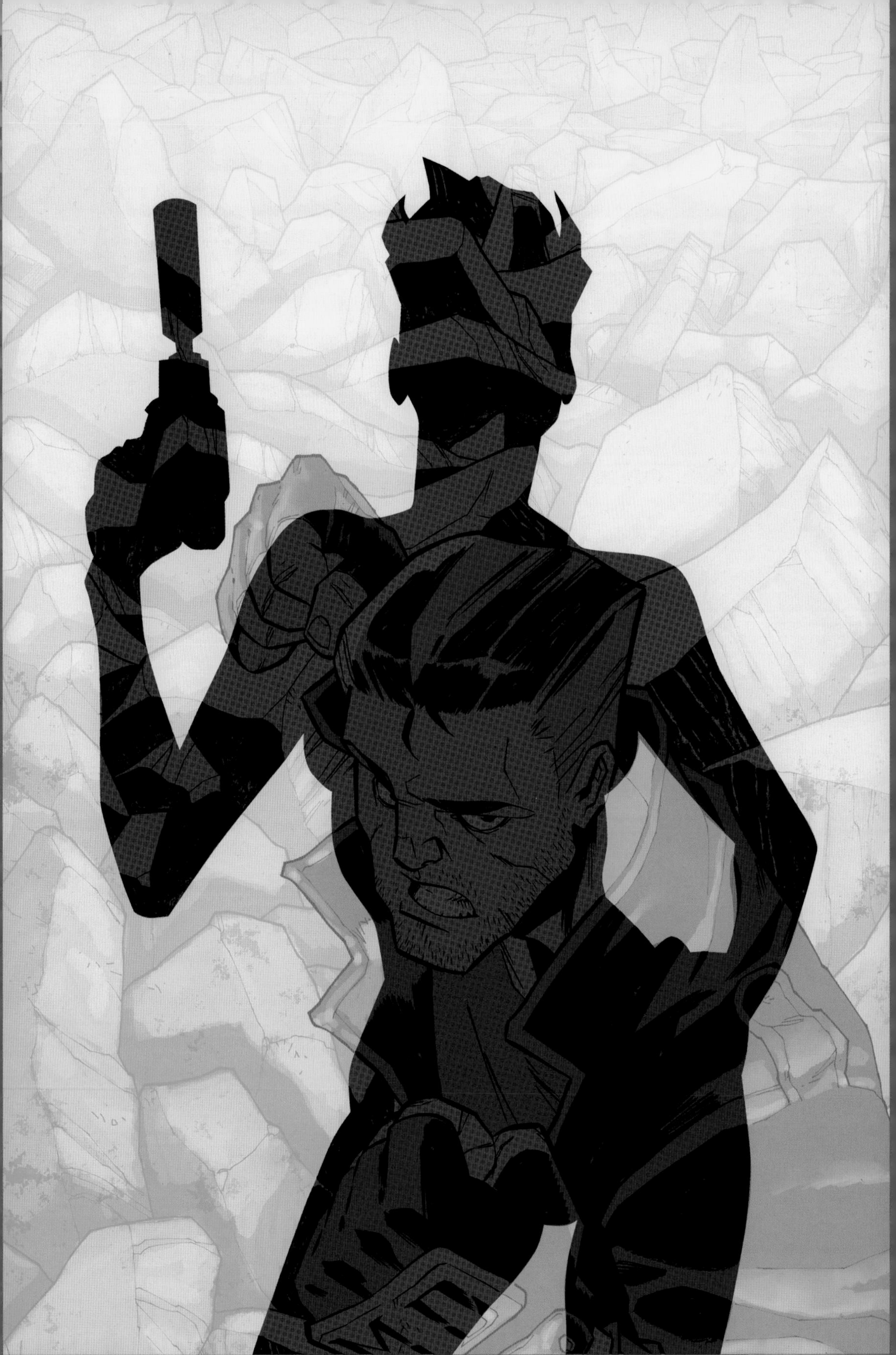

# PLANET OF THE APES

## SPECIAL 14 PAGE PREVIEW

# PLANET OF THE APES VOLUME ONE ON SALE NOW!

WRITTEN BY **DARYL GREGORY**     ART BY **CARLOS MAGNO**     COVER BY **KARL RICHARDSON**

2680 A.D.
THE CITYSTATE OF MAK.

...AND SO THE LAST OF MAN'S WEAPONS WAS PUT AWAY.

AND CAESAR *SEALED* THE ARMORY OF MANDEMUS.

TO THIS DAY, APES AND HUMANS HAVE LIVED TOGETHER IN FRIENDSHIP, HARMONY...

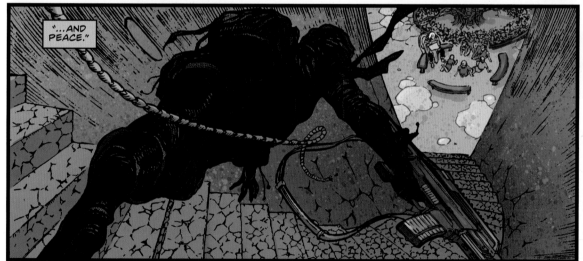

"...AND PEACE."

LAWGIVER!

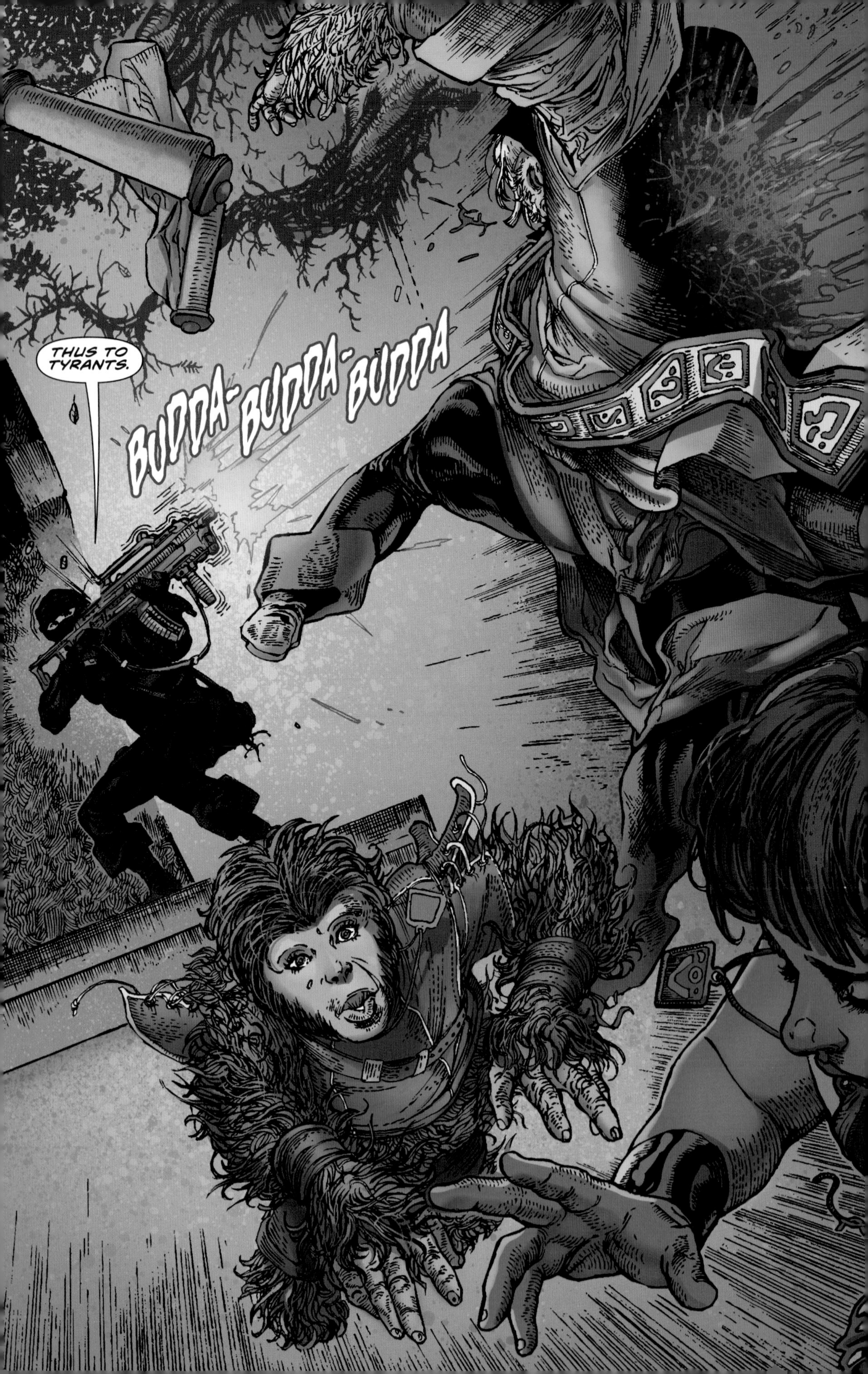
THUS TO TYRANTS.
BUDDA-BUDDA-BUDDA

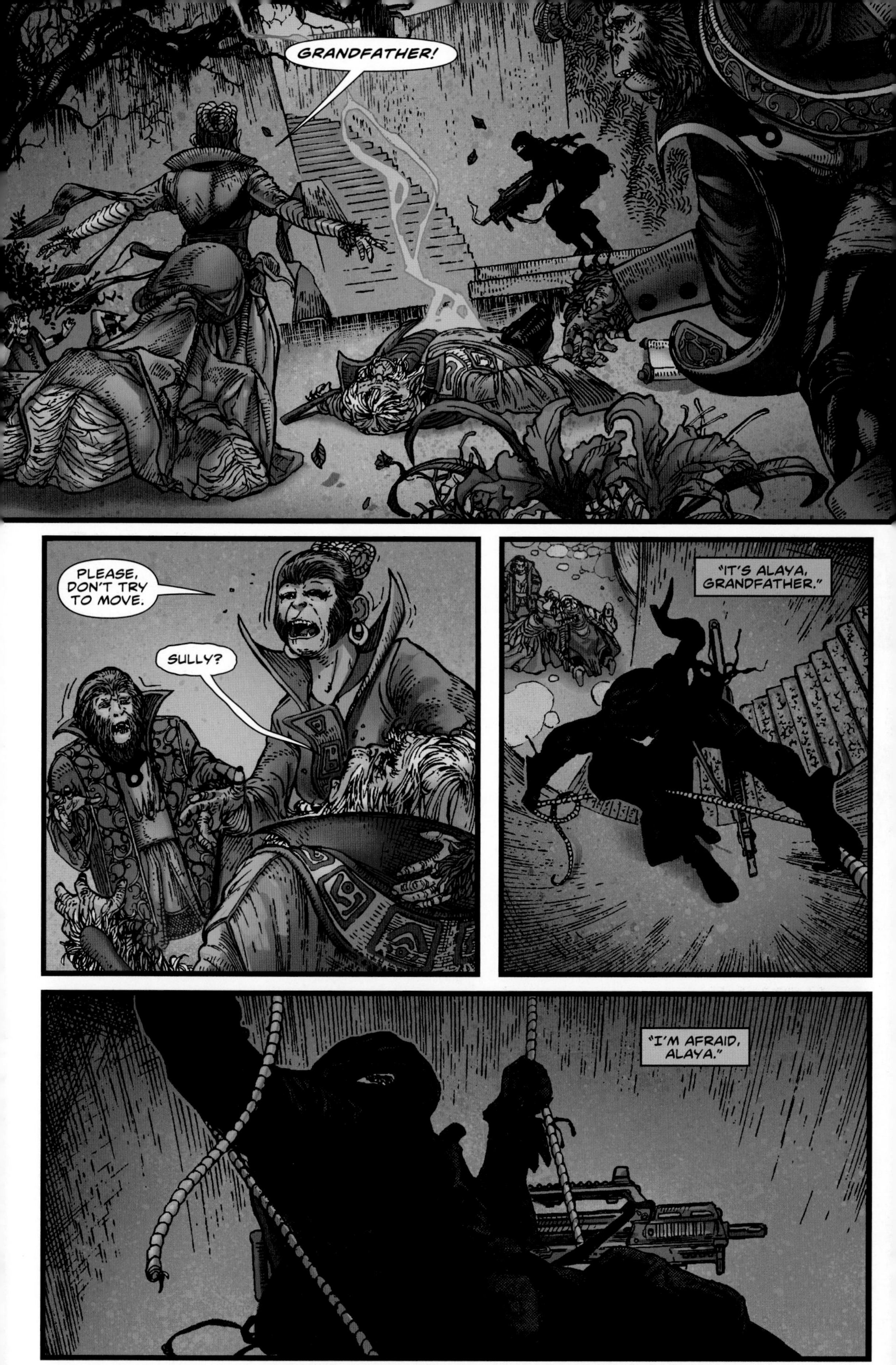
GRANDFATHER!
PLEASE, DON'T TRY TO MOVE.
SULLY?
"IT'S ALAYA, GRANDFATHER."
"I'M AFRAID, ALAYA."

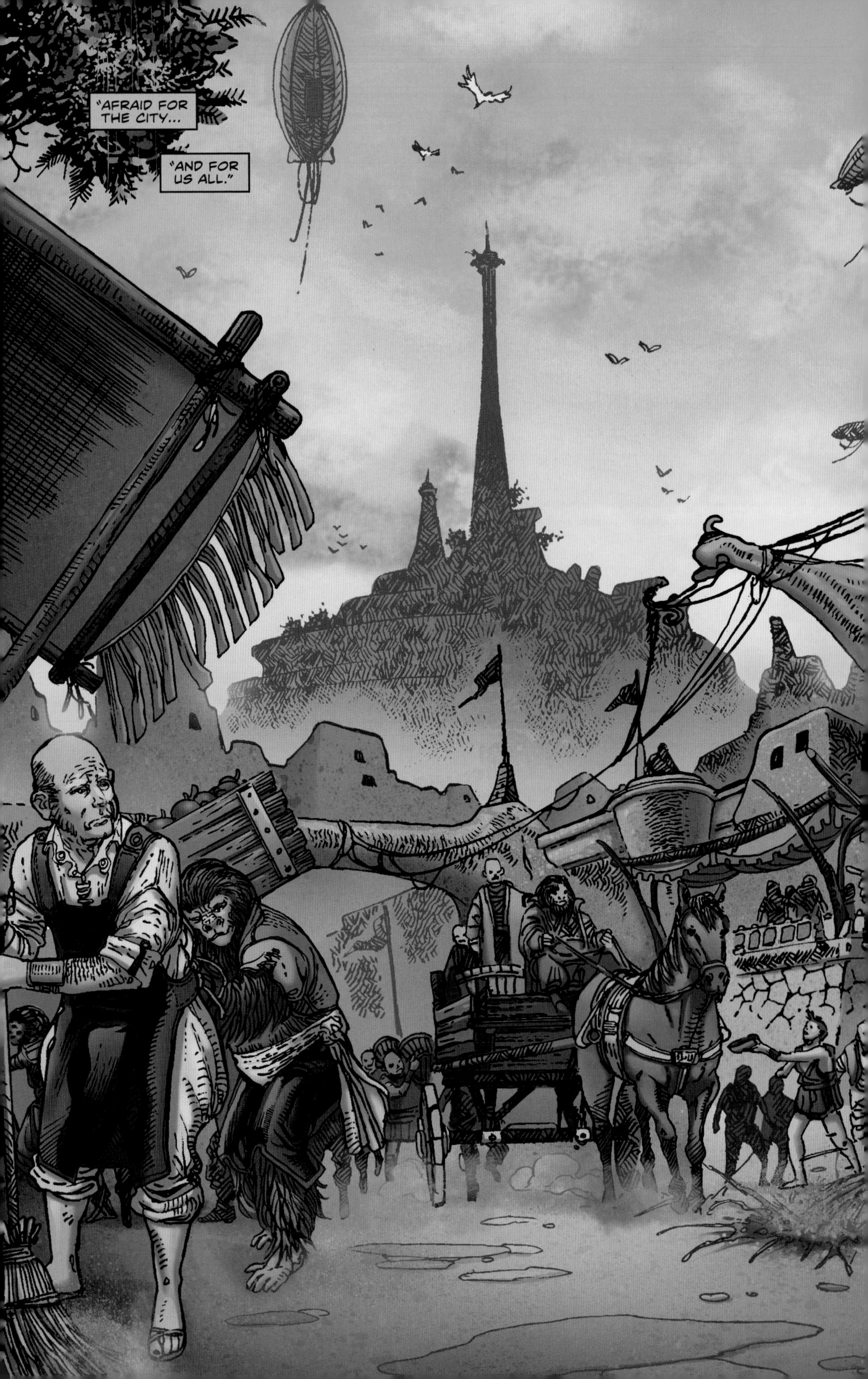
"AFRAID FOR THE CITY...
"AND FOR US ALL."

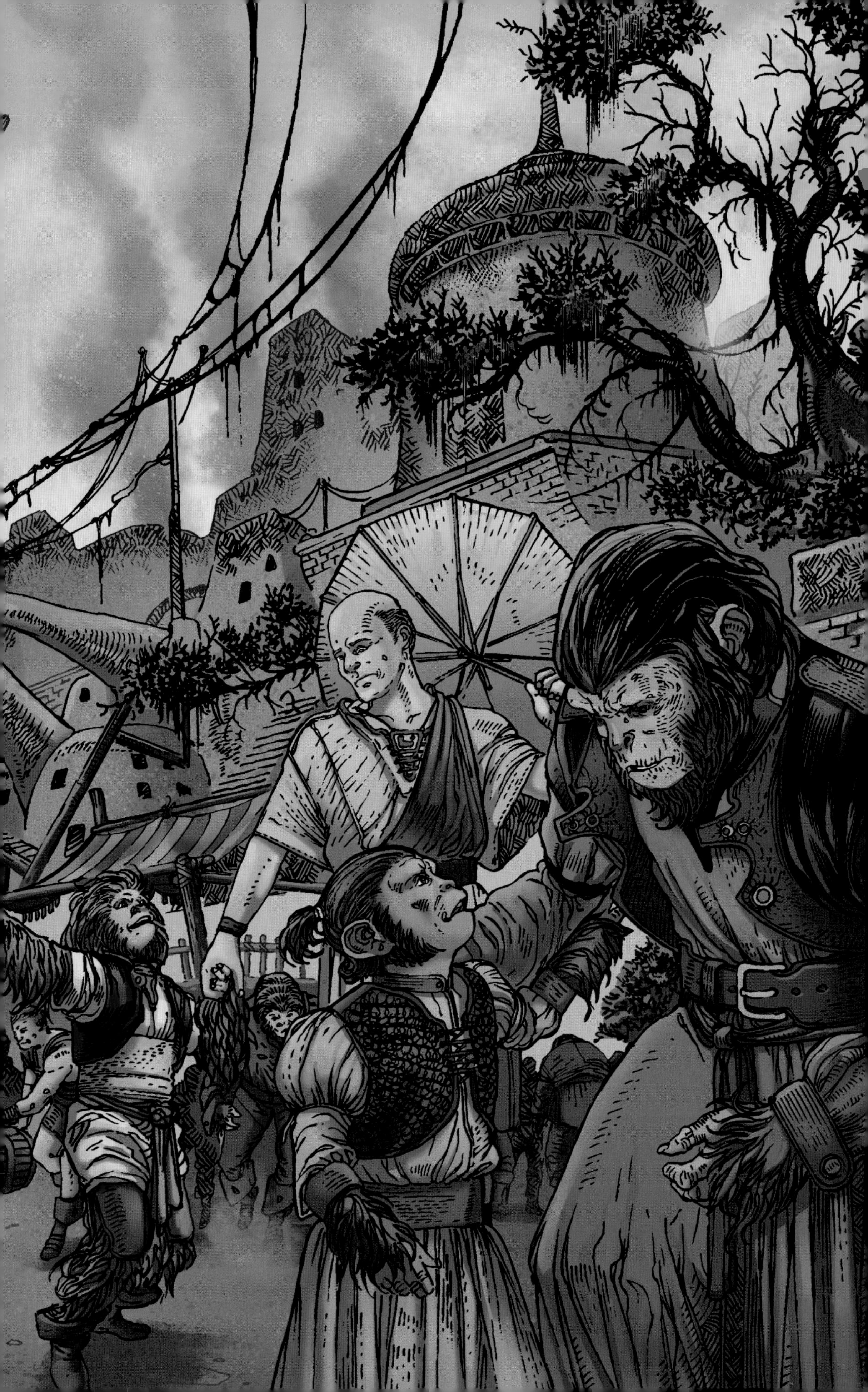

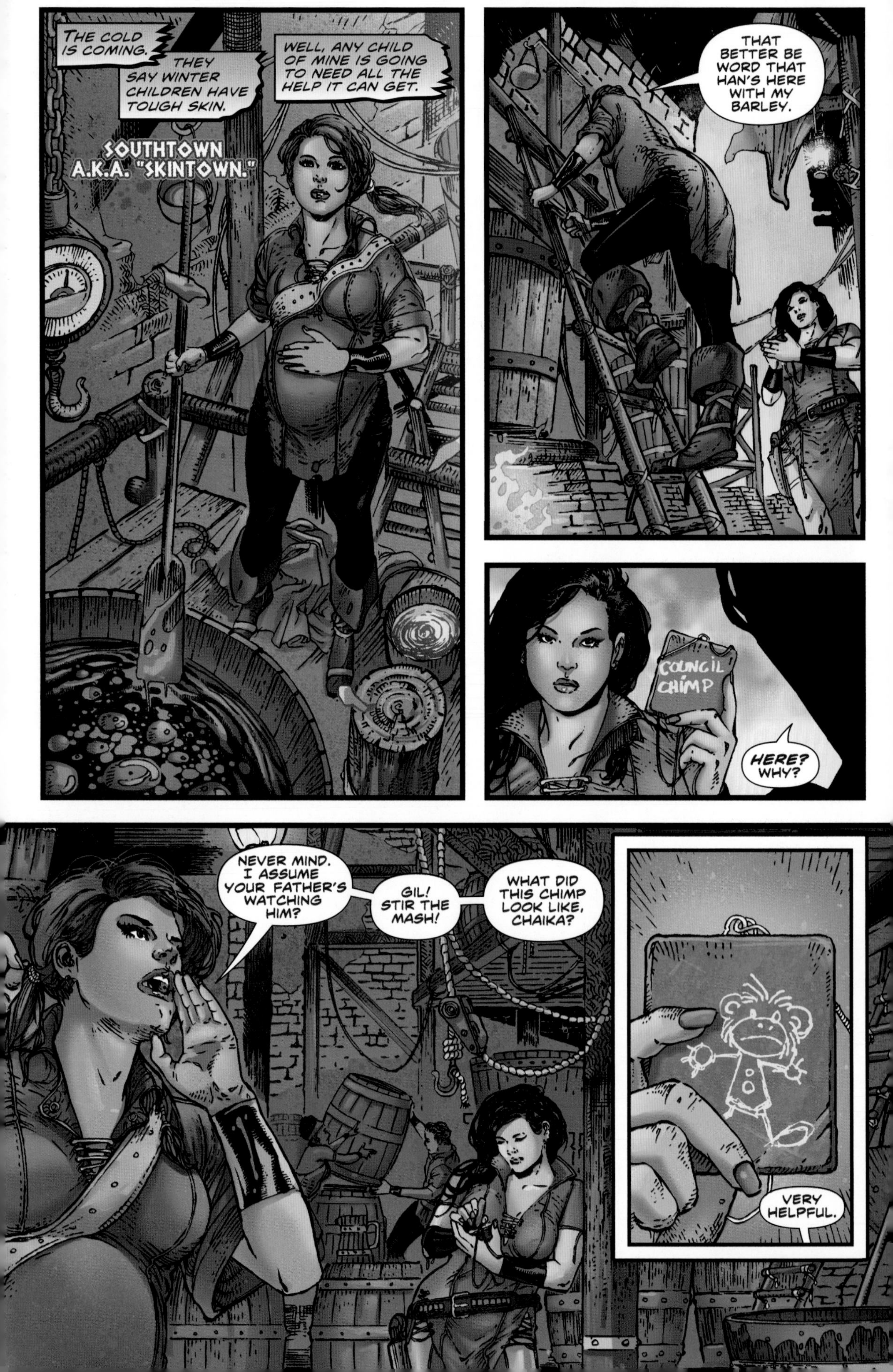
THE COLD IS COMING.
THEY SAY WINTER CHILDREN HAVE TOUGH SKIN.
WELL, ANY CHILD OF MINE IS GOING TO NEED ALL THE HELP IT CAN GET.
SOUTHTOWN A.K.A. "SKINTOWN."
THAT BETTER BE WORD THAT HAN'S HERE WITH MY BARLEY.
COUNCIL CHIMP
HERE? WHY?
NEVER MIND. I ASSUME YOUR FATHER'S WATCHING HIM?
GIL! STIR THE MASH!
WHAT DID THIS CHIMP LOOK LIKE, CHAIKA?
VERY HELPFUL.

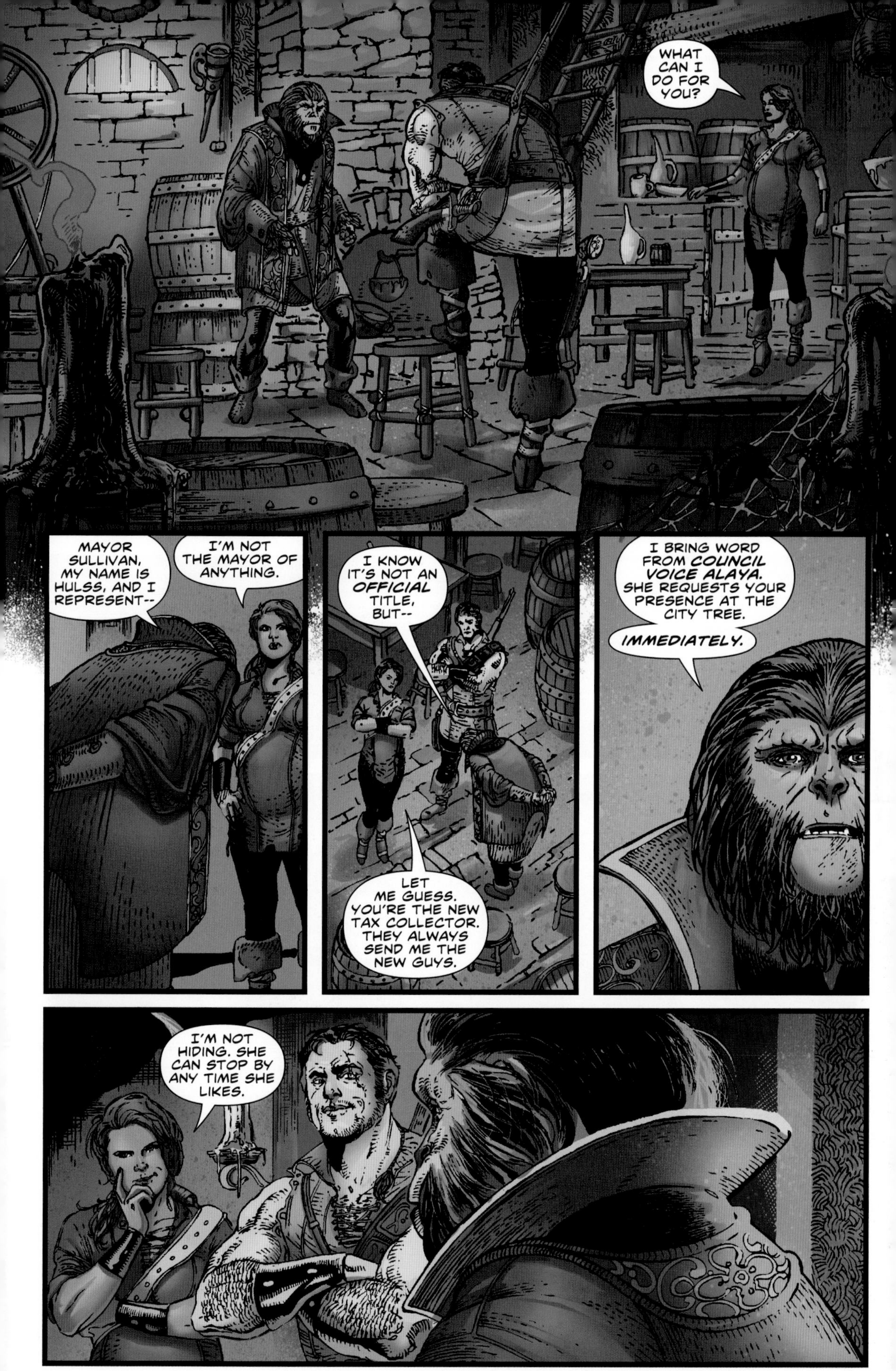
WHAT CAN I DO FOR YOU?
MAYOR SULLIVAN, MY NAME IS HULSS, AND I REPRESENT--
I'M NOT THE MAYOR OF ANYTHING.
I KNOW IT'S NOT AN *OFFICIAL* TITLE, BUT--
LET ME GUESS. YOU'RE THE NEW TAX COLLECTOR. THEY ALWAYS SEND ME THE NEW GUYS.
I BRING WORD FROM *COUNCIL VOICE ALAYA.* SHE REQUESTS YOUR PRESENCE AT THE CITY TREE.
*IMMEDIATELY.*
I'M NOT HIDING. SHE CAN STOP BY ANY TIME SHE LIKES.

COME *HERE*? TO *SKINTOWN*? YOU CAN'T EXPECT--

*WHAT* DID YOU SAY?

MY APOLOGIES-- *SOUTHTOWN*. IF YOU WOULD LET ME FINISH...

NOBODY'S STOPPING YOU.

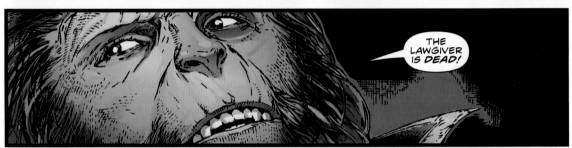

THE LAWGIVER IS *DEAD*!

WHEN DID THIS HAPPEN? WAS HE ALONE WHEN HE DIED?

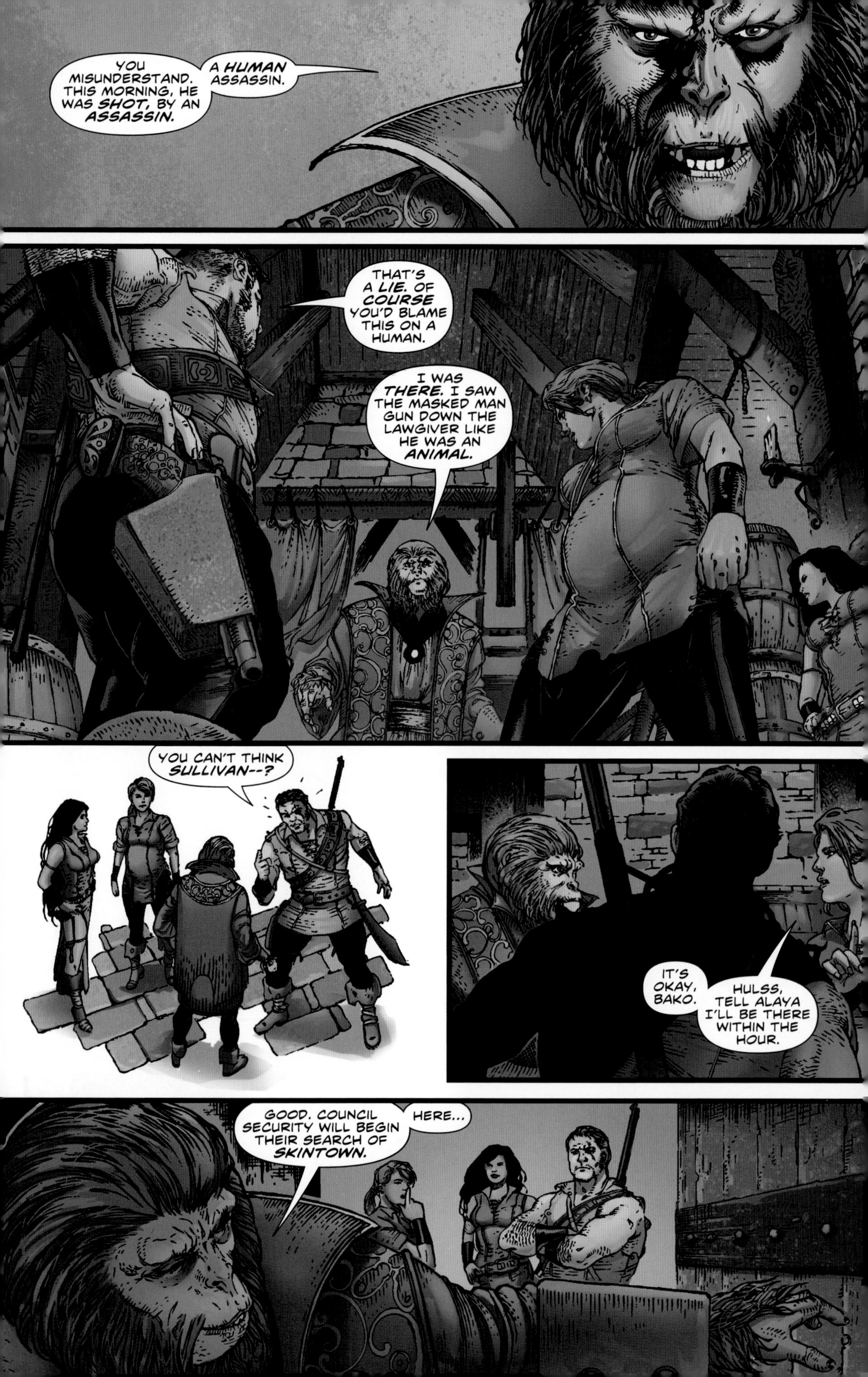
YOU MISUNDERSTAND. THIS MORNING, HE WAS SHOT, BY AN ASSASSIN.
A HUMAN ASSASSIN.
THAT'S A LIE. OF COURSE YOU'D BLAME THIS ON A HUMAN.
I WAS THERE. I SAW THE MASKED MAN GUN DOWN THE LAWGIVER LIKE HE WAS AN ANIMAL.
YOU CAN'T THINK SULLIVAN--?
IT'S OKAY, BAKO.
HULSS, TELL ALAYA I'LL BE THERE WITHIN THE HOUR.
GOOD. COUNCIL SECURITY WILL BEGIN THEIR SEARCH OF SKINTOWN.
HERE...

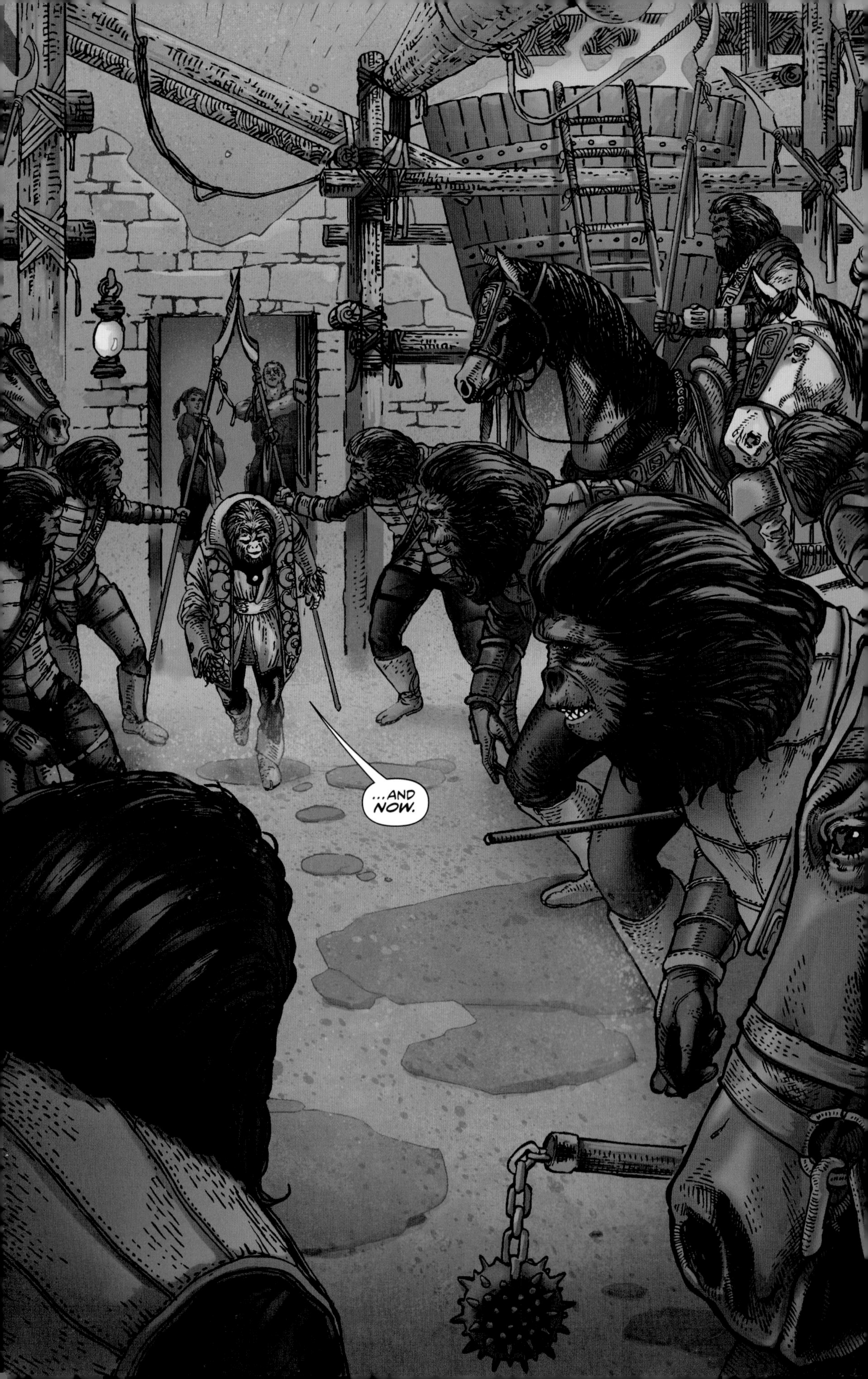
...AND NOW.

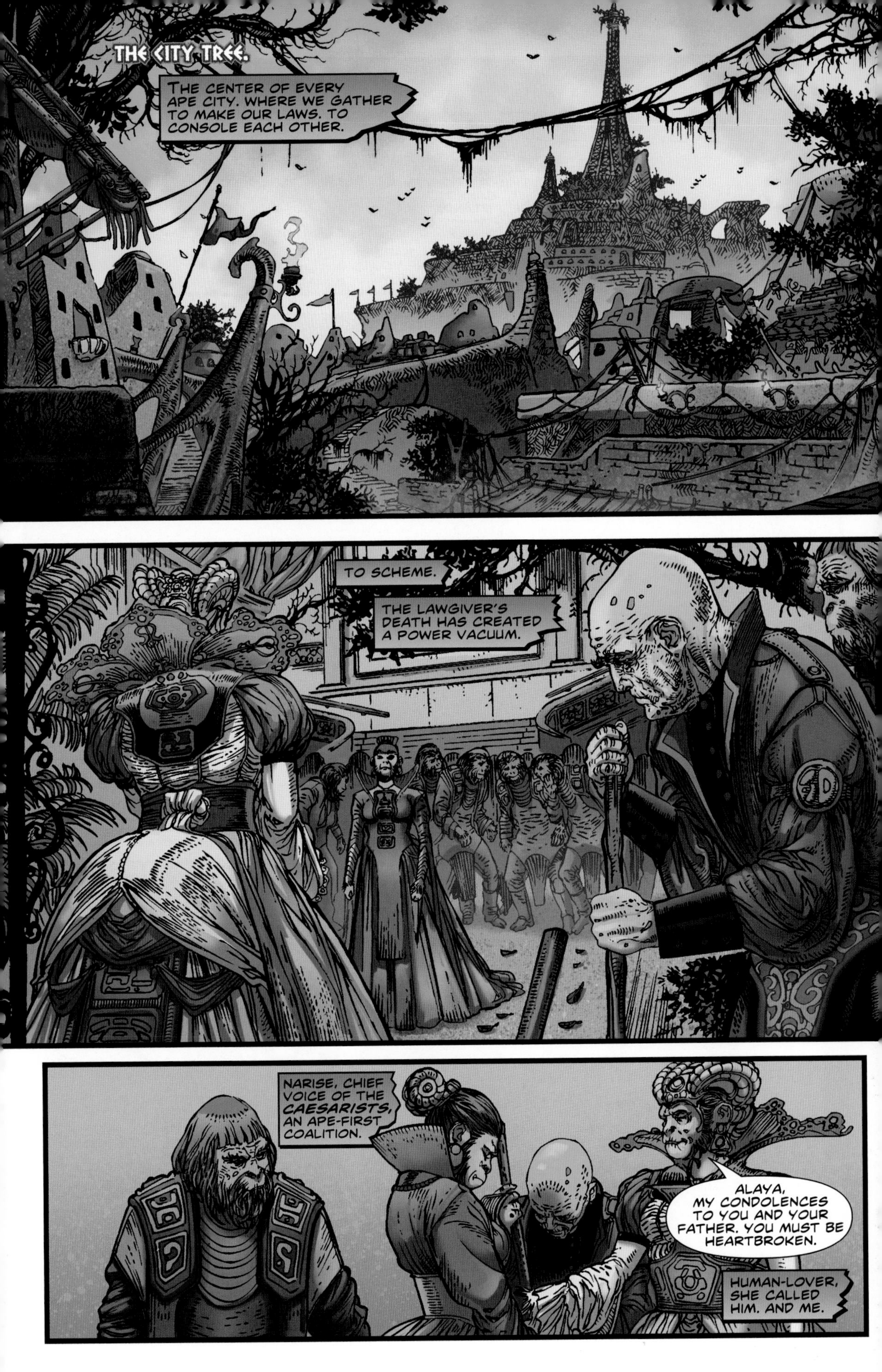
THE CITY TREE.
THE CENTER OF EVERY APE CITY. WHERE WE GATHER TO MAKE OUR LAWS. TO CONSOLE EACH OTHER.
TO SCHEME.
THE LAWGIVER'S DEATH HAS CREATED A POWER VACUUM.
NARISE, CHIEF VOICE OF THE CAESARISTS, AN APE-FIRST COALITION.
ALAYA, MY CONDOLENCES TO YOU AND YOUR FATHER. YOU MUST BE HEARTBROKEN.
HUMAN-LOVER, SHE CALLED HIM. AND ME.

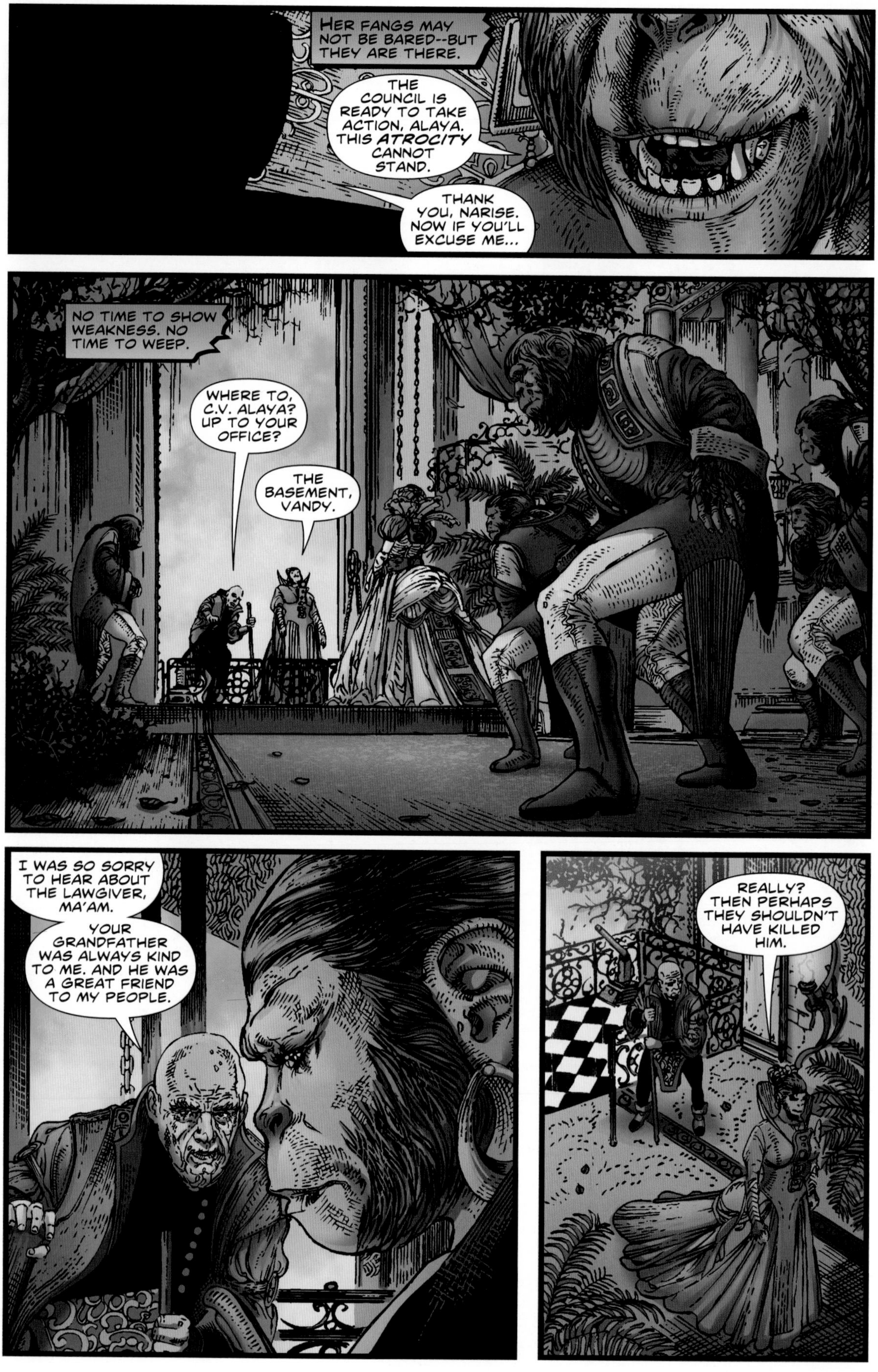
HER FANGS MAY NOT BE BARED--BUT THEY ARE THERE.
THE COUNCIL IS READY TO TAKE ACTION, ALAYA. THIS *ATROCITY* CANNOT STAND.
THANK YOU, NARISE. NOW IF YOU'LL EXCUSE ME...
NO TIME TO SHOW WEAKNESS. NO TIME TO WEEP.
WHERE TO, C.V. ALAYA? UP TO YOUR OFFICE?
THE BASEMENT, VANDY.
I WAS SO SORRY TO HEAR ABOUT THE LAWGIVER, MA'AM.
YOUR GRANDFATHER WAS ALWAYS KIND TO ME. AND HE WAS A GREAT FRIEND TO MY PEOPLE.
REALLY? THEN PERHAPS THEY SHOULDN'T HAVE KILLED HIM.

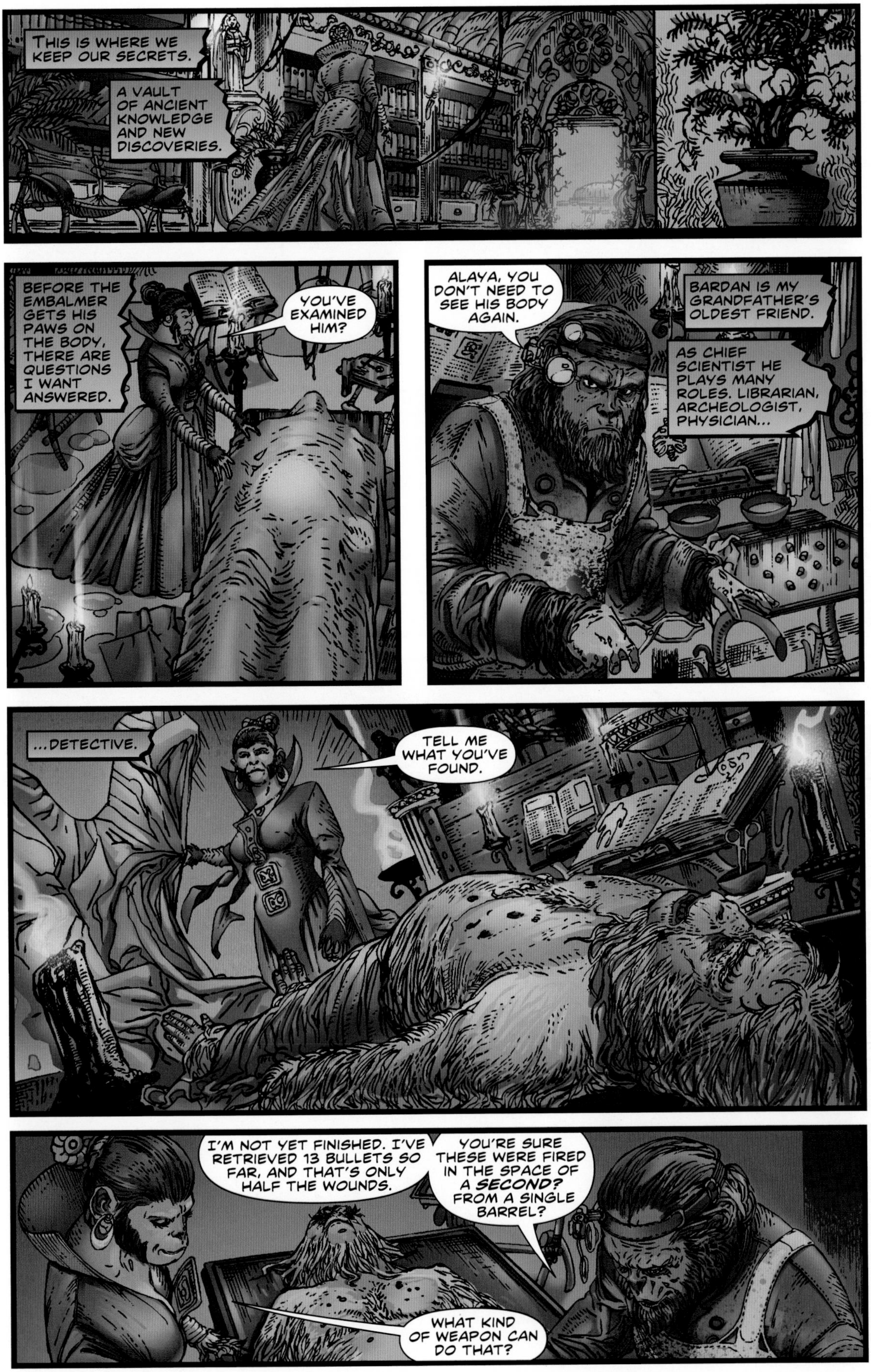
THIS IS WHERE WE KEEP OUR SECRETS.
A VAULT OF ANCIENT KNOWLEDGE AND NEW DISCOVERIES.
BEFORE THE EMBALMER GETS HIS PAWS ON THE BODY, THERE ARE QUESTIONS I WANT ANSWERED.
YOU'VE EXAMINED HIM?
ALAYA, YOU DON'T NEED TO SEE HIS BODY AGAIN.
BARDAN IS MY GRANDFATHER'S OLDEST FRIEND.
AS CHIEF SCIENTIST HE PLAYS MANY ROLES. LIBRARIAN, ARCHEOLOGIST, PHYSICIAN...
...DETECTIVE.
TELL ME WHAT YOU'VE FOUND.
I'M NOT YET FINISHED. I'VE RETRIEVED 13 BULLETS SO FAR, AND THAT'S ONLY HALF THE WOUNDS.
YOU'RE SURE THESE WERE FIRED IN THE SPACE OF A *SECOND?* FROM A SINGLE BARREL?
WHAT KIND OF WEAPON CAN DO THAT?

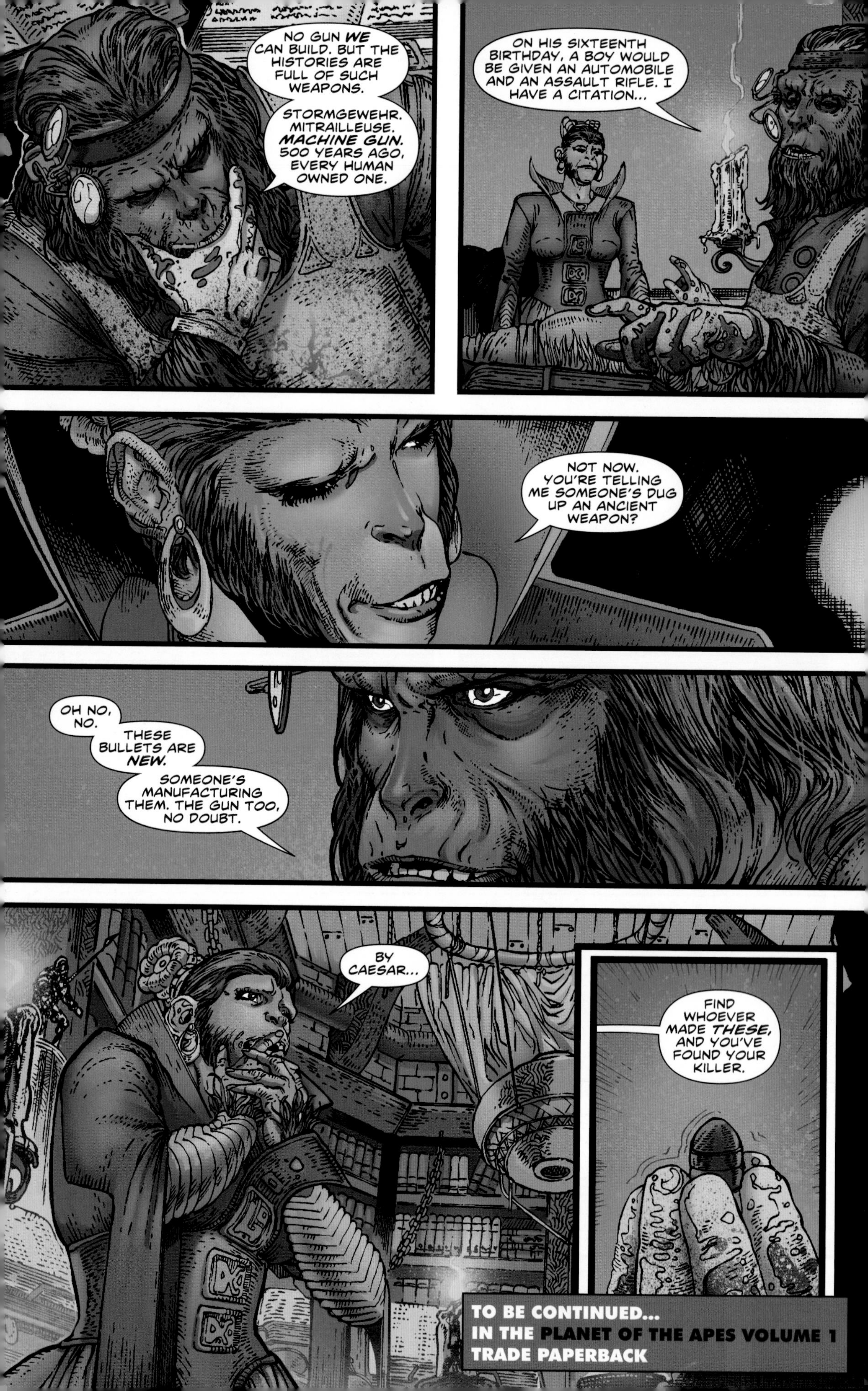
NO GUN *WE* CAN BUILD. BUT THE HISTORIES ARE FULL OF SUCH WEAPONS.
STORMGEWEHR. MITRAILLEUSE. ***MACHINE GUN.*** 500 YEARS AGO, EVERY HUMAN OWNED ONE.
ON HIS SIXTEENTH BIRTHDAY, A BOY WOULD BE GIVEN AN AUTOMOBILE AND AN ASSAULT RIFLE. I HAVE A CITATION...
NOT NOW. YOU'RE TELLING ME SOMEONE'S DUG UP AN ANCIENT WEAPON?
OH NO, NO.
THESE BULLETS ARE *NEW.*
SOMEONE'S MANUFACTURING THEM. THE GUN TOO, NO DOUBT.
BY CAESAR...
FIND WHOEVER MADE *THESE,* AND YOU'VE FOUND YOUR KILLER.
TO BE CONTINUED... IN THE PLANET OF THE APES VOLUME 1 TRADE PAPERBACK

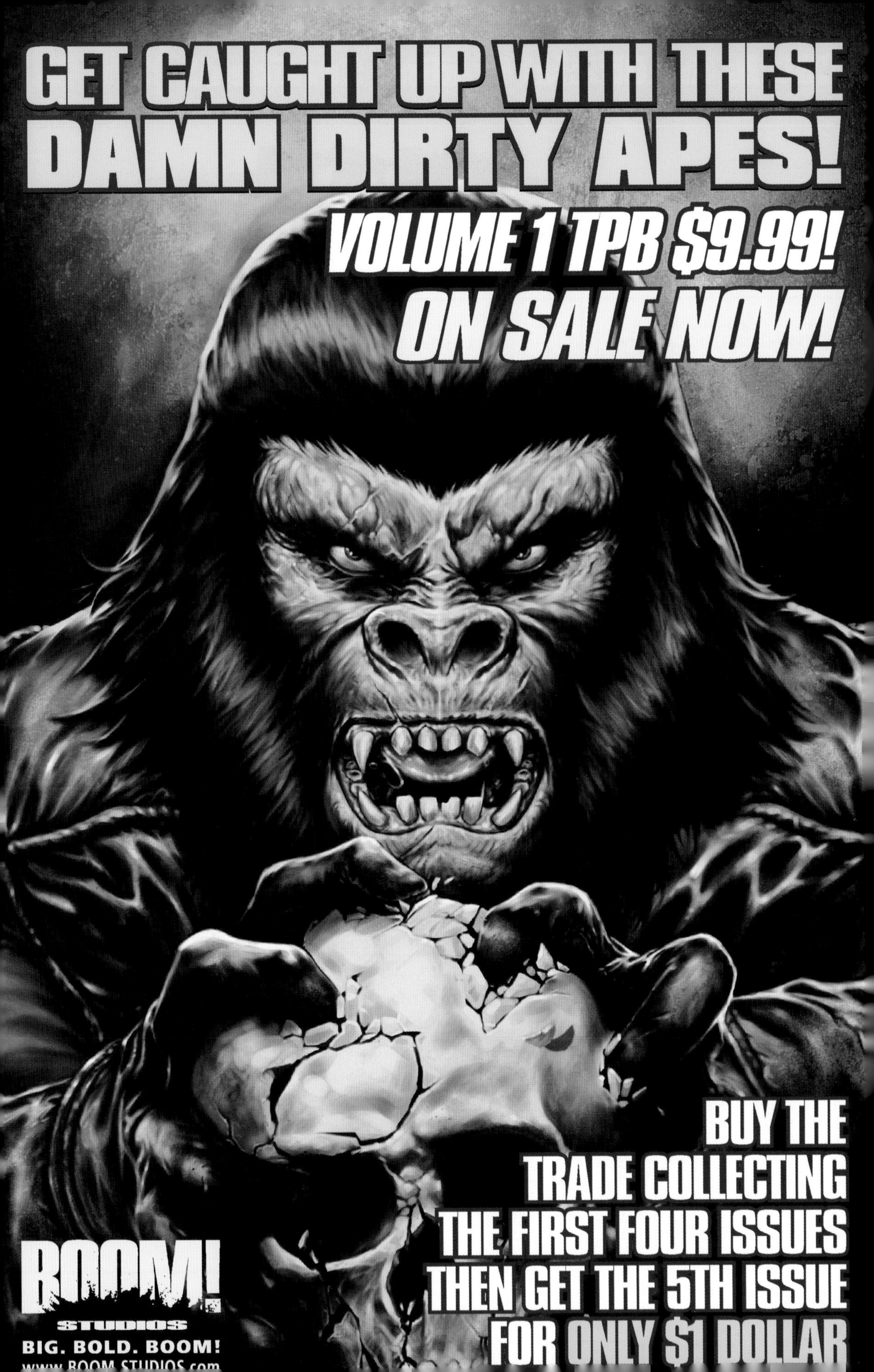
GET CAUGHT UP WITH THESE
DAMN DIRTY APES!
VOLUME 1 TPB $9.99!
ON SALE NOW!
BUY THE
TRADE COLLECTING
THE FIRST FOUR ISSUES
THEN GET THE 5TH ISSUE
FOR ONLY $1 DOLLAR
BOOM!
STUDIOS
BIG. BOLD. BOOM!
www.BOOM-STUDIOS.com

# CGC Is the Official Grading Service of  BOOM! STUDIOS

# You wouldn't buy...

... A DIAMOND WITHOUT CERTIFICATION

... A HOUSE WITHOUT AN INSPECTION

... A CAR WITHOUT A PROFESSIONAL'S OPINION

**CGC UNIVERSAL GRADE**
**9.8**
Irredeemable #1
Boom! Studios, 4/09
WHITE Pages
Mark Waid story
Peter Krause art
John Cassaday cover
0966865001
Afterword by Grant Morrison.

**CGC**

MARK WAID · PETER KRAUSE
IRREDEEMABLE
AFTERWORD BY GRANT MORRISON
BOOM! 1 2009 $3.9 COVE

## So, why buy comics without the expert's opinion?

When you purchase a comic certified by CGC, you know that it has been graded by the hobby's most experienced and trusted team, according to an established grading standard. Furthermore, every book graded by CGC undergoes a thorough restoration check by leading professionals. When restoration is detected, it's clearly noted on the certification label.

Once certified by CGC, every comic is encapsulated in a state-of-the-art, tamper-evident holder, providing superior protection and stability for long-term enjoyment. **For your comic books, you deserve certification from CGC, the only expert, impartial, third-party grading service. Get the expert's opinion!**

**CGC**
When a Comic Book becomes a Treasure

P.O. Box 4738  |  Sarasota, Florida 34230  |  1-877-NM-COMIC (662-6642)  |  www.CGCcomics.com

**An Independent Member of the Certified Collectibles Group**

# DEFINITIVE IRREDEEMABLE

## Deluxe slipcase oversized hardcover edition!

### COLLECTING THE FIRST 12 ISSUES!

Nominated for 3 Eisner Awards
and 2 Harvey Awards!

BOOM!
STUDIOS

# AVAILABLE NOW!

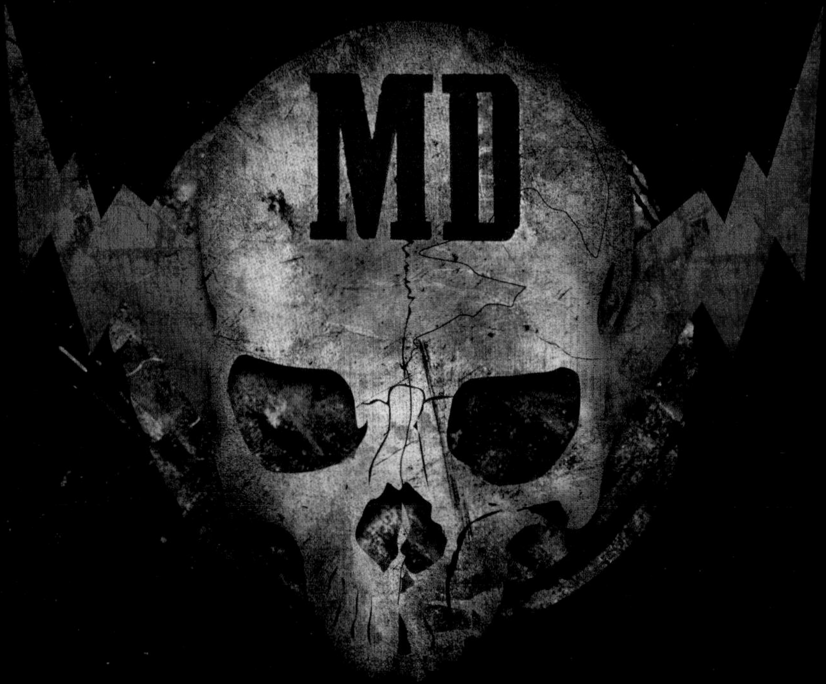
MD